Adjusting to Europe

Adjusting to Europe provides lively coverage of the impact of Europe on national policies. With contributions from some of the leading writers on European politics and public policy, it delivers a new and exciting analysis of the policy-making process.

The impact of the EU upon its member states has been profound in terms of regulatory powers yet its redistributive functions are negligible. *Adjusting to Europe* confronts the paradoxes of policy-making at the EU level not only from an institutional point of view, but also with a consideration of the context and styles of the policies.

The book begins with an introduction analyzing from a theoretical and empirical point of view the ways and means, and the extent to which national policies have been Europeanized. It is followed by a section on policy-making and policy styles within the EU, by country studies of British, German and French administrations, and by a final section that looks at the European impact on domestic policy by reference to specific policy areas, including social and industrial policy.

Yves Mény is director of the Robert Schuman Centre, at the European University Institute, Florence. **Pierre Muller** is director of research at the Centre National de la Recherche Scientifique (Centre de Recherches Administratives), Paris. **Jean-Louis Quermonne** is professor of political science at the Institut d'études Politiques in Grenoble, director of studies at the Fondation Nationale des Sciences Politiques and president of the Association Française de Science Politique.

European Public Policy Series
Edited by Jeremy Richardson, University of Essex
European Public Policy Institute, University of Warwick

This series provides accessible and challenging books on three aspects of European public policy:

- the European Union policy process and studies of particular policy areas within the EU;
- national and comparative policy studies with a significant interest beyond the countries studied;
- public policy developments in non-EU states.

Books in the series come from a range of social science disciplines but all have in common the objective of analyzing the dynamics of the policy-making and implementation process via empirical work guided by relevant theory, thus furthering our understanding of European integration. Books in the series are accessible beyond the academic and student market, to those who are directly involved in public policy within Europe.

Titles in the series include:

Democratic Spain
Reshaping external relations in a changing world
Edited by Richard Gillespie, Fernando Rodrigo and Jonathan Story

Forthcoming titles include:

Policy-making, European Integration and the Role of Interest Groups
Jeremy Richardson and Sonia Mazey

Regulating Europe
Giandomenico Majone

The European Commission
Policy styles and policy instruments
Jeremy Richardson and Laura Cram

Making Europe Green
Environmental policy-making in the European Community
David Judge, David Earnshaw and Ken Collins

Remaking Social Europe
Ricard Gomà

Policy-making in the European Union
Edited by Jeremy Richardson

Adjusting to Europe

The impact of the European Union
on national institutions and policies

Edited by
Yves Mény, Pierre Muller and
Jean-Louis Quermonne

London and New York

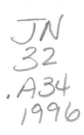

First published 1996
by Routledge
11 New Fetter Lane, London EC4P 4EE

Simultaneously published in the USA and Canada
by Routledge
29 West 35th Street, New York, NY 10001

Typeset in Times by LaserScript, Mitcham, Surrey
Printed and bound in Great Britain by
Mackays of Chatham PLC, Chatham, Kent

British Library Cataloguing in Publication Data
A catalogue record for this book is available from the British Library

Library of Congress Cataloging in Publication Data
Adjusting to Europe: the impact of the European Union on national institutions and policies/[edited by] Yves Mény, Pierre Muller, and Jean-Louis Quermonne.
(European public policy)
Includes bibliographical references and index.
1. Political planning – European Union countries. 2. European Union. I. Mény, Yves. II. Muller, Pierre, 1950– .
III. Quermonne, Jean-Louis. IV. Series
JN32.A34   1996
327.4–dc20   96–19654

ISBN 0–415–14410–8 (hbk)
ISBN 0–415–14409–4 (pbk)

Contents

Part III The European impact on domestic policies

Figures and tables

Contributors

Giuliano Amato, formerly Prime Minister of Italy, teaches at the European University Institute in Florence and is the chairman of the Italian anti-trust authority.

Elie Cohen is Directeur de Recherche at the Centre National de la Recherche Scientifique (CNRS) in Paris. He is the author of *L'Etat brancardier* (1989) and *Le Colbertisme high-tech* (1992).

Christian Lequesne is Chargé de recherche at the Fondation Nationale des Sciences Politiques (FNSP) in Paris. He is the author of *Paris–Bruxelles: comment se fait la politique européenne de la France* (1994).

Giandomenico Majone is Professor of Political Science at the European University Institute in Florence. His publications include *Evidence, Argument and Persuasion in the Policy Process* (1989) and *Europe: un Etat régulateur?* (1995).

Sonia Mazey is Lecturer in Politics at the University of Cambridge and Fellow of Churchill College. Her recent publications include *Lobbying in the European Community* (edited with J. J. Richardson, 1993) and *The State of the European Union* 3, *Building a European Polity?* (edited with C. Rhodes, 1995).

Yves Mény is Director of the Robert Schuman Centre at the European University Institute. His publications include *Government and Politics in Western Europe* (1990) and *La Corruption de la République* (1992). He has authored or edited several books about public administration and policies.

Pierre Muller is Directeur de recherche at the Centre National de la Recherche Scientifique and teaches at the Institut d'études politiques de Paris. He has co-authored with Bruno Jobert *L'Etat en action* (1987) and edited several books on public policy.

Jean-Louis Quermonne is Professor at the Institut d'études politiques de Grenoble and Directeur d'études et de recherche at the Fondation Nationale des Sciences Politiques (FNSP) in Paris. Among his publications the most recent are *Les Systèmes politiques occidentaux* (1986) and *Le Système politique de l'Union européenne* (1994).

Jeremy Richardson is Professor at the University of Essex. He has authored or edited many books, among them *Policy Styles in Western Europe* (1982) and *Lobbying in the European Community* (with Sonia Mazey) (1993). He is editor of *The Journal of European Public Policy.*

Dietrich Rometsch is research assistant at the Institut für europäische Politik in Bonn. He has published on the European Commission in the *Jahrbuch der europäischen Integration.*

Philippe C. Schmitter is Professor at Stanford University. He has authored or edited many books on neo-corporatism and democratic transition.

Helen Wallace is Professor at the University of Sussex and Director of the Sussex European Institute. She has published extensively on the politics and policies of the European Community.

Wolfgang Wessels is Jean Monnet Professor at the University of Cologne and Chairman of the Trans-European Policy Studies Association (TEPSA). he has published many articles and books on the process of European integration, most recently, *The European Union and Member States* (with Dietrich Rometsch, 1996).

Series editor's preface

There is still considerable debate and conflict about the nature of the European Union (EU) and its future direction. One only has to reflect on the difficulties encountered in many member states in ratifying the Maastricht Treaty to realize that this particular phase of the European integration process was a 'marketing disaster', as one observer put it. Europe's political elite had moved too far and too fast for the peoples of Europe. There is now a sense of gloom about the state of the EU and its economies. Conflict rather than consensus seems to be the norm, with serious divisions between member states and within member states, a growing sense of retreat into the defence of pure national interest and a reassertion of intergovernmentalism.

Yet the history of European integration has always moved in 'fits and starts', episodically moving between 'Europhoria' and 'Eurosclerosis'. We, therefore, need to take a longer-term view. In so doing, it is apparent just how much integration has taken place, despite no basic agreement about such fundamental concepts such as federalism and subsidiarity. Somehow, Europe seems to muddle through and to create gradually a rather 'productive' (in the sense of legislative output) policy-making system. Whether one is a Euro-sceptic or Euro-enthusiast, the fact is that there is an enormous corpus of European law. Even without monetary union and the further political integration that it would undoubtedly bring, Europeanization has had a major impact on the policy processes at the national level, on the behaviour of different policy actors, both public and private, and on the institutions of the member states. Even so, it would be silly to argue that national sovereignty has all but gone. The degree of Europeanization varies across sectors, and even in those policy areas where Europeanization has obviously gone very far the member states are still central actors and are deeply embedded in the Euro-level public process. Hence one of the most interesting questions today is how a balance is struck between continued integration and continued national sovereignty. Somehow both trends exist side by side.

In many ways this very broad question lies at the heart of this edited volume, which explores the nature of European public policy itself, the nature of the policy process and the various actors within it, and the possible emergence of a European political agenda. As the editors argue, the convergence of public policies in Europe is leading to 'a kind of co-operative federalism without a state'. Just how this rather odd political animal functions is addressed in the three parts of the volume, discussing the general processes by which Community and national interests can be articulated, the impact of Europeanization on three main national administrations, and the impact that Europeanization can have on domestic policies. Our hope is that the volume will make a significant contribution to our understanding of a key phenomenon reflected in the volume's title – namely how do different types of policy actors *adjust* to Europe?

Jeremy Richardson

Acknowledgements

The editors of this book wish to thank for their help and assistance in producing, translating and editing this book Adrian Favell, François D. Lafond, Julian Lindley-French, Martin Rhodes and Simon Towle. Our gratitude goes also to the staff of the Robert Schuman Centre of the European University Institute in Florence and in particular to Monique Cavallari and Annette Merlan, who were so helpful in the process of making this volume.

1 Introduction

Yves Mény, Pierre Muller and Jean-Louis Quermonne

In current debates about the transformations of the public sphere, public policy has come to take a pivotal role. Public policy is at the heart of the challenges which post-industrial societies now face: of how to make politics, as politics becomes increasingly identified with the craft of making policy and how to combine the conflicting requirements of efficiency and democratic legitimacy? On the one hand, the growing complexity of the problems to be addressed requires greater expertise. On the other, there is pressure from more and more individuals or groups to be involved in the process of decision-making.

From this point of view, the functioning of the institutions of the European Union casts light on a paradox in the domestic politics of its member states. The more public policy develops and diversifies as a means of regulation, the more the gap between society and government – between the citizens and the 'machinery' that implements policies – appears to widen.

The construction of Europe in particular exposes the transformations occurring in the public sphere. The peculiar form of European Community politics is, indeed, the product of specific types of policy-making. One might even suggest that the European Union is the by-product of the policy process in its most 'prosaic form', insulated for a long time from party politics. This raises two main questions, which are the guiding concerns of this volume:

1 Is a European sphere of public policy emerging as part of an embryonic European public sphere? This question can be phrased another way: is there a convergence taking place in the styles, modes of operation and content of public policy in the various member states? Is there, in other words, a 'common market in public policies'?

2 In what way are national policies (in their formula as much as their content) influenced by the policies of the European Union? Or, if some form of convergence can be established, is there a model of public policy

that is used as a reference? Is the policy style which is emerging in the European Union a precursor of the way in which future policies will be made in member states?

PUBLIC POLICIES IN EUROPE: A NEW DIVISION OF LABOUR?

How can unity be created from multiplicity? How can a common will be found from a starting point of different if not divergent interests? The founding fathers of Europe tried to respond to these questions – and these ambitions – by drawing on the most classic repertoire of political action: creating institutions, putting procedures into place and establishing principles of action (the 'four liberties') – all of which were directed predominantly towards the formulation of public policies. But not any kind of policies. As the European Economic Community was not a federal super-state, but a *sui generis* construction, and because it disposed of a budget that was only a tiny fraction of national budgets, the Community was bound to privilege regulatory policies. Using the classic typology of public policies developed by Ted Lowi (which distinguishes between constitutive, regulatory, distributive or redistributive policies), it is clear that regulatory policies constitute the core of EC political action. This choice – or one might say, constraint – is well explained by Giandomenico Majone, who shows how the characteristics of regulatory policies are the best adapted to the structure and properties of the European institutions:

> An important characteristic of regulatory policy making is the limited influence of the budget on the activities of regulators. The size of non-regulatory, direct-expenditure programmes is constrained by budgetary appropriations and, ultimately, by the size of government tax revenues. In contrast, the real costs of most regulatory programmes are borne directly by the firms and the individuals who have to comply with them.[1]

On the other hand, even if redistributive policies have recently become more important, they are still of modest size and are limited to certain sectors (notably agriculture and regional policy).[2] It is significant that, in contrast to the national governments, the social policy of the Community is quite marginal in terms of budgetary allocations, even if its regulatory dimension has a major impact – an influence that has been actively encouraged by some states (France and Germany, for example) but feared or rejected by others (Great Britain). The regulatory option is also strengthened by the juridical and structural weakness of the Community, and now the Union, when it comes to the implementation of the policies elaborated and decided in Brussels.[3] The European institutions may take decisions (or choose not to); but, while they can exert some control, they are prohibited from putting them into action.

This limitation of the room for manoeuvre of Community institutions is sometimes considered a congenital weakness, both because the Community budget appears derisory in comparison with the income and expenditure of each of the member states and because the limited scope for redistributive policies weakens the visibility and the legitimacy of the Parliament, Commission and Council of Ministers. In stark contrast with national *welfare* states, the Community is hardly more than a *regulatory* state. Moreover, the separation of the decision-making process from the process of policy implementation – a separation which has practically no equivalent in national systems of government – is the source of novel difficulties which have been well captured in Fritz Scharpf's discussion of the 'Joint Decision Trap'.[4]

However, before passing final judgement on the restricted nature of Community decisions, it would be useful to consider the full range of implications – both positive and negative – of these budgetary and institutional constraints. At least five consequences can be highlighted:

1   The 'confinement' of Community action to the field of regulatory policies invests the Brussels institutions with a crucial role which is not only substantive but also symbolic. The traditional division of the political process between decision-making and implementation privileges an elite which thinks and decides over and above the indistinct mass of subordinates or civil services: the policy-makers prevail over the implementers. The noble part of political work thus seems to have been elevated to the Commission or the Council of Ministers, to the detriment of the nation states, which, however, are no longer so willing to accept this loss of influence. Whatever the reality, the dominant perception at the national level (both in parliament and in public administration) is that nowadays national institutions are heavily constrained.

2   The exercise of *regulatory power* is made all the more possible by the fact that – in contrast to redistributive policies – it does not encounter budgetary limitations. For regulation hardly costs any more than the spending required for the functioning of the service and the publication of decisions. Regulatory decisions, in essence, are carried by the Official Journals of the EU and other administrative bulletins. From then on, the costs and expenses are externalized on to other actors: national public institutions generally, but above all economic actors and consumers, which have to transform a legal decision into concrete public policy. The examples of this are legion, but one will suffice. When the Community announced a number of norms concerning atmospheric pollution and imposed the catalytic converter on cars to reduce emissions of toxic gases,

it not only externalized the implementation of this policy but imposed all the costs on the car industry and, ultimately, consumers. The budgetary impact on the Community of a policy which convulsed an industry and redistributed benefits and costs among the actors involved was practically nil. This is something which Laura Cram has aptly labelled 'calling the tune without paying the piper'.[5]

3   The fact that regulatory policies are increasingly devised in Brussels profoundly transforms the process of decision-making and, in consequence, the way in which interests are structured. The search for the harmonization of rules within a community of states with disparate traditions and policies is an inexhaustible source of work for the Brussels regulatory machine. But since the legal harmonization of rules has turned out to be almost impossible, the Single Act has taken up the principle of jurisprudence adopted by the Court of Justice in the famous 'cassis de Dijon' case – the principle that any product circulating freely in one of the producing states must be accepted in all the member states. By sweeping away the jungle of protectionist regulation the Court of Justice shifted the onus of regulation at the Community level. The autonomy apparently given back to each national system (each may regulate as it wishes, provided that its rules are not in conflict with the principles and regulations of the Community, and provided that products and services are able to circulate freely) has created such problems for economic agents that they have become the most pro-active lobbyists for European regulation, thereby seeking to remove the uncertainties of fragmented markets or discordant national regulations. Thus the development of regulatory policies is not simply a by-product of bureaucratic expansionism. That said, the flow of regulations from the Commission remains impressive.

4   The central role of the Commission in the development of Community policies (in principle the Commission has a monopoly of the 'supply' side) does not derive exclusively from the institutional arrangements in Brussels. In fact, the pressure of demands for common regulations places it at the centre of the game, strengthens its position and reinforces its legitimacy – at least in the eyes of political elites and groups who see in the Commission a solution to their problems. (This is not to say that there are no costs attached to this 'centrality': notably the risk of being made a scapegoat by groups which lose their niche or their comparative advantage, or by governments only too happy to pass the blame for unpopular policies on to a technocratic authority.)

Community institutions in general, and the Commission in particular, therefore, play the role of a clearing house, where economic, political and social actors and interests converge. Thus European policy-making structures are characterized by a high degree of pluralism (Philippe C.

Schmitter, the theorist of neo-corporatism, is foremost among those who underline this particular trait), involving multiple pressure groups (Brussels-based lobby groups employ almost as many people as the Commission itself), intense and never-ending negotiation, continual interaction between the different national, transnational and – increasingly – local levels of the Community, and a constant search for equitable bargains for each of the member states involved.

This frame of action has challenged many national practices, disturbing not only certain privileged links between economic sectors and their bureaucratic interlocutors but equally traditional modes of national regulation (industrial policies, public services, etc.). Indeed, this complex and often unpredictable game not only upsets the rules. It also introduces new principles and categories ('subsidiarity', 'proportionality', 'good faith', etc.), modifies politico-administrative cultures (for example, the expansion of the role of the judge over that of the technocrat),[6] and sometimes breaks with deep-rooted tradition and practice by dismantling solidly established policy communities. In other words, this regulatory policy-making framework not only creates competition over rule-making between political and economic actors from different states. It also provides an ideal opportunity for actors to seek to impose measures that best suit the interests, practices and habits of the sector or country they represent. The choice of the catalytic converter as an answer to car pollution was not just a technical solution. It also represented the victory of German industry, which was best prepared to respond to the needs of the new market. In addition, negotiations in Brussels offer new opportunities to certain interests otherwise marginalized in national decision-making. Numerous interests (in the field of the environment, for example) are, paradoxically, represented better in Brussels than in their national capitals. Thus, in the never-ending conflict over rules, mastering the processes of Community decision-making becomes essential. Often, the most effective results are achieved through controlling the initial stages of the development of a policy: reports, commissions, and working groups thus become crucial venues for defining the nature of the problem to be addressed and the range of solutions to be favoured. By the time the dossier reaches the political level it is often too late to change course. The choice by that stage is often between acceptance and veto – if the latter is still a viable option.

It is obvious that this strategy has both benefits and costs. The advantages accrue to those leading countries which succeed in convincing the Community institutions and public opinion that their options or solutions are the best: the British, although they are isolated in certain sectors, have displayed great skill at this. Not only is their 'Community professionalism' recognized by everyone, but, what is more, the strategic choices that they have made in the past – privatization, deregulation, the opening of markets, etc. – have begun to appear more attractive to the Eurocrats and to their partners. It has perhaps been too often forgotten that 'policies' are also – and perhaps above all – words and ideas, and, as Majone reminds us, these play a crucial role in the creation of political reality and the decisions that are made. When France, in contrast, looks to protect the interests of Air France or Air Inter as far as it possibly can, it becomes the target of harsh criticism from numerous countries and even more numerous airlines. The idea of a national airline as a public service commitment to air travel is apparently no longer accepted. In this area of policy, France had to renounce the ambition of imposing its convictions upon its partners. To be sure, this is not a one-way game, and each partner can be both leader and follower by turns. But it means that, far from being controlled by a permanently dominant player (in the way that can sometimes happen at the national level), the game is fluid, unstable and often unpredictable.

One of the keys to the fluidity and dynamism of this game can be found in the ways different players use their comparative advantage. The advantage may derive from an effective legal structure, a dominant market position, or a precious national asset. Certain players without abundant resources may then be tempted into competitive deregulation – by having less stringent social regulations, or a greater tolerance of fraud, for example. Thus, Europe may well be affected by what Americans call the 'Delaware effect', after the state which, without any significant resources, was able to attract the headquarters of large American corporations to its jurisdiction. Its favourable conditions have levelled the corporate tax and legal system downwards, forcing other states to more or less align themselves with the lowest common denominator to avoid losing footloose corporations. This danger should not go unrecognized in Europe. Britain's refusal to sign the 'Social Chapter' of the Maastricht Treaty gave rise to the fear of 'social dumping'; tax havens exist even in the heart of the Community (Jersey, Monaco, Luxembourg); and tax systems are sometimes widely divergent, even if the harmonization of VAT and the general extension of the welfare state have eliminated the most glaring differences. However, a downward spiral of competition in Europe is countered by other factors that push for a rise in standards: protection of the environment, for example, has been improved, thanks to pressure from leading countries (Denmark, the Netherlands, Germany). The same goes for consumer protection or the strengthening of customs and norms at the level of the Community. In sum, a downward spiral of competition regulation is not inevitable.

To explain this apparently paradoxical situation, Majone puts forward two complementary interpretations, based on the transaction costs and the level of mistrust. By making the institutions of the Union in general, and the Commission in particular, responsible for the establishment of regulatory policies that may even go beyond those that are strictly necessary for a free market the national governments reduce the transaction costs that might flow from less strict formulations such as those produced by intergovernmental agreements. Distrust between the partners, moreover, explains the propensity of each to turn to the central player, the Commission, the actor most able in their eyes to protect them from the negative costs externalized by the various other players in the game. It is not otherwise possible to explain why so many initiatives come not from the Commission itself but from national governments, the Parliament, the Council of Ministers, or interest groups. The price that is paid for this is complexity: 'Regulatory complexity,' writes Majone, 'is in part another manifestation of the cascading effect of mutual distrust.'[7]

5   Because European policies are the outcome of complex compromises and interactions, and because the Community institutions have no infrastructure at their disposal, the implementation of policies gives back to the national actors a significant margin for manoeuvre. This is not peculiar to the Community. Everywhere, including a formally centralized state such as France, policy-makers are at the mercy of the implementers. The emperor often has no clothes when it comes to implementing his decisions. Except in areas where the administration has no discretionary power (i.e., if such-and-such conditions are found, such a service must be provided), policy-makers must always be conscious of the limitations on their power of intervention. Most policies are immediately reinterpreted and reformulated by the implementers, who, far from being passive, are in fact policy-makers in their own right – albeit at a less visible and more symbolic level.

The problem is even more acute with European policies, where the national actors responsible for implementation may be tempted to claw back at the base what they lost at the summit. The means of pursuing this passive kind of resistance are multiple: delay in the enactment of directives, lax interpretation, intentional or tolerated fraud, the corrupting of the original goals, ill will on the part of the judicial authorities, or even outright refusal to enforce the policy. But if the overall picture is taken into account it is remarkable how much the Community has been able to do in so many different fields, with such limited resources, with so few instruments of control, and without customs officials, policemen or enforcement agencies. The reasons may be found in the growth of institutional rules and the functioning of the market.

The rules that the treaties set up, and the interpretation given to them by the Court, have in effect turned all political actors into potential defenders of Community policies by offering them a means of recourse against the slowness and inaction of national public authorities. Although it is certainly not the case that each of the 300 million European citizens is a litigant in the making, all that is needed are a few committed legal applicants, well informed interest groups and some economic actors capable of taking on the costs of long court cases, in order to launch a challenge against the inaction or ill will of member states. In the short term Community policies are often badly applied; in the long term the changes that have been made are impressive.[8]

The functioning of the market also assists the application of Community policies, despite certain isolated cases of reluctance or resistance here and there. There is no need here to labour this point, so numerous are the examples: rules concerning the packaging of margarine, the uniform price of petrol, access for foreign airlines to French airports, the sale of foreign beer in Germany, or of sterilized milk in Great Britain, etc.

In short, not only is the European imprint ever stronger at the level of policy construction; it is also beginning to show in the implementation of policies, despite the obstacles. This situation is, moreover, destabilizing and innovative: it undoes the structure of old coalitions of interest and traditional circuits of decision-making; at the same time it creates new conditions, dealing new cards, and forcing changes and adaptation. Until the last few years, this evolution remained largely invisible. But now its consequences are appearing ever more clearly, because, according to certain analysts, the changes are profoundly altering the behaviour of public policy actors. These analysts are particularly alert to the fact that no domain of public policy can any longer be isolated from the European process, which has become an obligatory channel of influence for civil servants, political actors or representatives of interest groups. This is what one might call, in the words of Svein Andersen and Kjell Eliassen, the 'Europeanization' of public policies.[9]

Of course, this convergence of policies does not entail harmonization, but rather the progressive emergence of a bundle of common norms of action, the evolution of which escapes the control of any particular member state and yet decisively influences the behaviour of public policy actors. This creates a permanent challenge to national political systems, which are forced to adapt to a normative and strategic environment that they have as yet only partially mastered.

Indications that such a process of convergence is in progress can be found at three levels. In the first place, a transformation of the process of public policy agenda-setting can be observed, with the emergence of a

European political agenda. The second point of convergence can be found in *the forms of interest representation*, with the corporatist system of representation threatened by more open and competitive modes of representation. Finally, a spectacular convergence *of the modes of operation* of various actors involved in public decision-making should be noted.

THE EMERGENCE OF A EUROPEAN POLITICAL AGENDA

The emergence of a European political agenda is the most obvious development and one that is stressed by the greatest number of observers. Here it is covered by the chapters devoted to industrial and competition policies. Until recently, national public policy actors (politicians, civil servants, interest groups) more or less dominated the formulation of public policy issues. It was at the national level that each country defined the problems it faced and the way in which they were approached. It is now evident that, in an ever growing number of sectors, the process of problem definition has shifted, to a greater or lesser extent, to the European level. As a consequence, it is in the proceedings of the Union's official institutions that the terms and conditions of public intervention will be formulated in future.

This change became apparent early on in the field of agriculture and the upheavals created by the reform of the common agricultural policy. During the 1980s the pace at which new problems were added on to the political agenda (the struggle against overproduction, or consideration of the environmental impact of certain forms of modern agriculture) progressively began to escape strictly national-level actors. It has been well noted how, during the long and difficult negotiations over the reform of the CAP, the French Minister of Agriculture, as well as the professional organizations in the sector, was constantly put on the defensive by the Commission's proposals for reform.[10]

The case of environmental policy is similar, although, unlike agriculture, this sector did not figure among the initial responsibilities of the Community. Well before the signing of the Single Act, which officially conferred authority in this matter to Europe, a series of directives systematically mapped out the landscape of environment policies affecting the transport of dangerous materials, the quality of air and water, and so on.[11] 'European norms' thus became an obligatory reference for national policy-makers, as well as a strategic resource for environmental actors. The 'European' nature of the norms allows them to supersede internal national debates and gives them a *sui generis* dimension. Other policy sectors are also influenced by the process of enlarging the Community agenda on environmental issues. In this way, intervention by the Commission to impose the use of catalytic converters constrained the car industry to seriously modify its strategy.[12]

More generally, all the policies connected, at close or long range, with the creation of a single market are also affected. Via a 'spill over' effect, the recognition by the member states of this macro-objective is accompanied by *de facto* acceptance – if not always with good grace – of the capacity of the European authorities to add a multitude of related problems to the agenda. The most spectacular case has been that of competition policies, which have enjoyed a veritable renaissance during the 1980s. At first sceptical, the member states soon had to take account of the activism of the Commission, in monitoring mergers and alliances[13] as much as in scrutinizing state intervention with public aid.[14] Other sectors have been equally affected by the extension of the Community agenda (e.g. regional policy, telecommunications, etc.).

In a general way, public action concerning industry is increasingly defined at the European level and it has become obvious, for most actors involved, that industrial policy must be shaped in Brussels. Should a system of indirect aid be developed, along the lines of US government intervention, in support of certain sectors such as aerospace? To what extent must aid be sector-specific? The debate continues, not only between different national approaches, but also between DG III (Industry) and DG IV (Competition). In the end, with the entry into force of the Maastricht treaty, even the policies that are the prerogative, the hard-core functions, of the nation state – such as immigration – have begun to be influenced, and not only by the intergovernmental Schengen agreement. Two observations can be made on this point.

1   Although the process has been under way for some time, the broadening of the Community policy agenda has drastically accelerated since the publication of the 'White Paper' on the completion of the internal market and the Single Act; and one cannot but admire, with Giandomenico Majone, the subtlety of this 'domino effect' which has extended Community prerogatives in the name of a great, neo-liberal-inspired, free market.[15] From a rather different perspective, Andrew Moravcsik has now effectively demonstrated that the extension of the internal market has been linked with the extension of majority voting in the Council of Ministers.[16]

2   This extension of the Community agenda, and the transfer to the European level of agenda-setting, does not mean, however, that there is a consensus on how problems should be dealt with. This is hardly the case at the level of the nation state, let alone at that of the Community. Yet it is also clear that Europe is ever more the site of debate, the place where

issues are formulated, where different interpretations confront one another, and where different actors engage in conflict or negotiation and where solutions are defined. It is increasingly evident that Europe shapes the intellectual and normative framework of public policy. This overall frame of reference is structured around two fundamental norms, which go well beyond their immediate significance, and define the overall conception of public policy-making. These are the norms of the market (partially offset by social policies) and the norm of subsidiarity which, little by little – but not without conflict – is penetrating national systems of public policy.[17]

It remains to be seen how agenda-setting in the Community works. The literature on this question reveals its highly competitive nature. Whilst, at the national level, an actor or coalition of actors may hope to reduce access to political agenda-setting, it is much more difficult to imagine this at the Community level, given the diversity of the interested parties and the fluidity of the mechanisms of negotiation.

As a result, agenda-setting at the European level is a much more risky and uncertain process than at the national level: it is never known exactly which issue is going to emerge, or who will bring it up and how,[18] even if, formally, the Commission takes the initiative in formulating the policies, which are then submitted to the Council of Ministers for approval in liaison with the European Parliament.[19]

This situation is one that creates openings but also uncertainty for the various players. They must in some way be permanently on guard in order to not be caught napping by the sudden appearance of a new project that they 'didn't see coming'. The current evolution of the decision-making system of the Community, which reinforces the political role of the Council of Ministers to the detriment of the Commission and allows a genuine right of amendment to the European Parliament, will extend this dual character of openness and uncertainty, by multiplying the points of access to the Community agenda.

Given these developments in European policy-making, what is occurring at the national level? This question takes us on to the second point of convergence noted above.

A NEW SPACE FOR THE REPRESENTATION OF INTERESTS

This second form of convergence is related to the modes of interest organization. Here again the 1980s were a turning point in the way in which an entirely new and separate forum of representation emerged, as seen in the growth of the number of lobbyists in Brussels, estimated in 1992 at several thousand.[20] This development is clearly linked with the transformation of the European political agenda: quite apart from attempting to influence policy-making directly, it would be impossible today for interest groups to remain ignorant of Community decisions and initiatives.

Despite this, 'Euro-groups' have not replaced national interest groups, which, increasingly, integrate the European dimension into their strategies and seek to make themselves felt at all levels of the decision-making process.[21] Even traditionally active groups like COPA (the farmers' organization) or UNICE (the employers' organization) have not fully replaced their national affiliates within the European institutions. National identities have not been erased: far from it, when compared with European sectoral identities, which remain largely inchoate. This fact is underlined, for example, by the persisting conflicts between British and French farmers, or the divergence of interests between car makers in the north of Europe and those in the south.

All the same, it does not mean that Euro-groups have no role to play. To a certain extent they contribute, often with difficulty, to reconciling the differences between national approaches when faced with proposals emanating from the Commission. However, their principal role is to provide information to their national affiliates. Experience shows that, particularly for the 'heavy' players such as big business, it is more effective to use several simultaneous channels of action: a presence within the union or professional organization at the European level, lobbying by a permanent representative at Brussels, and intervention via the inter-mediary of national administrations, which the actor will try to persuade to share the same point of view on the discussions under way.[22] This has three important consequences.

1   As Philippe Schmitter shows, the form of interest organization that prevails at the level of the Union is more indicative of a pluralist than of a corporatist logic.[23] The relations that are established between these groups and the institutions of the European Union – and particularly with the Commission through its network of committees – are less stable, more open, but also more competitive and uncertain than forms of representation at the national level. This observation is congruent with what has previously been said about the political agenda.

2   It is difficult to define these forms of Community representation and organization. The concept of networks has been suggested as a tool. But the concept of a *policy network*, like the concepts associated with it (policy community, issue network, epistemic community . . .), while stimulating, is also debatable. The reality is that this is a new game the rules of which are not yet fully written.[24]

3   The third question raises the question of convergence: are we witnessing a kind of 'contamination' of modes of interest representation at

the national level by the forms of representation more typical of the European level? There is an observable opening up of the game, in which actors are now able to use the European level either to bypass the national system of representation or to mobilize supplementary resources. It is certain that actors which are able to diversify their levels of intervention, and which can anticipate changes in the Community agenda, increase their playing power in the national negotiations quite spectacularly. The ecologists, but also firms such as the French subsidiary of British Airways, TAT, in its struggle against the national company Air Inter, are good cases in point.

But is a progressive transformation of the national rules of the game via imitation of the 'Community method' likely to occur? While, for the moment, different national forms of representation are not under threat, it is clear that the development of more competitive and open forms of representation in the Community is tending little by little to change the rules of the game at two key levels: between the state and interest groups and in both national and intergovernmental negotiations.

NEW MODES OF DECISION-MAKING

From this, a third dimension of convergence emerges which is inseparable from the others: convergence in the operational modes of decision-making processes[25] and, further, in the ways in which governments act and in conceptions of state/society relationships. At the European level, the decision-making process is characterized by several specific elements.

1 It is characterized by *uncertainty*, due to the absence of stable forms of leadership.[26] According to the sector and the particular moment in time, the configuration of the system of actors may vary, restructuring itself in terms of alliances and modes of governance. Beyond the institutional aspects linked with new forms of co-operation between the three principal actors (the Commission and its network of committees, the Council of Ministers, COREPER and the Parliament), it is the absence of any leadership in the decision-making process which is most striking. Given the collegiate organization of the Commission, the ambiguous status of the Council of Ministers – which is both an organ of political co-operation and a legislative authority – and the role of the European Parliament in influencing decisions, rather than making them, it is very difficult to establish the exact locus of Community power. It is clearly more a system based on compromise than a traditional nation state form of decision-making.

At times it will be the influence of the President of the Commission or of a commissioner that is dominant; at others, the key role in decision-making will be played by a member state, or a coalition of member states.

Here, as elsewhere, complexity and uncertainty go hand in hand. The Community system may thus be described as a system of decision-making with variable geometry, in which the position of different actors changes according to the process in question or the issues at hand. One might even suggest that this system of decision-making provides a good example of James March's 'garbage can' model.[27]

2   Then there is the *openness* of the process, linked with the fact that access to the circles of decision-making is generally easier than at the national level.[28] Even if it is no longer appropriate to describe it as a 'lightweight' administration, the Commission has not turned itself into a governmental bureaucracy of the traditional type. The key point here is expertise. Whilst national administrations tend to have a monopoly of the legitimate expertise that may be called upon – even if the monopoly is often shared with a world of professional interests – the Commission seeks to master such expertise by multiplying formal and informal contacts with the various partners in its orbit. And the Commission is not the only institution doing this, given that the number of committees of experts – who nowadays prepare the work of the Council under the auspices of COREPER – is greater than the number of working groups which gravitate around the Commission itself.

3   The *opacity* of the process, to the extent that, paradoxically, the functioning of the system seems less readable the more open it becomes.[29] This can be explained by the fact that the rules of the game are not yet stabilized – which encourages openness – and often appear to be fluid and 'unspoken'.

This paradox of Community decision-making, at once open and opaque, derives from the fact that the construction of European policies is an infinitely more complicated process than policy-making at the national level, because the acceptability and legitimacy of the norms decided on are constantly being questioned. To rely on internal expertise is thus practically inconceivable, without running the considerable risk that the decision will be rejected or, quite simply, not applied in practice. On the contrary, the network of committees that exists enables the integration of a multitude of public and private partners at every stage of decision-making, including those who will be given the responsibility, at a later stage, of implementing the policies at the member-state level.

The more or less informal creation of a cast of actors with access to decision-making takes place through this process, a cast whose selection is based on poorly known, or even obscure, criteria. It seems that the process of seeking and counter-posing different types of expert advice works like a mechanism for selecting an elite that is both politico-administrative and drawn from 'civil society' (with representatives of different lobbies, professional or otherwise). It creates a universe of more or less stable networks based on certain conflictual or co-operative relationships. This universe of networks has its own language, its own codes and modes of operation, creating a *de facto* barrier to 'outsiders'.[30] This is the root of the paradox: since the rules are less precise, the system is more open, and easier to penetrate, than bureaucratic, corporatist national systems. But as the rules of the game are not formalized, all kinds of co-optation, indeed all kinds of coalition, would appear to be possible.

But are traditional modes of decision-making at the national level, based on a stable interface between the administration and representatives of well defined sectors, giving way to more complex, more competitive, and therefore more unstable, forms of exchange? Indeed, the success of 'partnership'-based forms of action, both at the national level and in the strategies of local communities, suggests that they are. This is most evident within Community programmes. When, for example, the EURO-FORM programme was set in motion by the French Minister of Agriculture, the way in which 'local teams' were selected as partners for the programme differed appreciably from traditional means of doing so, which usually involves a monopoly of representation by professional agricultural organizations. Although more open in certain respects – since these programmes are not reserved for official 'organizations' – the way in which the selection process took place was also relatively opaque, the criteria of choice remaining for the main part informal.

Undoubtedly, the same could be said about the procedures involved in the LEADER programme. This set about targeting the rural actors by creating 'local action groups' of political and socio-professional representatives, but largely bypassed the traditional circles in charge of national and regional development. The same holds for the BRITE EURAM programme, which made companies eligible for aid which did not have access to support via existing national channels.

Although still limited, this convergence in the operational modes of public intervention and forms of interest representation has important implications. It does not mean that the styles of public policy particular to each member state are going to disappear, any more than conflicts of interest or divergent points of view. But it is something more than a conjectural development; indeed, it amounts to the emergence of a common sphere of mediation at the European level.

FROM PUBLIC SPHERE TO POLITICAL SYSTEM

Several questions are raised by the claim that convergence is occurring in the sphere of European public policies. Here, two will be mentioned in particular. The first directly concerns the comparative study of national and Community policies. Can it be said, beyond the fact of convergence, that a genuinely European sphere of public policy is beginning to form? The second extends the subject from 'policies' to 'politics' proper and asks whether we are witnessing the emergence of a distinctly European political model.

Comparative analyses, taking as their model the classic federal state, are unable to come to terms with the European system. Where one might expect to find two public spheres superimposed on one another, there is a very blurred picture in which the two levels of public policy are instead entangled and indistinct. This entanglement has diminished the space reserved for powers that are exclusive either to the Community or to the member states, and has expanded the domain in which the two exercise their powers concurrently.

Consequently, if such a thing exists, the European public sphere must be seen first and foremost as an economic space. And, in so far as that space is politicized, it resembles not a new planet as such but a nebula that is still partly in fusion. The difficulty of characterizing this new entity can be accounted for by two of its particular traits. The first concerns the fact that the Community's field of action does not follow the clear rules concerning the separation of powers that characterize a classic federal state. Indeed, the Community's zone of influence is defined by the process of 'spill over' and the principle of subsidiarity. And while no sector of public policy is impervious (at the level of the state) to the influence of European processes, no bundle of common European policies is able to mark itself off as an 'exclusive concern' of the Community, even in sectors as highly Europeanized as agriculture, competition or external trade.

The second trait is a result of the extreme complexity of Community decicion-making. The multiple forms of expertise involved tend to overwhelm the representation of interests. And the absence of a separation of powers within the 'triangle of institutions' ensures more room, as has been noted, for the search for compromise over the exercise of powers of arbitration.[31] As Marc Abélès has stressed,

> when they are put in European terms, problems are often more difficult to resolve than when they are posed within a national context. At the European level they involve a far greater number of parameters and resist being reduced to Manichaean terms to please this or that electorate. In this sense, compromise becomes an essential element of political practice.[32]

As a result, the standard methods of institutional analysis appear ill adapted to the mapping out of a nascent European public sphere. And one of the central lessons of this volume is the need, therefore, to fall back on something else, preferably the 'toolbox' of public policy research.

The application of public policy methods of analysis to Europe tends to verify the still embryonic nature of the European public sphere, and reveals it to be a far from unified political power. In other words, the convergence of public policies in Europe and their tight interweaving are, in the absence of an arbitrating voice at the summit, leading to a kind of co-operative federalism without a state. Yet this co-operative federalism finds its roots, not in the American model, but in the political practice of continental European states. For some time now it has been visibly reminiscent of Switzerland, Germany or Belgium;[33] it even appears today in the decentralized political practice of certain nation states. To use Habermas's definition in this context, the presence and the influence of the citizen – if not his or her participation in the process of decision-making – is indeed making itself increasingly felt,[34] and the Union may yet still become a political sphere with a greater degree of legitimacy.

But is this observation sufficient for us to pass without pause from the study of public policy to that of actual political power? Does the recognition of convergence in public policy in Europe suggest the emergence as such of a European political model?[35] On this point it is wise to remain sceptical.

As regards the content of policies, it is true that the recognition of a global European reference point may indeed facilitate a common political culture. Yet there is strong national resistance in numerous sectors to the harmonization of member-state policies. In order to obstruct or delay this process, these member states invoke their own national specificity: the importance of the public sector in France or Italy, the resistance of the British Conservatives to a single currency, or, indeed, the compromise, endorsed by the Commission, giving preference to the mutual recognition of legislation over the harmonization of policies.

On the other hand, as regards the process of decision-making, the implementation of the Treaty of Rome initiated a 'specific Community method',[36] recognizable by its three principal components: the Commission's monopoly on proposing legislation, the Council of Ministers' powers of decision-making, and the consultation procedure of Parliament. And after 1987 the implementation of the Single Act and preparations for the single market witnessed the triumph of this method, strengthening the use of qualified majority voting within the Council and then conferring the power of amendment on the Parliament. This was so successful at the time that it was possible to see a complete system of networks emerging through the way in which the method functioned.

However, it would seem that, by reinforcing intergovernmental procedures and provoking a Euro-scepticism that has denounced its technocratic nature, the Maastricht Treaty has destroyed the credibility of this method. In any case, at a time when priority is being given to the enlargement of the Union, first to EFTA member states, then later to the countries of central and eastern Europe, it is by no means certain that the 'Community method' can remain intact. Moreover, originally conceived for a union of six countries, it was difficult even to adapt to a Europe of twelve; and hence, it is highly likely that in a Union of fifteen, then twenty, and perhaps even thirty states, it would soon reach the limit of its practicality. But what could replace it?

In present circumstances, the concepts put forward by certain contributors to this volume provide only provisional paths for reflection, whether it be the notion of 'organized anarchy' borrowed from James March, the idea of the 'condominio' (Philippe Schmitter), or the reference to automatic regulation (Elie Cohen). The members of the intergovern- mental conference planned for 1996 under the Maastricht Treaty will therefore need to show some powers of innovation: unless they simply extend the Community method – as has already been done in the enlargement of the Union to fifteen – or allow Europe to become a mere free-trade zone, it is difficult to see how they will manage without drawing on the source of inspiration provided by the federalist model.

It is evident that there is no longer any question of transposing the precedent of the USA, as envisaged by the founding fathers of Europe at the beginning of the 1950s. The disparate cultural paths of the two continents are too far apart to allow parallel political development based on the model of a federal state. Despite this, thanks to the entanglement of public policies in Europe and the base provided by integrated economies, one can discern the emergence of co-operative federalism without a state. And whatever the prejudices that a certain, often ill informed, political class has about the idea of federalism, the European version is highly original, and that should allow the European Union to remain distinctive.[37]

There remains the most difficult problem for a Union aiming to extend to around thirty member states: to find institutions capable of functioning within a framework whose geometry is ever-changing. The exemptions that have been allowed to Great Britain and Denmark at Maastricht give only the haziest idea of what this may entail. And the reconciliation of the existence of a 'hard core'[38] of members at the heart of Europe with a less integrated periphery almost amounts to squaring the circle. On the other hand, it can be taken as given that any remotely realistic European political model will have to allow an important role to the national governments. Consequently, any 'constitution' of the European Union must recognize their power of choice, as much at the head of the executive (as the increasing interventionism of the European Council seems to forebode, and as the creation of a European Security Council may well illustrate) as within the legislature (as must be the case if the Council of Ministers evolves towards the kind of status enjoyed by the German Bundesrat). The advent of a full-time presidency of the European Council, besides, ought to reinforce this tendency, especially if it is one day to be combined with the presidency of the Commission.

Formalized in this way, such a model, which incorporates a strong dose of intergovernmentalism, would clearly be distinct from the federal model of the USA. Other elements, which underline the specificities of the European case, may well contribute to the overall balance of the model: for example, the formation of an interparliamentary network linking action by national parliaments with that of the European Parliament, or indeed the emergence of independent regulatory agencies such as the future central bank. As for the future of the European Union as an overall political system, it is directly related to the capacity that states will or will not have to overcome the syndrome of Euro-scepticism. And the emergence of such a system may be obstructed, or permanently delayed, if it is forced to slide towards the lowest common denominator that the idea of a zone of free exchange would represent.

If, on the contrary, the European Union succeeds in finding the path towards a custom-built political model, Community policies, by attaining the status of full public policies in their own right – that is, by linking control of implementation with the power of regulation – will thereby achieve the requisite convergence with policies at the national level. This would be the stage at which genuine coherence is attained, fulfilling the ambitions of the policy of economic and social cohesion launched by the Commission under Jacques Delors. At that moment, to add a strictly methodological point, approaching the construction of Europe via the study of public policies will have found its full vindication.[39]

It remains true, however, that the European institutions will be increasingly confronted with a singularly difficult challenge: that of achieving legitimacy. In democratic states, governments base their legitimacy on elections and redistributive policies. At the moment, these two political and financial resources are not fully developed, jeopardizing the stability and the progress of the European project as well as being detrimental to public opinion. European public policy has been and remains an exclusively elite affair. The masses have yet to be included: in other words, we still await the creation of truly public sphere, capable of uniting democracy with governability.[40]

ACKNOWLEDGEMENT

This introduction was translated by Adrian Favell.

NOTES

1 G. Majone, 'Cross-National Sources of Regulatory Policy-making in Europe and the United States', *Journal of Public Policy*, 1991, vol. 11, 1, p. 96.
2 The importance of these policies has grown in relative terms down the years, to the point where structural policies, which represented 17 per cent of the Community budget in 1988, will represent 33 per cent in 1999 if the 'Delors Package II' is applied. Cf. Jean-Charles Leygues, *Les Politiques internes de l'Union européenne*, Paris, LGDJ, 1994, p. 57. All the same, the Community budget remains limited in comparison with national budgets. It represents 'less than 1.3 per cent of the Gross Domestic Product of the Union, or about 4 per cent of the combined expenditures of the central governments of the member states'.
3 On the development of and the paradoxes involved in these regulatory policies, see G. Majone, 'The Development of Social Regulation in the European Community: Policy Externalities, Transaction Costs, Motivational Factors', *Aussenwirtschaft*, 1995, vol. 50, I, pp. 79–110.
4 Fritz W. Scharpf, 'The Joint Decision Trap: Lessons from German Federalism and European Integration', *Public Administration*, 1988, vol. 66, pp. 239–78.
5 L. Cram, 'Calling the Tune without paying the Piper? Social Policy Regulation: the Role of Community Social Policy', *Policy and Politics*, 1993, vol. 21, 2, pp. 135–46.
6 Henri Oberdorff, 'Des incidences de l'Union européenne et des Communautés européennes sur le système administratif français', *Revue de droit public*, 1995, vol. 1, p. 25; Jacques Ziller, *Administrations comparées: les systèmes politico-administratifs de l'Europe des Douze*, Paris, Montchrestien, 1993.
7 G. Majone, 'Cross-national Sources of Regulatory Policy-making', p. 89.
8 Renaud Dehousse, *La Cour de Justice des Communautés Européennes*, Paris, Montchrestien, 1994, coll. Clefs.
9 Svein S. Andersen and Kjell A. Eliassen, 'The EC as a New Political System', in *Making Policy in Europe: the Europeification of National Policy-making*, London, Sage, 1993.
10 François-Gilles Le Theule and David Litvan, 'La réforme de la PAC: analyse d'une négociation communautaire', *Revue française de science politique*, Octobre 1993, vol. 43, 5, pp. 755–87.
11 David Vogel, 'The Making of EC Environmental Policy', in Svein S. Andersen and Kjell A. Eliassen, *Making Policy in Europe*, p. 124.
12 Andrew McLaughlin and Jordan Grant, 'The Rationality of Lobbying in Europe: Why are Euro-groups so Numerous and so Weak? Some Evidence from the Car Industry', in Sonia Mazey and Jeremy J. Richardson (eds), *Lobbying in the European Community*, Oxford, Oxford University Press, 1993.
13 Hervé Dumez and Alain Jeunemaître, *La Concurrence en Europe*, Paris, Seuil, 1991.
14 On this point see Chapter 9 by G. Amato.
15 Giandomenico Majone, 'Déréglementation ou re-réglementation? La conduite des politiques publiques dans la Communauté européenne depuis l'Acte

unique', in Bruno Jobert (ed.), *Le Tournant néo-libéral en Europe*, Paris, l'Harmattan, 1994.

16 Andrew Moravcsik, 'Negotiating the Single European Act', in Robert O. Keohane and Stanley Hoffmann (eds), *The New European Community: Decision-making and Institutional Change*, Boulder, Westview Press, 1991.

17 Pierre Muller, 'Entre le local et l'Europe. La crise du modèle français de politiques publiques', *Revue française de science politique*, April 1992, vol. 42, 2, pp. 275–97.

18 Sonia Mazey and Jeremy J. Richardson, 'Transference of Power, Decision Rules and Rules of the Game', in *Lobbying in the European Community*, p. 19.

19 Andy Smith, 'La Commission européenne au travail: missions, méthodes et sens du jeu', contribution to the study workshop *Premières approches de l'émergence d'un milieu politico-administratif européen*, Grenoble, Institut d'études politiques, 19 December 1993.

20 Svein S. Andersen and Kjell A. Eliassen, 'Complex Policy-making: Lobbying in the EC', in *Making Policy in Europe*, pp. 38–9.

21 Wyn Grant, 'Pressure Groups and the European Community: an Overview', in Sonia Mazey and Jeremy J. Richardson, *Lobbying in the European Community*.

22 David Spence, 'The Role of the National Civil Service in European Lobbying: the British Case', in Sonia Mazey and Jeremy J. Richardson, *Lobbying in the European Community*, p. 48.

23 Philippe C. Schmitter, 'Representation and the Future Euro-polity', *Staatswissenschaften und Staatspraxis*, March 1992, vol. 2, pp. 379–405.

24 See Patrick Le Galès and Mark Thatcher (eds), *Les Réseaux de politique publique*, Paris, L'Harmattan, 1995.

25 Jean-Louis Quermonne, *Le Système politique de l'Union européenne*, Paris, Montchrestien, 1994, 2nd edition, coll. Clefs.

26 Christian Lesquesne, *Paris–Bruxelles: comment se fait la politique européenne de la France*, Paris, Presses de la FNSP, 1994.

27 Michael D. Cohen, James D. March and John P. Olsen, 'A Garbage Can Model of Organizational Choice', *Administrative Science Quarterly*, 1972, vol. 17, pp. 1–25.

28 Svein S. Andersen and Kjell A. Eliassen, 'Policy-making and the Institutions in the EC', in *Making Policy in Europe*, p. 19.

29 Martin Donnelly, 'The Structure of the European Commission and the Policy Formation Process', in Sonia Mazey and Jeremy J. Richardson, *Lobbying in the European Community*, p. 74.

30 Concerning the telecommunications sector, see Godefroy Dang-Nguyen, Volker Schneider and Raymund Werle, 'Networks in European Policy-making: Europeification of Telecommunications policy', in S. S. Andersen and K. A. Eliassen, *Making Policy in Europe*.

31 Pascal Lamy, 'Choses vues d'Europe', *Esprit*, October 1991, p. 67.

32 Marc Abélès, 'A la recherche d'un espace public européen', *Pouvoirs*, April 1994, vol. 69, p. 125.

33 Maurice Croisat, 'Le fédéralisme d'aujourd'hui: tendances et controverses', *Revue française de droit constitutionnel*, 1994, vol. 34, pp. 451–64.

34 Jürgen Habermas, *L'Espace public*, with a previously unpublished preface by the author, Paris, Payot, 1993.

35 Jean-Louis Quermonne, 'Existe-t-il un modèle politique européen?', *Revue française de science politique*, April 1990, vol. 40, 2, pp. 192–211.

36 Jean-Louis Quermonne, *Le Système politique de l'Union européenne.*
37 Ibid.
38 Claus-Dieter Ehlermann, 'Increased Differentiation or Stronger Uniformity?'
     Working paper, Robert Schuman Centre series, European University Institute,
     1995.
39 Giandomenico Majone, *L'Europe, un Etat régulateur?* Paris, Montchrestien,
     1995, coll. Clefs.
40 Simon J. Bulmer, 'The Governance of the European Union: a New
     Institutionalist Approach', *Journal of Public Policy*, 1993, vol. 13, 4,
     pp. 351–80.

Part I

Articulating the Community and national interests

2 Some alternative futures for the European polity and their implications for European public policy

Philippe C. Schmitter

Before one can even speculate about what public policies are likely to emerge at the level of Europe, or how they are likely to be processed and implemented, one must have an inkling about what kind of polity the European Community/Union is going to become. No one doubts that the EC/EU will be the dominant political institution at the supranational level in the future – especially with virtually every European country trying to become a member – but what will 'it' be? How closely will it resemble the forms of political combination that we are used to dealing with, i.e. the nation state and the international organization? Or, will it be something significantly different, something that will rely upon an unprecedented format of stable governance and legitimate authority?

THE EMERGENCE OF NOVELTY

The guiding theme of this chapter is that the formation of Europe will *not* be a 're-run' of the processes and policies that earlier made the nation state the predominant political institution of Europe – and, subsequently, the world. Nor can it be confined to the status of a 'confederation' or a 'regional intergovernmental organization', even one of unprecedented scope and powers. The EC/EU is well on its way to becoming something new – and that should have major implications for both the actors and the processes of policy-making at all levels: supranational, national and sub-national.

One of the greatest weaknesses of contemporary political science is that its vocabulary is thoroughly contaminated by the (usually implicit) assumption that, whatever the actors or the actions, they are taking place within the confines of a sovereign nation state or of an interstate system formed by such units. It seems self-evident to most observers that for the foreseeable future this particular form of political life will continue to dominate all others, spend most publicly generated funds, allocate most resources, enjoy a unique legitimacy and furnish most people with a distinct and overriding identity. However, we may recognize that the sovereign nation state is under assault from a variety of directions – within and beyond its borders – its 'considerable resilience' has been repeatedly demonstrated and seems to be indelibly entrenched in the ways that we think about politics.[1]

But what if the probable outcome were not the outright demise of the state's peculiar brand of 'high politics' and its replacement by the 'higher politics' of a new sovereign supranational Euro-state? What if something qualitatively different were evolving that would blur the distinction between 'high' and 'low' politics and eventually produce a new form of multi-layered governance without clear lines of demarcated jurisdiction and identity?

Try just to imagine a polity that did not have the following: (1) a locus of clearly defined, unchallengeable supreme authority; (2) an established, central hierarchy of public offices; (3) a defined and distinct sphere of competence within which it could make decisions that were binding on all; (4) a fixed and continuous territory over which it exercised authority; (5) exclusive recognition by other polities, membership of international organizations and the capacity to conclude international treaties; (6) an overarching identity and symbolic presence for its subjects/citizens; (7) an established and effective monopoly over the legitimate means of coercion; (8) a unique capacity to impose its decisions directly upon intended individuals and groups; and (9) the sole power to control the movement of goods, services, capital and persons within its borders – but which *did* have the capability to take decisions, resolve conflicts, produce public goods, co-ordinate private behaviour, regulate markets, hold elections, respond to interest pressures, generate revenue, allocate expenditure and even to declare and wage war! If you could do all this, you would have succeeded in at least mentally superseding the limits imposed by the nation state upon habitual ways of thinking about politics and would have begun to glimpse the emerging properties of the EC/EU, although it might still be difficult to imagine how such a 'post-national, unsovereign, polycentric, non-coterminous, neo-medieval' arrangement could possibly be stable in the longer run.

THE ABSENCE OF CONGRUENCE

But how can we be sure what these emergent properties are? And what should we call them? Admittedly, the Treaty of Rome, the Single European Act and the subsequent Maastricht Accord – the major founding documents of the emerging Euro-polity – are not much help. Unlike the constitutions of nation states, they do not commit their members to a consistent and certainly not a definitive institutional design. However, if we combine their dispositions with other, less formal, arrangements that have been literally written into the integration process from the start, we may be able to glimpse what this unprecedented (and perhaps unwanted) form of political domination will look like.

Its core lies in *the growing dissociation between authoritative allocations, territorial constituencies and functional competences.* In the classic model of the state (but not invariably in their praxis), the exercise of public authority in different functional domains is coincident or congruent with a specific and unique territory.[2] When one arrives at its physical borders, the legitimate exercise of coercion in all these domains ends. The polity on the other side has, in principle, no right to command obedience in any domain on one's own side – and there probably exists no superordinate entity exercising authority over both sides.

But what if either the functional or the territorial domains (and even more if both) were not congruent with the same, singular authority? What if there were a plurality of polities at different levels of aggregation – national, sub-national and supranational – that overlapped in a given domain? Moreover, what if these authorities did not have exclusive functions or well established hierarchical relations, but negotiated with each other in some continuous way to perform common tasks and resolve common problems across several domains? What, in other words, if there were no sovereignty, no definitive centre for the resolution of conflicts or the allocation of public goods – just a process? And what if the participants in this process were not just a fixed number of nation states, but an enormous variety of sub-national units and networks, supranational associations and movements and transnational firms and parties?

THE NEED FOR A NEW LEXICON

We need a whole new political vocabulary in order to label such developments – initially, at the level of discrete and novel arrangements as they emerge in the on-going practice of EC/EU institutions and, eventually, at the level of general configurations of authoritative decision-making and policy implementation once they begin to form a relatively stable polity.

The first need is already being fulfilled on a daily basis by 'Euro-speak', the *Volapuk intégré* that is constantly being invented to describe *ad hoc* or *de jure* solutions to Community problems. Originally, these expressions had a distinctively neo-functionalist cast, e.g. *l'engrenage, le 'spill-over', la méthode communautaire, l'acquis communautaire* and *la supranationalité*, but recently they have increased greatly in number and seem to be emanating more and more from European jurisprudence or treaty provisions, e.g. 'subsidiarity', 'proportionality', 'additivity', 'complementarity', *transparence, compétences*, 'direct effect', 'unanimity', 'qualified majority', 'co-responsibility', 'transposition', *géometrie variable, juste retour*, 'mutual recognition', 'home-country control', 'co-decision', 'pooled sovereignty', 'opting out', 'opting in', 'economic and social cohesion', 'sustainable convergence', 'Euro-compatibility', 'balanced support', and so forth. There are even a few terms which seek to describe the process of integration as a whole and/or its eventual outcome, e.g. *comotilogie*, the way in which Commission drafts are subjected to an extensive exchange of views among national administrators, interest representatives and Eurocrats until a consensus is reached and a policy proposal put forth; *troika*, the system of collective executive power through which the President of the Council of Ministers during the six-month term in office of his/her country is associated with the preceding and succeeding presidents; 'concentric circles', the assumption that all institutional developments within the EC/EU revolve around a single administrative core, i.e. the Commission in Brussels, and eventually leads to accretions of its *compétences*.

My hunch is that the second need, i.e. for labels to identify the general configuration of authority that is emerging, can be fulfilled by simply aggregating inductively items from Euro-speak as they are invented and take hold. These may provide valuable hints about particular properties of the integration process, but they cannot be expected to add up to a coherent description of its possible outcome. Heretofore, the *porte-manteau* term for this has been 'federation'. Not only does this common label disguise a fairly wide range of institutional formats, but it also strongly implies the existence of an orthodox sovereign state at its core – regardless of how political authority and identity may be shared among its sub-national territorial constituencies.[3]

THE EXPLOITATION OF IDEAL TYPES

In order to provoke discussion, I propose to resort to the creation of ideal types, rather than attempt to piece together constructive types from existing efforts at state-building or regional integration. Moreover, I will give the results of this deductive exercise neo-Latin appellations – the better to remind the reader of the novel arrangements they represent. The central assumption of Figure 2.1 is that all forms of modern politics are rooted in representation. Where the units of authority have grown larger in area and population, and more heterogeneous in social and economic interests, rulers and ruled have relied increasingly on regularized

Territorial constituencies

		variable tangential egalitarian differentiated reversible	fixed contiguous hierarchical identical irreversible
Functional constituencies	variable dispersed shared overlapping	CONDOMINIO	CONSORTIO
	fixed cumulative separate coincident	CONFEDERATIO	STATO/ FEDERATIO

Figure 2.1 Territorial and functional elements in the formation of polities

mechanisms of indirect participation to communicate with each other. *Grosso modo*, these linkages conform with two different principles of aggregation: the *territorial* and the *functional*. Various intermediaries – parties, associations, movements, clienteles, notables – identify with the constituencies formed by these principles and represent their interests *vis-à-vis* the authorities. It is this mix of territorial and functional constituencies, along with their corresponding relations of authority and accountability, that defines the type of polity.

And the merging Euro-polity is no different. It began with a dual bias: (1) toward channelling the representation of territorial interests exclusively through the national governments of member states; and (2) toward privileging the development of functional representation through transnational, European-level interest associations. The deliberate neo-functionalist strategy of Jean Monnet *et cie* was to concede the former as inescapable (if eventually mutable) feature of the international system and to build gradually and surreptitiously upon the latter. After some initial successes, this failed for a variety of reasons and the ensuing period of 'intergovernmentalism' from the mid-1960s to the mid-1980s saw even the functional interests being transmitted largely through territorial channels.[4] Since then, the mix of functional and territorial constituencies/authorities at various levels has shifted significantly within the EC/EU, giving rise to the present uncertainty about the eventual outcome.

Stato/federatio

According to Figure 2.1, for the stato/federatio form to predominate at the European level, both types of constituency should be coincident or coterminous with each other. The territorial boundaries of their authority would be fixed for ever and would surround a physically continuous space. Membership would be irreversible – either because central authority would be deployed to prevent partial defections from specific norms or because outright secession would become too costly for the welfare of the citizens. National and sub-national units might not disappear – especially in the federalist versions of this outcome – but each would have an assured and identical status within an overarching hierarchy of authority. On the functional side, there would be a fixed allocation of competences among a variety of separate agencies operating within a cumulative division of labour – normally co-ordinated through a common budgeting process. Given the characteristics of existing nation states, the most likely sub-species of stato to emerge in Europe would be something akin to the *Politikverflechtung* and 'co-operative federalism' practised by the Swiss and the Germans, hence the label stato/federatio.[5]

Confederatio

A confederatio would be a more loosely coupled arrangement in which the identity and role of territorial units was allowed to vary, while the distribution of functional constituencies and competences was rigorously fixed and separate in order to protect members from encroachment by the central authorities. In it, there need be no presumption of territorial continuity and no established hierarchy of internal authority. Members would retain their autonomy and be relatively free to enter and exit. Each could negotiate its own differentiated relation to the unit as a whole but, once a member, would be strictly bound to contribute to the few, cumulative and coincident functions devolved upon central institutions, e.g. common currency, liberalization of trade flows, environment protection, traffic control, weather forecasting, and/or collective security. Historically, such policies have been short-lived, viz. the United States from 1781 to 1789, Switzerland from 1815 to 1848 or Yugoslavia from the death of Tito in 1980 to 1991. They proved either incapable of defending their varied and dispersed territories from encroachment by others or of redistributing resources among themselves to prevent the defection of their members. With the recent changes in international security and material welfare, such a solution may be more viable than in the past.

Consortio

The consortio is a form of collective action practised more by consenting firms than consenting polities. In it, national authorities of fixed number and identity agree to co-operate in the performance of functional tasks that are variable, dispersed and overlapping. They retain their respective territorially based identities, form a relatively continuous spatial bloc and accept positions within a common hierarchy of authority, but pool their capacities to act autonomously in domains they can no longer control at their own level of aggregation. There seem to have been relatively few salient historical examples of this type, given its implications for national sovereignty, but one suspects that a detailed investigation of the bilateral relations between any two contiguous states would reveal a large number of 'regional' commissions and task forces designed to cope with specific problems without endangering the international status of their participants. Once these are proliferate enough to interact and stimulate each other, it may be accurate to speak of a consortio having replaced strictly state-like relations, say, between the United States and Canada or Norway and Sweden.

Condominio

Finally, the condominio would be the most unprecedented, even unimaginable, outcome of all, since it would be based on variation in both the territorial and the functional constituencies. Precisely what the state system had taken so long to fix into a coincident interrelation would be sundered and allowed to vary in unpredictable ways. Instead of a Eurocracy accumulating organizationally distinct but politically co-ordinated tasks around a single centre, there would be multiple regional institutions acting autonomously to solve common problems and produce different public goods. Moreover, their dispersed and overlapping domains – not to mention their incongruent memberships – could result in competitive, even conflictual, situations and would certainly seem inefficient when compared with the clear demarcations of competence and hierarchy of authority that (supposedly) characterize existing nation states. While it seems unlikely that anyone would set out deliberately to create a condominio – and no long-lasting historical precedents come to mind – one can imagine a scenario of divergent interests, distracted actors, improvised measures and compromised solutions in which it just emerges *faute de mieux* and rapidly institutionalizes itself as the least threatening outcome. According to my admittedly biased and speculative reading of the Maastricht Treaty, this may even be the most probable trajectory of the EC/EU – unless emergent trends and subsequent events deflect its course in the near future.

THE IMPRECISION OF THEORY

None of the prevailing theories of integration can predict which (if any) of the above four ideal types will be closest to the Euro-polity that is emerging. All focus on process, not outcome. All presume integration will eventually lead to some kind of stable institutionalized equilibrium, but fail to specify how and when this can be expected to occur.

Neo-functionalists, by defining the process largely in terms of the transfer of sovereignty to a single, more encompassing, 'regional' centre of authority and, thereby, focusing attention on the alternatives of intergovernmentalism and supranationalism, seemed to imply that something like a stato/federatio was the probable outcome – provided, of course, the mechanisms of *l'engrenage*, transnational interest politics and *l'eurocracie* were sufficient to overcome the propensity to inertia and self-encapsulation.[6] Neither they nor the neo-realists seemed to have imagined that the EEC/EC might end up somewhere between these two extremes.[7]

Ironically, their predecessors – the pure nationalists – might have pointed them in a different direction. David Mitrany insisted on what he called 'technical self-determination':

> the function determines its appropriate *organs*. It also reveals through practice the nature of the action required under the given conditions, and that way the *powers* needed by the respective authority. The function, one might say, determined the executive instrument suitable for its proper activity, and by the same process provides a need for the reform of the instrument at every stage.[8]

Following this premise, Mitrany went on to deny 'the habitual assumption . . . that international action must have some overall *political authority* above it' (p. 75) and, in effect, provided a sketch for what we have called a consortio at the global level.[9]

What neither Mitrany nor others seems to have imagined is the possibility that not just functional domains might vary, but so might also the resource base, governance arrangements and levels of commitment across territorially defined participants. The very fact that Europe began its integration 'at sixes and sevens' should have alerted theorists to this likelihood. Since then varying sub-sets of member states have either threatened or actually gone ahead on their own, most notably in the area of monetary co-operation within the 'Snake' and the EMS, and more recently in internal security with the Schengen agreement. The Maastricht Treaty opens up whole new possibilities of 'variable geometry', some of which may be lodged in relatively autonomous Eurocratic bodies and may even be beyond the jurisdiction of the European Court of Justice.

The processes of 'association' and 'enlargement' have always introduced an element of ambiguity in defining exactly what were the territorial limits of EC authority – and the new agreement on the European Economic Area (EEA) makes this issue even more complicated by compelling non-member states to adopt Euro-norms and obey Euro-directives without having been full participants in the process of negotiating them.

If this were not difficult enough to comprehend, a whole new dimension of the territorial question is emerging, namely, 'subsidiarity' or what level of aggregation should be relevant in deciding and implementing which EC policies. Until recently, everyone took it for granted that the natural and irreducible spatial consequences were defined by sovereign nation states – in their existing and highly unequal configuration.[10] This is how voting quotas, financial contributions, nominations of European Commissioners and Judges, seats on the Council of Ministers, and so forth are distributed. Indeed, the orthodox assumption held that the creation of the EC actually served to strengthen the role of nation states over lesser political units.[11]

Subsequent changes from below in the territorial distribution of authority within these states[12] and from within in the magnitude and distribution of Community regional funds[13] have resulted in a veritable explosion of attention by sub-national political units to the integration process. Regions, provinces, municipalities, and even whole 'unrepresented nations' (e.g. Catalans, Welsh, Basques and Bretons) have opened up quasi-embassies in Brussels and sought to establish direct contact with EC officials to influence the distribution of structural funds and the direction of sectoral policies. They have been forming associations, alliances and commissions across national borders and pressing for the special status of 'Euro-regions' that group adjacent units from different countries.[14] It would obviously be premature to suppose that this flurry of activity and the creation of informal channels of sub-national representation will succeed in 'outflanking' the heretofore dominant position of national member states within the EC/EU, and eventually drive the outcome toward a *condominio* in which varying and overlapping scales of territorial aggregation would interact with varying and overlapping domains of functional competence, although the recent insertion into the Maastricht Treaty of a 'Committee of Regions' does somewhat enhance that probability.[15]

THE IMPACT ON PUBLIC POLICY

Neither the Single European Act nor the Maastricht Treaty is self-implementing. Nor, as we have suggested, does either embody a coherent design. Their eventual impact upon the Euro-polity and its policies will depend on a series of supervening conditions and events, not least of which will be the growing politicization of EC/EU issues. Heretofore, the dominant strategy has presumed a relatively low level of visibility and controversiality and the gradual incorporation of specific, not to say specialized, categories of interest. European policy-making has had its periodic crises (and extricated itself from them with agonizing compromises and complex package deals), but they took place out of sight from mass publics. Now that the process of national ratification of the Maastricht Treaty has broken that barrier, it may be difficult to return to business as usual. Even the issue of enlargement, which has been handled in such an 'intergovernmental' fashion in the past, has recently stirred unprecedented passions at the national level. And if such controversy surrounds the admission of four new rich countries and the shift in the minimal blocking coalition from twenty-three to twenty-seven votes, try to imagine what it is going to be like to attempt to incorporate an even more numerous set of relatively poor eastern European countries!

Within the framework of the 1996 intergovernmental conference, the EC/EU faces the major unresolved issue of revising its institutional format. There are already indications that this deadline may be brought forward. Politicization and enlargement – not to mention growing evidence of problems in the implementation of existing policies and the blatant failure of efforts at foreign policy co-ordination with regard to Bosnia-Herzegovina – are putting great strain on existing arrangements. It is not inconceivable that the legitimacy of the entire enterprise could be at stake.

Nevertheless, certain features of Euro-policy-making seem relatively well established and likely to survive whatever format is eventually chosen:

1   *There will be no single dominant style of policy-making, for the simple reason that there will be no single Europe.* In each of the multiple, partial and overlapping 'Europes' that are emerging there will be a distinctive style of collective action, depending on the mixture of territorial units and functional constituencies involved. The choice will not be limited to either of the two 'classic' formulas: a 'diplomatic' style characteristic of confederatii or a 'federal' style characteristic of territorially decentralized stati. Whatever the style, it should be more flexible, heterogeneous and issue-specific than corresponding national styles.

2   *Whatever emerges, it will not so much resemble the policy style of any of the existing national member states as constitute something novel.* It will be directed more by the shifting functional and territorial imperatives of the newly emergent polity than by the nationally ingrained habits and preferences of the policy-makers and administrators that compose it. This is for two reasons: first, the absence of a hegemonic member able to

impose its 'style' in a given arena either by the virtue of the superiority of its resources or of its problem-solving capacity;[16] second, the enormous increase in the scale of governance will impose a logic of its own beyond the capabilities of any previous nation state apparatus.[17] One should never forget that the 'polity space' of an integrated Europe will be demographically larger and culturally and linguistically more diverse than that of the United States.

3   Unless the EC/EU manages to acquire a significantly greater direct capacity to generate its own revenues and to implement its distinctive policies, i.e. to become more like a state than heretofore, *national and sub-national administrations will continue to determine the style of face-to-face authoritative interaction with individual firms and citizens*. European directives and regulations may come to occupy an increasing role in fixing broad policy objectives (and in bringing about their much needed convergence, *pace* the Single European Act), but their effective implementation will still depend on the *bonne volonté* of a very divergent set of national, provincial and local agencies. Under these conditions, the burgeoning 'implementation deficit' could prove to be even more negative than the much more talked about 'democracy deficit'.

4   Whatever the mix of national styles or functional imperatives, *European policy-making is likely to be dominated for the foreseeable future by a strong dose of* comitologie, *i.e. by a process of protracted negotiation in committees located at different levels of aggregation*. Voting and especially minimal winning coalitions will be rare, except sporadically at the highest levels; compromise among all the participants will be the usual decisional norm, regardless of formal rules. Calculations of proportionality in relation to intensity of interest (known as 'Sankt Proportius' in the Austrian jargon) and reciprocity in relation to successive issues ('log-rolling' in American terms) will ease acceptance. A great deal will depend upon complex and highly specialized systems of consultation, especially with the socio-economic interests most directly affected. These have been and will continue to be granted privileged access – although not necessarily through their European peak and sectoral associations. There is very convincing evidence that specific firms and even individual businessmen have found their way to the corridors of power in Brussels. Even though politicization will bring an increase in demands for 'transparency', the whole process will remain relatively opaque to wider publics. Whether *comitologie* among experts and representatives will suffice in its various territorial and functional configurations to ensure legitimacy by the citizenry is an open (and crucial) question. So far the 'democracy deficit' has generated much discussion, but little effective mobilization – and even if it were filled, say by increasing the *compétences*

of the European Parliament – the Commission and other Euro-executive agencies would still be likely to have to rely heavily on the information and compliance of specialized interest representatives.

5   *In the future an increasing proportion of EC/EU conflicts will take place not within Community/Union institutions, but between them.* Each specialized agency with its stipulated functional domain and its specific membership will be tempted to resolve internal disputes between interests by appropriating the benefits for itself and passing on the costs to other European agencies. In the absence of any strong and disciplined pan-European political parties, and of anything resembling a Euro-government responsible to a single party or coalition of parties or a more serious role for the Euro-Parliament – and, especially, if the Commission's monopoly over the introduction of new policies is weakened – it will become increasingly difficult to ensure compatibility between the policies pursued at the European level. Three mechanisms of collective decision-making, however, could emerge to ensure that consortio and condominio-type solutions do not degenerate into utter incoherence:

1   *Hegemony.* Some country or, more likely, core area that is a prominent member of all conceivable 'Europes' could assert its dominance and impose its solutions to the eventual conflicts of *compétence* and interest that are bound to emerge between relatively independent European institutions. The Franco-German axis is the obvious candidate for this, although it has become increasingly fragile in the aftermath of German reunification and would have to surmount significant differences in national administrative styles and structures of interest intermediation.

2   *Verrechtligung.* Inter-agency conflicts could be converted into issues of law and turned over to the European Court of Justice for adjudication. To a certain extent this is already happening although in the future its efficacy will depend upon the willingness of all members of all European institutions to accept the supremacy of a common body of Community law – even in functional domains where they have no say in the elaboration of the rules. The recent treaty creating the European Economic Area establishes an important precedent in that direction.

3   *Parliamentarization.* If the European Parliament's *compétences* were substantially increased and if all members of whatever European institutions were compelled to become members and abide by its decisions, an overarching legislative process could intervene to ensure a minimum of policy coherence. This is to leave unresolved the complex issue of the apportionment of seats and voting rights across a varied *gamme* of issue arenas – not to mention the fact that 'parliamentary sovereignty' is by no means a well established norm in all European national polities.

If, as I suspect, an integrated Europe will move increasingly in the direction of either a consortio or a condominio, it will have to break new ground, probably by combining all the above. The usual solutions of strict issue demarcation in a confederatio or of a hierarchical inter-agency co-ordination in a federatio will simply not be available. The closest approximation in existing practice would be the *Politikverflechtung* that characterizes the 'co-operative federalism' of Germany and Switzerland.[18]

The European Community/Union is still an *objet politique non-identifié* and it will be some time before we can discover for sure what type of polity it is going to become. The contest between territorially bound nation states and functionally defined industrial and service sectors is still unresolved. There are even assertive sub-national regions openly demanding greater representation and aggressive transnational firms discreetly establishing privileged access. The options are still open, although if the past is any guide the outcome will be a compromise, a second-best mixture of competing ideals and interests that no one wanted initially, but everyone (or almost everyone) is prepared to live with. The fact that the general public continues to remain national (or sub-national), has little or no identification with Europe as such, and tends to regard the policies of EC/EU as excessively remote and opaque casts a giant shadow over the entire process. It is one thing to imagine a compromised arrangement that member governments and associated interests could live with momentarily; it is quite another to imagine one that individual citizens would accept as legitimate in the long run.

Some type of Euro-polity will emerge during the coming decade. The point of no return has passed, in my view. A reversion to national political autonomy, economic autarchy and/or regional insecurity within the previous state compartments is not viable and probably would not be tolerated by the citizenries. In other words, the race between the nation state and some form of supranational authority may be over, but we are not sure what the attributes of the winner will be. Until we are, it will be very difficult to predict who the actors in European policy-making will be and by what processes they will be able to make binding and legitimate public decisions.

ACKNOWLEDGEMENTS

This chapter is excerpted, revised and then extended from a longer manuscript on 'Interests, Functions and Powers: Emergent Properties and Unintended Consequences in the European Polity' which will be published in Gary Marks and Peter Lange (eds), *The Emerging Euro-polity*, New York, Cambridge University Press, forthcoming.

NOTES

1 For a particularly eloquent defence of its 'limited but real powers', see Stanley Hoffman, 'Reflections on the Nation-state in Western Europe Today', *Journal of Common Market Studies*, September–December 1982, vol. 21, 1–2, pp. 21–38. Also Donald J. Puchala, 'The European Common Market and the Resilience of the Nation State', *Il Politico*, 1988, vol. LIII, 3, pp. 447–66, where it is found, even after the signing of the Single European Act, that 'the weight of evidence tends to lie on the side of [European integration's having] strengthened states' (p. 461).

2 And in the nation state model these domains are supposed to be coterminous, with a distinct and unique national identity based on a common language, culture, descent group or 'community of fate' [*Schicksalsgemeinschaft*].

3 From this perspective the British allergy to the 'F word', which seems so ridiculous to a North American or German, is well founded. What the British are objecting to is the possible emergence of a state, i.e. any political form – however decentralized or deconcentrated – that accumulates sovereign powers within a single set of institutions at the European level. Cf. the discussion between Ian Davidson, 'New Era for EC Family', and Martin Wolf, 'Federalism before a Fall', *Financial Times*, 3 December 1991. Samuel Brittan has attempted to clarify the terms of discussion for the British and concludes that the 'true dividing lines are between different ideas on the role of the state rather then between countries or between federalists and nationalists'. 'Let Fools Contend about the Forms', *Financial Times*, 21 November 1991.

4 For a brief account of the failure of Euro-corporatism, see Philippe C. Schmitter and Wolfgang Streeck, 'Organized Interests and the Europe of 1992', in N. J. Ornstein and M. Perlman (eds), *Political Power and Social Change*, Washington, D.C., AEI Press, 1991, pp. 46–67.

5 Alberta Sbragia pays special attention to the Swiss and German versions of federalism because they accord a prominent and guaranteed role to sub-national political units in their respective upper Houses of parliament in her 'Thinking about the European Future: the Uses of Comparison' in A. Sbragia (ed.), *Euro-politics*, Washington, Brookings Institutions, 1992, pp. 257–92. Fritz Scharpf has explicitly explored the parallels between the German federal system and the EC in his 'The Joint Decision Trap: Lessons from German Federalism and European Integration', *Public Administration*, autumn 1988, vol. 66, pp. 239–78. For the historical lessons Switzerland has to offer see Ernst-Wolfgang Böckenförde, 'Die Schweiz. Vorbild für Europa?', *Neue Zürcher Zeitung*, 14–15 December 1991; Charlotte Murert, 'The Swiss Pattern for a Federated Europe', in *International Political Communities*, Garden City, NJ, Anchor Books, 1966, pp. 149–74.

6 Although Ernst B. Haas was careful to avoid this assumption in his *Beyond the Nation-State*, where he defined as his dependent variable 'the process of *increasing* the interaction and the mingling so as to obscure the boundaries between the system of international organizations and the environment provided by their nation-state members' (p. 29). In their *Europe's Would-be Polity*, Englewood Cliffs, Prentice Hall, 1970, Leon Linberg and Stuart Scheingold admit candidly that 'we have no concept of a termination state for the Community' (p. 138).

7 In all fairness, I should note Donald Puchala's effort to delineate a 'concordance system' which resembles something approaching my confederatio type; Leon Lindberg's and Stuart Scheingold's discussion of a 'sector integrated supranational system' which is close to the consortio type and Ernst B. Haas's musings on 'regional communes' (also a consortio) and 'asymmetrical regional overlap' (perhaps something like my condominio): Donald Puchala, 'Of Blind Men, Elephants and International Integration', *Journal of Common Market Studies*, March 1972, vol. 10, 3, pp. 267–85; Leon Lindberg and Stuart Scheingold, *Europe's Would-be Polity*, pp. 307–10 (where the concept is credited to Walter Yondorf); Ernst B. Haas, 'The Study of Regional Integration: Reflections on the Joy and Anguish of Pretheorizing', in Leon Lindberg and Stuart Scheingold (eds), *Regional Integration: Theory and Research*, Cambridge, Harvard University Press, 1971, p. 31.

8 David Nitrany, *A Working Peace System*, London, Royal Institute of International Affairs, 1943, pp. 174–212.

9 Mitrany himself rejected the 'regional fallacy', i.e. the idea that functional problems could best be tackled by a sub-set of states characterized by their (alleged) cultural homogeneity or physical propinquity. Indeed, he expressed the fear that a united Europe might very well reproduce on a larger scale the historical pathologies of its component members and agreed that there 'is no special reason to believe that a federal Europe would suddenly be guided exclusively by sweet reasonableness and self-restraint', *A Working Peace System*, pp. 174–212.

10 There is one very important exception to this generalization. From early on, the German *Länder* insisted that they must be informed and participate at least indirectly in the deliberations of the Council of Ministers on issues assigned exclusively to them by the constitution of the Federal Republic. Rudolf Hrbek and Uwe Thaysen (eds), *Die Deutsche Länder und die Europäische Gemeinschaften*, Baden-Baden, Nomos, 1986.

11 L. J. Sharpe, 'Fragmentation and Territoriality in the European State System', *International Political Science Review*, July 1989, vol. 10, pp. 223–38.

12 Cf. S. Tarrow, P. Katzenstein and L. Graziano (eds), *Territorial Politics in Industrial Nations*, New York, Praeger, 1978; Yves Mény, *Dix ans de régionalisation en Europe: bilan et perspectives (1970–1980)*, Paris, Editions Cujas, 1982; Michael Keating, *State and Regional Nationalism: Territorial Politics and the European State*, London, Harvester Wheatsheaf, 1988.

13 For the overview, see Gary Marks, 'Structural Policy in the European Community', in A. Sbragia (ed.), *Euro-politics*, pp. 191–224.

14 For an illuminating analysis of how new bargaining arrangements are emerging between sub-national and national units, see Leonardo Parri, 'Territorial Political Exchange in Federal and Unitary Countries', *West European Politics*, July 1989, vol. 12, pp. 197–219.

15 For some appropriately critical remarks on the likelihood of the emergence of a 'Europe des Régions' rather than a 'Europe des Etats', see Gary Marks, 'Structural Policy in the European Community', in Alberta Sbragia (ed.), *Euro-politics*, pp. 212–24, and his 'Structural Policy, European Integration and the State', unpublished paper, March 1991. Also Jeffrey Alexander, 'Sceptical Reflections on a Europe of Regions: Britain, Germany and the ERDF', *Journal of Public Policy*, 1991, vol. 10, 4, pp. 417–47. One of the most obvious impediments is the very asymmetrical fashion in which regional governance is

distributed across national polities in Europe. Great Britain, for example, completely lacks this intermediate layer (although the issue of devolution of authority to Scotland did emerge during the last elections). Portugal and Greece have only recently begun to experiment with regionalization in order to attract more EC funds. Unfortunately for the issue of economic and social cohesion, it is invariably the most developed internal regions that are the best equipped and most eager to exploit the Brussels connection. For the most enthusiastic endorsements of this idea, see Riccardo Petrella, *La Renaissance des cultures régionales en Europe*, Paris, Editions Entente, 1978; Georges Pierret, *Vivre l'Europe . . . autrement. Les régions entrent en scène*, Paris, Jean Picollec, 1984; Jean-Pierre Raffarin, *'92 Europe: nous sommes tous des régionaux*, Poitiers, Projets Editions, 1988; Colin Ward, 'All Power to the Regions!', *New Statesman and Society*, 6 December 1991, pp. 30–2; Wolfgang Clement, 'Auf dem Weg zum Europa der Regionen', in J. J. Hesse and W. Renzsch (eds), *Föderalstaatliche Entwicklung in Europa*, Baden-Baden, Nomos, 1991, pp. 15–28.

16 I leave aside the early stages of the integration process in which the French administrative style was clearly hegemonic – for both reasons. Not only has the prestige of the statist, *grandes écoles*, approach declined (along with French administrative performance), but enlargement has greatly augmented the variety of available policy styles. Also, to the extent that the outcome of integration becomes less 'concentric', i.e. less co-ordinated by the Commission in Brussels, the EC/EU institutions dispersed throughout Europe should be expected to acquire at least some of the administrative traits of the places where they will be located.

17 For a discussion which argues that the shift in scale is one of several factors that have affected the emerging system of European interest representation and that is driving it in the direction of a more pluralist, American-style outcome than is at present characteristic of any of the member states of the EC/EU, see Philippe C. Schmitter and Wolfgang Streeck, 'Organized Interests and the Europe of 1992'.

18 Fritz Scharpf is responsible for initiating the concept of *Politikverflechtung*. See F. W. Scharpf, B. Reissert and F. Schnabel (eds), *Politikverflechtung. Theorie und Empirie des Kooperativen Föderalismus in der Bundesrepublik*, Kronberg, Scriptor, 1976. He has explicitly explored the parallels between the German federal system and the EC in 'The Joint Decision Trap: Lessons from German Federalism and European Integration', *Public Administration*, autumn 1988, vol. 66, pp. 239–78, and further developed the implications of the model in 'Kann es in Europa eine stabile föderale Balance geben?', in R. Wildenmann (ed.), *Staatswerdung Europas? Optionen für eine Europäische Union*, Baden-Baden, Nomos, 1991, pp. 415–28, and in 'Autonomieschonend und gemeinschaftsverträglich: Zur Logik der Europäischen Mehrebenenpolitik', Cologne, MPIFG Discussion Paper 93/9 (1993). For some of the historical lessons Switzerland has to offer, see Ernst-Wolfgang Böckenförde, 'Die Schweiz. Vorbild für Europa?', *Neue Zürcher Zeitung*, 14–15 December 1991, and Charlotte Muret, 'The Swiss "Pattern for a Federated Europe"', in *International Political Communities*, Garden City, NJ, Anchor Books, 1966, pp. 149–74.

3 EU policy-making

A garbage can or an anticipatory and consensual policy style?

Sonia Mazey and Jeremy Richardson

UNCERTAIN AGENDAS, SHIFTING NETWORKS AND COMPLEX COALITIONS

Our purpose in this chapter is to analyze one aspect of the state-like characteristics of the EU – the role that interest groups play in the EU policy process. Our hope is that this 'window' will enable us to begin to determine whether the EU policy process has begun to develop some stable 'decision rules' or whether the process is more akin to an unpredictable 'garbage can' model of decision-making.[1] We believe that the European Commission at least has a 'procedural ambition' which may lead to the emergence of a more predictable and stable 'European policy style'. The Commission may be moving towards a more 'mature' form of bureaucratic behaviour which emphasizes a more regularized and predictable relationship with organized interests.

It is possible to present two contrasting pictures of the EU policy process. Some of the institutional developments and behavioural patterns in the EU policy process are quite familiar to students of national policy-making. In terms of institutional structures, there is a heavy concentration of power, in the policy *formulation* process, within the bureaucracy – namely the Commission. As we have argued elsewhere,[2] the Commission constitutes a kind of *bourse*, acting as a market for policy ideas and innovation within the EU policy process. Thus, there is no doubt that the bulk of lobbying effort is directed at the Commission, just as at the national level civil service departments and administrative agencies are generally the most common target of interest groups. The unwritten rules of lobbying within the EU are also quite similar to those at the national level. The most successful groups are those that exhibit the usual professional characteristics – namely sufficient resources, good advance intelligence of intended policy change, and strong contacts with bureaucrats and politicians. Above all, they have the ability to provide policy-makers with sound technical advice. The key resource for any group is a reputation for expertise and reliability. It is no surprise, therefore, that one of the main features of the EU policy process is increasing resort to the use of committees of various kinds as institutions for the formation of policy. One consequence of this trend is that consultation with groups is also becoming increasingly institutionalized and regularized. The concentration of policy formulation in the hands of a bureaucracy and the nature of the 'rules of the game' may mean that certain types of groups are likely to be more successful than others. Moreover, there are some peculiar EU institutional features – particularly the continuing importance of the member governments – which may reinforce the existing bias evident in the national policy process in favour of technically expert and well resourced producer groups. Multinational firms in particular enjoy some special advantages because of their technical expertise and their ability to co-ordinate lobbying across the member states. In addition, the opportunities such firms have to relocate their operations (in contrast to trade unions, for example) provide them with a most effective sanction which may be used against both national governments and the EU itself.

Despite these familiar features, the EU policy process exhibits a unique, fluid decision-making process, in which the power relations between even the key institutions are not yet stabilized. In consequence, the policy agenda in most sectors is very unpredictable – hence our reference to the 'garbage can' model. The institutional and political complexity of the EU means that notwithstanding the privileged position of certain interests noted above, 'windows of opportunity' can readily be created by a range of diverse actors.[3] Thus, the EU presents an unusual combination of opportunity structures and a highly competitive market for ideas. The EU policy process may therefore appear to be a rather good (or bad!) example of the Cohen *et al.* 'garbage can' model of decision-making. This model is based upon an analysis of 'organized anarchies' – organizations characterized by problematic preferences, unclear technology and fluid participation. As the authors argue, there are two phenomena crucial to an understanding of anarchy in organizations. The first is the manner in which organizations make choices without consistent, shared goals. The second is the way in which members of an organization are activated. In practice, 'an organization is a collection of choices looking for problems, issues and feelings looking for decision structures in which they might be aired, solutions looking for issues to which they might be the answer, and decision-makers looking for work'.[4] In terms of the EU policy process, the garbage can model may be applicable to such a system of uncertain agendas, shifting networks and complex coalitions.[5]

The EU also exhibits extreme jurisdictional disputes between different parts of what is supposed to be a unified bureaucracy (the Commission) and the usual problems caused by the difficulty of achieving horizontal co-ordination. Whereas at the national level there are usually unified recruitment and training procedures with bureaucrats drawn from a pool of recruits with a common cultural and educational background, the EU has not yet created a unified bureaucratic culture or operational style. Thus, the Commission's procedural ambition is undermined by differing procedural styles.

An equally significant system characteristic is that the other main 'pillar' of consultation is still manifestly weak and underdeveloped – namely the hundreds of 'Euro-groups' purporting to represent genuinely European interests. The reasons for the patchy development of effective European-level interest articulation structures, which are essential to the emergence of a genuinely European (or at least EU)-level process of interest intermediation, are all perfectly understandable. For example, the structural characteristics of sectors such as banking or retailing in the fifteen member states are often very different. These variations produce different interest group structures and, more important, different policy objectives. For effective European-level associational structures to emerge, a reasonable level of mutual self-interest, willingness to co-operate and to make sacrifices in the common interests of the group are needed. Where potential or actual members of Euro-level groups are in such intense competition with each other in the market place and – equally important – where there exist alternative lobbying options to participating in a Euro-group – it is not surprising that many European federations simply do not work effectively as channels of interest group representation. However, there may be a trend towards specialization within the Euro-associations (the European Chemical Industry Council being a good example of such a development), thus enabling them to mobilize technical, coherent advice to the Commission more quickly. As the EU's own bureaucracy itself becomes more specialized, so will the organizational structures of those interest groups with which it deals. Intra-organizational specialization within Euro-groups may reduce the need to build very broad coalitions across an industry as a whole. The resort to specialization within the Commission, the Council of Ministers and the European Parliament is a common response by policy-makers faced with complex problems. The tendency for policy-makers to seek ways of 'unpacking' issues of high political salience and/or of a cross-national nature into more 'manageable' problems which can be processed away from the glare of publicity as 'technical' issues is, again, quite familiar at the national level.

Finally, there is the problem of institutional instability within the EU policy process. Both their powers and the relationships between EU institutions are still subject to change. The basic 'decision rules' are subject to dispute in three respects. First, we do not yet know how the new arrangements (the co-decision procedure) between the Council of Ministers, the Commission, and the European Parliament will work over time.[6] Second, the further extension of qualified majority voting has important implications for the policy-making process, as it further undermines the possibility of interests relying on national channels for influencing EU policy. Thus, it forces interests to play at least a two-level game.[7] More generally, it is a rule change which may have the effect of accelerating the transfer of allegiance away from the nation state towards the European Union, as originally suggested by the neo-functionalists. This rule change also strengthens the incentive for national governments themselves to engage in complex Euro-coalition building, an activity involving messy trade-offs between different policy problems. Third, the whole question of subsidiarity, and the resulting caution shown by the Commission – and, more recently by the European Court of Justice – about openly pressing for further EU policy developments means that the level at which policies will be determined is now more uncertain. Any changes in the level of decision-making for particular policy problems will cause a redistribution of costs and benefits between interests. We may expect some unusual coalitions to emerge in this situation, as it is not clear that national governments which are enthusiastic about the 'repatriation' of some powers to the nation state will enjoy the support of some of their traditional 'national' clients. European policy integration has gone so far in some sectors – often pressed by the groups themselves in keeping with the neo-functionalists' predictions – that the disbenefits of a reversal will be quite apparent and will be resisted by many interest groups. A coalition of interest groups and some EU institutions – notably the European Parliament – may prove to be an effective 'ratchet' preventing any significant reversal of the Europeanization of policy-making witnessed in recent years. Little wonder, therefore, that it can be difficult to model the European policy process when most players are involved in a complex and shifting series of 'nested games'.[8] Our argument, however, is that these nested or multi-level arena games all tend to shift the focus of players' behaviour to the European level. Europeanization of policy-making in western Europe may have already achieved a critical mass and momentum to convince most organized interests that Brussels is a permanent and increasingly important feature of their organizational environment. Even within the problematic Euro-associations referred to above, recognition of the overriding need for Euro-level solutions to their members' problems may prove an effective counterweight to their centrifugal tendencies. As

Europeanization accelerates, most policy actors recognize that some means has to be found of regularizing and institutionalizing such activity.

THE EUROPEAN COMMISSION–INTEREST GROUP INTERFACE

The absence of a clearly identifiable government or governmental party at the Euro-level leaves the Commission largely responsible for EU policy initiation, especially as the EU edges towards the status of a 'mature' state where much of the basic framework of major policies is already in place. In this situation, one of the scenarios suggested by Habermas may indeed come to pass, i.e. 'the state seems forced to abandon the substance of power in favor of an efficient way of applying available techniques in the framework of strategies that are objectively called for'.[9] More recently, Majone has argued that the broad nature of contemporary policy-making is changing. According to this view, the new features are: the rediscovery of efficiency as a primary policy goal; a new awareness of the strategic importance of policy credibility; and increasing willingness to delegate important policy-making powers to technocratic bodies enjoying con- siderable political independence.[10] As Majone also notes, the role of independent, expert bodies is increasing at the international as well as at the national level. (Majone cites the European Commission, the future European central bank and the World Trade Organization as examples of such bodies.) The Commission will, therefore, retain its attractiveness as a target of lobbying, both in terms of agenda-setting and in terms of the processing of issues increasingly perceived as 'technical' in nature. As European integration shifts from the 'big ideas' of the EC's founding fathers towards the politics of expertise, the Euro-polity may witness the scientization of politics as suggested by Habermas.[11]

From the outset, in the early years of the Community, the High Authority began to exhibit those bureaucratic characteristics identified by Downs.[12] Its administrative reorganizations between 1954 and 1955 resulted in a more effective, but more traditionally structured, bureaucracy. Members of the High Authority involved in the policy-making process became increasingly enmeshed in cross-cutting relations with organized interests and national administrations.[13] This pattern has continued over the years. In responding to increased interest group mobilization at the European level, the Commission's approach to consultation may appear to have been pragmatic and unplanned. Busy officials often lack detailed technical expertise themselves and lack knowledge of the different systems and problems in the fifteen countries of the EU. They also need to be cognizant of the external dimension of the EU's activities and of the effect that EU policies may have on non-EU interests which are important economic actors within the EU. Commission officials therefore have to find means of both tapping sources of expertise beyond member state governments and of mobilizing support (and heading off opposition) from interests directly affected by EU policy proposals. In classic Downsian fashion, the Commission has proved adept at constructing supportive clientele groups! Moreover, current pressure for more accountability and greater democratic control over EU policy-makers will merely intensify the Commission's desire to mobilize interest group support. The more the EU opens up channels of democratic accountability – for example, by further increasing the powers of the European Parliament – the more the Commission will be driven to seek to accommodate key interest groups quietly in the policy formulation phase for fear that disaffected groups will seek to mobilize support elsewhere, within national governments, in the European Parliament or even with other European (and global) institutions. After all, what better justification for Euro-policy initatives than that the 'affected' interests want them!

Although unplanned, the Commission's relations with outside interests are underpinned by a clearly articulated 'procedural ambition' – that wherever possible the interface between officials and interests should be via the relevant Euro-associations for each particular policy area. Where such groups do not exist, the Commission itself has been active in helping to create and sustain them – again a familiar bureaucratic response in most Western democracies. In a number of cases, direct and indirect funding is provided, both to sustain the groups and to facilitate interchange between policy professionals (public and private). The Commission, though not endowed with big budgets to dispense, often manages to 'massage' the agenda-setting process in a rather subtle and skilful way by bringing the affected interests together at an early stage in the policy process. By this means, policy ideas can be launched and changes in the climate of opinion engineered. Problems can be legitimized, a common perception of what may be achieved can be developed and coalitions in favour of policy change can be constructed.

Nevertheless, the inherent weakness of Euro-groups has meant that officials unwittingly undermine the development of effective Euro-groups by frequently consulting national groups and individual firms direct. Often only the latter possess the information necessary for the Commission to formulate policy effectively. One needs to remember the mundane but crucial point that the pace of policy-making within the Commission itself is usually quite frenetic. Meta-policy-making designs are soon abandoned at midnight when a directive has to be redrafted by the next morning! Groups which can provide solutions rather than problems at the eleventh hour have an excellent opportunity to exercise considerable influence at this crucial stage of the policy process – policy formulation.

Bearing in mind that there is no governing party with a party programme and ideological 'baggage' limiting the initiative of officials, we perhaps need to pay more attention to the early stages of the EU policy process, where the agenda is being set.[14] Majone's observation that 'policy ideas matter most when public choice is about issues of efficiency – how to increase aggregate welfare – rather than about the redistribution of resources from one group to another',[15] is particularly apposite to the EU policy process. As he notes, the shift from redistributive to efficiency concerns is one of the distinguishing features of the political transformations of the past decade. As the Commission cannot rely on a majoritarian government to impose its electoral programme on the 'legislature', it usually has to demonstrate that there will be collective efficiency gains to the EU as a whole. As Majone notes, 'argument and persuasion are needed to discover opportunities for collective gains and to elicit support in favour of the most efficient ways of exploiting some opportunities'.[16] In the deliberation process, EU officials place considerable emphasis on practicability and hence listen to groups that know where the shoe will pinch at the national level. If such groups can be persuaded of the need for a Euro-level solution, it is more difficult for national governments to resist the policy proposed.

Within this complex administrative and multi-cultural decision-making environment, most officials appear to have developed a *modus operandi* which may have at least the rudimentary elements of a European policy style. An underlying characteristic of this style is openness to pressure group activity. This extreme bureaucratic openness is one reason for the sometimes quite radical shifts in policy direction as directives pass through several drafts following conflicting representations from interests in different member states. Just as agenda-setting is unpredictable and participation is extensive, so are policy outcomes until the final whistle is blown. Extreme permeability and open access have to be managed in a way consistent with effective problem-solving. The bureaucratic solution is to resort to familiar consultation structures and processes, such as advisory committees and informal consultation with interests in the developmental phases of policy-making. This procedure is also the best means of 'risk avoidance' and may help avoid too many 'U turns' at later stages of the policy process. Such strategies are commonplace at the national level. In Britain, for instance, Henderson argued, officials tend to protect themselves 'by making sure that at every stage of the policy process the right chairs had been warmed at the right committee tables by the appropriate institutions, everything possible has been done and no one could possibly be blamed if things go wrong'.[17] The proliferation of consultative procedures and structures at the Euro-level may well reflect similar bureaucratic concern, especially post-Maastricht, when European integration is politically controversial. By this means, big issues are also transformed into specific policy problems that can be processed by policy specialists, be they interest group representatives, so-called 'independent experts', or national officials. However, as an issue is processed via the EU policy machinery it may pass through a series of filters which gradually exclude certain types of interests. Interest groups themselves appear to recognize this process; some groups deliberately concentrate on agenda-setting activities, in acknowledgement of their limited capacity to influence later stages of the policy process.[18] At the detailed technical level – particularly in such areas as standard-setting – we may, therefore, see the beginnings of capture by specific narrow interests. Officials from most policy-oriented DGs habitually use various advisory bodies (e.g. expert groups, expert committees, industry groups) and regularly convene seminars, workshops, and conferences of the 'relevant' interests in order to seek views and advice. More important, they also use these structures to see if some viable consensus can be reached on what practical solutions should be adopted. We should not be surprised by this 'logic of negotiation'.[19] Officials in Brussels know, as do officials at the national level, that interest associations can be simultaneously a source of help and of trouble. It makes sense to bring those interests together in some *ad hoc* or permanent structure in order to define problems, devise possible solutions and mobilize support from those who 'matter' for successful implementation. Thus there are estimated to be some seventy-five consultative committees helping the Commission in its pre-legislative consultation 'amounting to a sort of formalisation of the consultation process'.[20] The Commission is in charge of the process of committee formation, and although some of the committees are of state officials, it is common for them to consist of representatives of private interests such as companies, trade federations, trade unions, consumer organizations, etc.[21]

NATIONAL GOVERNMENTS AND INTEREST GROUP CO-ORDINATION

If, as we argue, the role and importance of interest groups in the EU policy process is central, a question arises over the decision-making role and significance of national governments at the European level. To what extent is the (generally pluralistic) model of EU policy-making presented here consistent with intergovernmental models of EU policy-making? None of the above discussion should lead us to underestimate the role of official state actors in the shape of Ministers from governments, their permanent representatives in Brussels on COREPER, and their representatives on the many working groups and committees set up by the Commission. However, national governments often act as agents, with their 'principals' being national firms and interests. The French position on GATT and the British government's opposition to further increases in social costs in the labour market are two obvious examples of such activity. Where proposed Euro-regulations threaten national interests it is common for national governments to reflect this agency/principal relationship. The relationship between national interest groups and national governments can of course vary, reflecting existing national styles. Those countries which have a long tradition of government/group consultation and which have developed effective co-ordinating mechanisms within their national administrations may be advantaged in the EU policy process. One of the paradoxes of the process of European integration is that at the political level Britain is often perceived as the 'awkward' partner[22] yet when it comes to the process of co-ordinating its EU policy Britain is seen as something of a Rolls-Royce machine.[23] Similarly, Britain appears to be building upon the long traditions of group integration in the policy process[24] in trying to improve co-ordination of Brussels lobbying between itself and its 'clients'. Following a review of the implementation of EU law in Britain, the government concluded that even greater efforts need to be made in order to produce a more effective British (not just British government) lobbying effort. It is already commonplace for panels of business representatives, enforcers and government officials to meet on a regular basis between meetings of EU Council working groups.[25] The aim is to bring the British government and 'its' interest groups (usually favoured groups) even closer together in response to the Europeanization of the policy process. Thus, 'Ministers and officials should therefore have the confidence to be open about the difficulties they sometimes face in Brussels, and should be prepared to make use of business contacts and networks in reinforcing the UK negotiating position'.[26] In a similar way, the strong (often neo-corporatist) traditions of government/group relations in Germany also facilitate effective co-ordination of German lobbying in the EU, reflecting the 'privileged position which the business associations enjoy in the public policy-making process'.[27] Despite the fragmented nature of the German bureaucracy, 'the sectoral policy communities of public and private interests add additional political weight through concerted transnational activities'.[28] In France, where co-ordination between the state and interest groups has not always been effective, the then Minister for European Affairs, Edith Cresson, set up in 1988 a number of 'mobilization groups' (*groupes d'étude et de mobilisation*) based on major EU policy areas and designed to facilitate the exchange of information between groups, officials, and ministers at the national level.[29]

There is, however, an alternative view of this seemingly generalized attempt to create a symbiosis between government and industry at the national level. This trend may reflect the increasing weakness of national governments as single actors in the EU policy process as much as a desire on the part of governments to help their chosen 'clients'. Nothing could make a national government more isolated in the EU policy process than opposition from both the other member states *and* its own client interests. There are some indications that strains are already emerging between some national groups and their governments (and indeed between national administrative agencies and national governments) when the former begin to act independently in Brussels. Many national groups, because of their increased involvement in transnational networks, are often much better informed of EU policy developments at the crucial early stage than are their national representatives in COREPER and their national ministries back home. They have a better intelligence system, more effective transnational coalition-building strategies and are often better resourced in Brussels, where the best intelligence is gathered. The real threat to national-level relations is when groups develop a very strong Euro-focus, view the nation state as decreasingly relevant to the furtherance of their interests and develop the means to influence the Euro-policy process in their own right. This is precisely the situation of many multinational (and indeed national) companies, which now pursue European and global rather than national strategies. One should not be surprised that the Europeanization of the governmental affairs activities of large corporations follow the Europeanization of their product and marketing strategies. The cost savings arising from the standardization of products across regions such as Europe can be realized only if regional regulation exists. Moreover, given current trends towards economic globalization, we may even predict that the EU itself may eventually be challenged as an independent policy-making system.[30] Similar regionalization and globalization incentives also exist for voluntary groups promoting issues such as the environment, women's rights and consumer interests. Nation states may therefore be trapped in the type of 'two-level game' described by Putnam:

> At the national level, domestic groups pursue their interests by pressuring the government to adopt favorable policies and politicians seek power by constructing coalitions among those groups. At the international level, national governments seek to maximize their own ability to satisfy domestic pressure, while minimizing the adverse consequences of foreign developments.[31]

FROM GARBAGE CAN TO DECISION RULES

Policy-makers (both public and private) habitually prefer order to chaos, predictability to uncertainty, and negotiated environments to garbage can situations. For example, a common theme of business group representations to the 1996 intergovernmental conference is that the EU's decision-making rules are too complex and unpredictable.[32] Policy-makers also turn to familiar models when trying to solve problems. It is, therefore, unsurprising to discover that European policy-makers draw upon established practices and traditions of problem-solving. The standard operating procedures which seem to be emerging at the Euro-level have long traditions in western and northern European states. Over twenty years ago, Martin Heisler and Robert Kvavik summarized the nature of the 'European polity' model, as 'A decision structure characterised by continuous, regularised access for economically, politically, ethnically and/or subculturally based groups to the highest levels of the political system'.[33]

Clearly, the EU is still a very long way from a stable policy process in terms of institutional arrangements and formal rules. However, the old suggestion by the neo-functionalist theorists that groups would play a key role in the integration process may have renewed relevance if one takes account of more recent – particularly post-Single Act and post-Maastricht – developments. There is evidence that organized interests are increasingly active in pressing for standardization, harmonization, and for a 'level playing field' in Europe. It would be wrong, of course, to see this interest group pressure as necessarily leading to more European integration. However, in discussing the concept of 'Community sentiment', Ernst Haas suggested that two of the six conditions for this sentiment to flourish are that:

> Interest groups and political parties at the national level endorse supranational action and in preference to action by their national government . . . [and] Interest groups and political parties organize beyond the national level in order to function more effectively as decision-makers *vis à vis* the separate national governments or the central authority and if they define their interests in terms larger than those of the separate nation state from which they originate.[34]

His formal definition of political integration is as follows: 'Political integration is the process whereby political actors in several distinct national settings are persuaded to shift their loyalties, expectations and political activities toward a new centre, whose institutions possess or demand jurisdiction over the pre-existing nation states.'[35] Available evidence[36] suggests that we are witnessing that process at work and that interest groups are often active in pressing for wider EU jurisdiction over the existing nation states. Interest groups have, therefore, developed very considerably in their integrative role from the rather limited role described by Lindberg in 1963. At that time, he saw 'most EEC-level interest groups as merely liaison groups with essentially secretarial functions and no role to play in co-ordinating national group views'.[37] He suggested that interest groups:

> would be of limited significance for political integration, unless participation in them comes to represent a fundamental restructuring of expectations and tactics. To what extent have collective needs at the regional level taken priority over national differences? Do the necessities of 'international lobbying' force compromise of initial positions? Do interest officials become more 'Europe-minded'?[38]

His answer to these and other questions was very guarded, reflecting the relatively early stages of the development of Euro-lobbying in the early 1960s. His caution was in part based on the fact that, at that time, 'the vital interests of relatively few are as yet directly affected by decisions of the Community institutions'.[39] Crucially, however, he argued that,

> one can expect that over time the necessity for lobbying will force groups to emphasize collective needs rather than national differences. Such a development can be expected as the central institutions of the EEC become more active, as the types of actions taken involve the harmonization of legislation and the formulation of common policies (rather than the negative process of . . . barriers to trade), and as . . . groups become aware that their interests can no longer be adequately served at the national level alone.[40]

Groups in most policy sectors have recognized that supranational decisions are now inevitable and that it is often in their interest to engage in anticipatory activity in order to influence the shape and direction of European-level policy solutions. Increasingly, groups themselves have recognized the logic and momentum of the greater Europeanization of solutions. Now that Euro-legislation has attained critical mass in many policy areas they are beginning to play a very significant role in the process of European integration, as predicted by the neo-functionalists.

We are, however, left with the major problem of how best to conceptualize what now exists at the European level, having identified certain trends in the policy process. Traditional theories of European integration (such as neo-functionalism) help in understanding the historical process of integration itself, but do not necessarily help us to 'model' the contemporary policy process. They seem more useful in helping to explain how we got here rather than how the system is working now. National policy-making models – such as pluralism, corporatism, neo-corporatism and particularly 'policy network' and 'policy community' approaches[41] are helpful in describing some aspects of this multi-faceted process. However, as Gerhard Lehmruch has suggested, more complex conceptualizations of the structure and process of interest intermediation beyond, say, corporatism are attracting increasing attention. He argues that the metaphor of policy networks and typologies of economic governance may contribute to a better understanding of the role of the state or of administrative strategies in the emergence and dynamics of national and sectoral configurations in interest intermediation.[42] His proposal is that we should begin to analyse what he calls the 'configurative' aspect of interest intermediation: 'It is a structure made up of complex linkages between organizations, agencies, and other institutions the dynamic of which is not always sufficiently understood by isolating specific elements or relationships.' These linkages should be seen as hanging together in complex 'configurations'. Furthermore, he argues, to delineate a 'policy network' approach in combination with an emphasis on institutionalization may be a further step in trying to understand these configurative dynamics. Understanding the variability of policy networks is suggested as particularly important in the analysis of attempts to remodel patterns of state intervention.

We do not yet know quite what form this institutionalization will take, but it is a reasonable prediction that some form of institutionalization will take place in order to render the system of European-level intermediation manageable. It seems unlikely that decision-making in the Commission will shift significantly from the sectorized and segmented approach which has developed so far, although the environmental case does suggest that even sectorization can be eroded. EU policy is likely to continue to emerge from sectoral networks of some kind. The evolution of these networks is still under way and we would expect a multiple model of EU policy-making to continue, in which interests play an increasingly important role but in which policy-makers make increased efforts to 'manage' the system. Moreover, as always, institutions and ideas will be as important as policy networks in determining policy outcomes. The core of the policy process is likely to remain Commission-based, sectorally structured and linked with a complex and often rather incoherent issue network of groups or organizations across Europe and beyond. Only for certain types of problems, or at certain stages of the policy process, will well defined, tightly drawn 'policy communities'[43] develop.

Thus, the EU policy process will remain difficult to characterize.

Different policy problems may produce different kinds of politics.[44] At times the process may resemble intergovernmentalism and at other times some kind of 'managed pluralism' or even corporatism. Even for the same policy issue the process might be rather episodic, with each 'episode' presenting a different kind of politics. The key to understanding the variability of this process may lie in knowing more about the origin of policy ideas, the way in which they are transmitted and absorbed across a range of different actors, and the interaction between 'expertise' and 'interest'. Our own focus on the interface between the EU bureaucracy and interest groups can capture only part of this complex process. Our purpose has been to argue that, at the Euro-level, all is not chaos; decision rules are emerging and the policy-making process is becoming less like a garbage can. We recognize that, on any given issue, a multiplicity of actions is involved. As Sabatier suggests, when analysing the policy process we need to include other potential influential actors – such as journalists, analysts, researchers.[45] According to his analysis, we need to view 'advocacy coalitions' (rather than formal organizations or free-floating actors) as the key units.[46] In a key passage he argues:

> Within the subsystem, it is assumed that actors can be aggregated into a number of advocacy coalitions composed of people from various organizations who share a set of normative and causal beliefs and who often act in concert . . . conflicting strategies from various coalitions are normally mediated by a third group of actors, here termed 'policy brokers', whose principal concern is to find some reasonable compromise which will reduce intense conflict.[47]

The origin and nature of these causal beliefs is of special relevance to the analysis of the EU, bearing in mind our earlier comments regarding the apparent unpredictability of the EU's agenda-setting process. As Adler and Haas note, the main theoretical question of international politics is 'Where do expectations come from?'[48] Their answer is not too dissimilar to Sabatier's advocacy coalition approach – it is to suggest the key role, at the transnational level, of 'epistemic communities'. Epistemic communities exert influence on policy innovation by (1) framing the range of political controversy surrounding an issue, (2) defining state interests and (3) setting standards.[49] The shift in the nature of the international telecommunications regime is an oft-cited example of policy changes reflecting changes in the nature of epistemic communities – in that case from one dominated by concern for domestic monopolies and bilateral agreements to one dominated by concern for competition and a shift of jurisdiction to trade institutions that serve new political constituencies.[50] These epistemic communities consist of '*networks of professionals with recognized expertise and competence in a particular domain and an authoritative claim to policy relevant knowledge within that domain or issue area*'.[51] Thus, as demands for human interpretations of social and physical phenomena increase, so epistemic communities emerge as possible providers of information and advice. 'The members of a prevailing community become strong actors at the national and transnational level as decision-makers solicit their information and delegate responsibility to them.'[52] At the level of the EU – a kind of transnation state – the conditions for the emergence of these complex advocacy coalitions and epistemic communities appear to be present, as epistemic communities are thought most likely to emerge under conditions of uncertainty. The shift in the locus of power to the EU is creating a policy system whose main characteristic is likely to be a small professional bureaucracy (the Commission) developing ever closer relations with a complex *mélange* of other policy actors. Agendas will be defined and issues processed within these at best translucent worlds of experts and interests who coalesce around particular policy problems. The emerging 'European policy style', at least at the micro-level, is likely to emphasize bargaining, complex coalition building and consensus building in supranational policy-making arenas distant from conventional institutional settings familiar at the level of the nation state. Yet the fundamental nature of this policy style may exhibit features which are familiar at nation-state level in western Europe. In terms of policy style,[53] the EU policy process is likely to be *anticipatory*, largely because the Commission will always be seeking to launch new policy initiatives designed to further the long-term goal of European integration. The process is also likely to be *consensual*, largely because the integration process itself would be jeopardized if too many policies were merely imposed rather than negotiated. Witness, for instance, the retreat by the Commission following the widespread public perception of Maastricht as a treaty too far. This policy style is likely to involve the identification and early mobilization of those interests that matter and the creation of long-term institutional structures. Within these structures, interests are brought together with other key actors such as independent experts, policy entrepreneurs, national officials and, increasingly, extra-European actors. The inherent logic of this system will be to shift the EU policy style over time from garbage can to a stable set of decision rules.

ACKNOWLEDGEMENTS

This chapter forms part of a research project on lobbying in the European Community, funded by the ESRC, the main results of which are to be published in Mazey and Richardson, *Policy-making, European Integration and the Role of Interest Groups*, London, Routledge, 1996. We would like to thank Guy Peters and Albert Weale for commenting on an earlier draft.

NOTES

1 Michael D. Cohen, James D. March and John P. Olsen, 'A Garbage Can Model of Organisational Choice', *Administrative Science Quarterly*, 1972, vol. 17, pp. 1–25.
2 Sonia Mazey and Jeremy Richardson, 'Interest Groups and Representation' in the EC Paper presented to the ECPR Joint Workshop Sessions, Madrid, April 1994.
3 John Kingdon, *Agendas, Alternatives and Public Policies*, Boston, Little Brown, 1984.
4 Michael D. Cohen *et al.*, 'A Garbage Can Model', p. 2.
5 Jeremy Richardson, 'EU Water Policy-making: Uncertain Agendas, Shifting Networks and Complex Coalitions', *Environmental Politics*, 1994, vol. 4, 4, pp. 139–67.
6 David Earnshaw and David Judge, 'Early Days: the European Parliament, Co-decision and the European Union Legislative Process post-Maastricht', *Journal of European Public Policy*, 1995, vol. 2, 4, pp. 624–49.
7 Robert D. Putnam, 'Diplomacy and Domestic Politics', *International Organization*, 1988, vol. 42, 3, pp. 427–60.
8 George Tsebelis, *Nested Games: Rational Choice in Comparative Politics*, Berkeley, University of California Press, 1990.
9 Jürgen Habermas, *Towards a Rational Society: Student Protest, Science, and Politics*, London, Heinemann, 1971, p. 64.
10 Giandomenico Majone, 'Public Policy: Ideas, Interests and Institutions', in Robert E. Goodin and Hans Dieter Klingermann (eds), *New Handbook of Political Science*, Oxford, Oxford University Press, 1996.
11 Fürgen Habermas, *Towards a Rational Society*, pp. 62–80.
12 A. Downs, *Inside Bureaucracy*, Boston, Little Brown, 1967.
13 Sonia Mazey, 'Conception and Evolution of the High Authority's Administrative Services (1952–58): from Supranational Principles to Multinational Policies', in Roger Morgan and Vincent Wright (eds), *Yearbook of European Administrative History*, Baden-Baden, Nomos, 1992, p. 12.
14 Sonia Mazey and Jeremy Richardson (eds), *Lobbying in the European Community*, Oxford, Oxford University Press, 1993; Guy Peters, 'Models of Agenda Building: is the European Community Different?', *Journal of European Public Policy*, 1994, vol. 1, 1.
15 Giandomenico Majone, 'When does Policy Deliberation Matter?', *Politische Vierteljahresstiftung*, autumn 1993, p. 1.
16 Giandomenico Majone, 'When does Policy Deliberation Matter?', p. 10.
17 P. D. Henderson, 'Two British Errors: their probable Size and some possible Lessons', *Oxford Economic Papers*, 1977, vol. 29, 2, pp. 159–205, at p. 89.
18 Sonia Mazey and Jeremy Richardson, 'Environmental Groups and the EC: Challenges and Opportunities', *Environmental Politics*, 1992, vol. 1, 4, pp. 109–28.
19 A. G. Jordan and J. J. Richardson, 'The British Policy Style or the Logic of

Negotiation?' in J. J. Richardson (ed.), *Policy Styles in Western Europe*, Hemel Hempstead, Allen & Unwin, 1982.

20 Market Access Europe, *Brussels – the Tip of the Iceberg. The Role of Committees in the EC's Decision-making System*, Brussels, Market Access Europe, 1993.

21 Ibid.

22 Stephen George, *An Awkward Partner: Britain and the EC*, Oxford, Oxford University Press, 1990.

23 Sonia Mazey, 'The Adjustment of the British Administration to the European Challenge', Unpublished Conference Paper, presented to meeting on 'European Administrative Modernization', Perugia, July 1992.

24 Jeremy J. Richardson (ed.), *Pressure Groups*, Oxford, Oxford University Press, 1993, pp. 86–9.

25 Department of Trade and Industry, *Review of the Implementation and Enforcement of EC Law in the UK*, London, Department of Trade and Industry, 1993, p. 4.

26 Department of Trade and Industry (DTI), *Review of the Implementation*, p. 7.

27 Kohler Koch, 'Germany: Fragmented but Strong Lobbying', in M. P. C. M. Van Schendelen (ed.), *National, Public and Private EC Lobbying*, Aldershot, Dartmouth, 1993, pp. 23–48, at p. 27.

28 Ibid., p. 33.

29 Monon, *Agir pour ne pas subir*, Paris, Ministère des affaires européennes, 1989, p. 22.

30 William D. C. Coleman and Geoffrey R. D. Underhill, 'The Single Market and Global Economic Integration', special issue of *Journal of European Public Policy*, 1995, vol. 2, 3.

31 Robert D. Putnam, 'Diplomacy and Domestic Politics', p. 434.

32 Sonia Mazey and Jeremy Richardson, 'Agenda-setting, Lobbying and the Intergovernmental Conference 1996', in Geoffrey Edwards and Alfred Pijpers (eds), *The European Union and the Agenda of 1996*, London, Longman, 1996.

33 M. Heisler and R. Kvavik, 'Patterns of European Politics: the "European Polity" Model', in Martin Heisler (ed.), *Politics in Europe: Structures and Processes in some Postindustrial Democracies*, New York, David McKay, 1974, p. 48.

34 Ernst Haas, *The Uniting of Europe – Political, Social, and Economic Forces 1950–57*, Stanford, Stanford University Press, 1958, pp. 9–10.

35 Ibid., p. 16.

36 Justin Greenwood, Jürgen R. Grote and Karsten Ronit, *Organised Interests and the European Community*, London, Sage, 1992; R. C. P. M. Van Schendelen, *National Public and Private EC Lobbying*; Svein S. Andersen and Kjell A. Eliassen, *Making Policy in Europe: the Europeification of National Policy-making*, London, Sage, 1993; Sonia Mazey and Jeremy J. Richardson, 'The Commission and the Lobby', in Geoffrey Edwards and David Spence (eds), *The European Commission*, Harlow, Longman, 1994, pp. 169–201.

37 Leon N. Lindberg, *The Political Dynamics of European Economic Integration*, Stanford, Stanford University Press, 1963, pp. 287–8.

38 Ibid., p. 99.

39 Ibid., p. 99.

40 Ibid., p. 101.

41 Jeremy Richardson, 'Actor-based Models of National and EU Policy-making:

Policy Networks, Epistemic Communities and Advocacy Coalitions', in Hussein Kassim and Anand Menon (eds), *The EU and National Industrial Policy*, London, Routledge, 1996.

42 Gerhard Lehmbruch, 'The Organization of Society, Administrative Strategies and Policy Networks – Elements of a Theory of Interest Systems', in Roland M. Czada and A. Windhoff-Heritier, *Political Choice – Institutions, Rules, and the Limits of Rationality*, Frankfurt, Campus, 1991, p. 122.

43 J. J. Richardson and A. G. Jordan, *Governing under Pressure: the Policy Process in a post-Parliamentary Democracy*, Oxford, Martin Robertson, 1979.

44 T. Lowi, 'American Business, Public Policy, Case Studies and Political Theory', *World Politics*, 1964, vol. 16, 4, pp. 677–715.

45 Paul A. Sabatier, 'An Advocacy Coalition Framework of Policy Change and the Role of Policy Orientated Learning therein', *Policy Sciences*, 1988, vol. 21, pp. 129–68, at p. 138.

46 Ibid., p. 158.

47 Ibid., p. 133.

48 Emanuel Adler and Peter M. Haas, 'Conclusion: Epistemic Communities, World Order, and the Creation of a Reflective Research Program', *International Organization*, 1992, vol. 46, 1, pp. 367–90, at p. 371.

49 Ibid., p. 375.

50 Peter F. Cowhey, 'The International Telecommunications Regime: the Political Roots of Regimes for High Technology', *International Organization*, 1990, vol. 44, 2, pp. 169–99, at p. 169.

51 Peter M. Haas, 'Introduction: Epistemic Communities and International Policy Co-ordination', *International Organization*, 1992, vol. 46, 1, pp. 1–35, at p. 3, emphasis added.

52 Ibid., p. 4.

53 Jeremy Richardson (ed.), *Policy Styles in Western Europe*, London, Allen & Unwin, 1982.

Part II

Adapting national bureaucracies

4 Relations between the European Union and the British administration

Helen Wallace

British European policy is passing through a particularly difficult period. Policy has become highly politicized, not for the first time since British accession to the European Community. Parliamentary pressures have become as acute as at any point in the past twenty-five years. There is a sharp contrast between the declared ambition of the Prime Minister to place Britain 'at the heart of Europe' and the British government's startling isolation from its counterparts elsewhere in the EC. This was polarized in March 1994 in the controversy around the issue of enlargement, so long and so consistently a primary goal of British policy, when it seemed that the government's secondary objective of protecting its opportunities to obstruct unwelcome EC proposals would displace its primary objective of advancing enlargement. The management of policy is dominated by the tones and discourse of 'high Gaullism' – in its odd British variant – and it comes from a government that is at an unprecedentedly low ebb in terms of popular esteem.

So we first have to distinguish the conjunctural from the underlying patterns. British policy stems from a party that is deeply divided on many issues, but for which the European issue has become a touchstone of wider divergences. Indeed, to all intents and purposes the government has been behaving as if it were a fragile coalition, but deprived of the codes of conduct and underpinning mechanisms that make coalitions a 'normal' and manageable feature of politics in so many other European countries. The specificity of the problems makes it very hard to generalize about the UK in terms of either policy content or policy management. Moreover the results of intra-party and intra-Cabinet negotiation represent the product of tense and ill managed disagreement and cannot easily be said to be more widely representative of British opinion or of the reflexes of the British government in a more structural sense. Yet the impact of the arguments and the consequential marginalization of the British in the European

Union of course has a wider and more far-reaching impact on the way in which British policy is defined and pursued. So it is not only an ephemeral feature of the political cycle.

To set British policy in context thus requires not only an assessment of the underlying features of the British government, but also some explanation of the reasons why so many of the British political class remain so ill at ease with the concepts and the practices of European integration. But it should be noted that the story is not all one of negative factors or of reticence and maladroitness in the day-to-day practice of Community business. On the contrary, British public officials at their best – and many of the very best work on European dossiers – are among the most skilled practitioners in the European Union; they can and do bring their skills to bear in developing constructive EC policies and legislation, as well as from time to time in blocking European developments. British ideas have contributed to the adoption of valuable new European policies and remain pertinent to continuing debates about the future adaptation of European policies to changing circumstances.

EMBEDDED CHARACTERISTICS OF THE BRITISH ADMINISTRATION

It cannot be stressed too much that the traditions of British government remain rooted in the assumption that governmental responsibility is exercised collectively by a single party through the processes of the Cabinet and the co-ordination of policy between departments. The codes of conduct and the working practices of the official are tied to this assumption. Government is supposed to act in a unified way, with differences of emphasis and of perspective, but not of approach, emanating from different departments. Departments do not have rigidly defined and demarcated spheres of responsibility and indeed tasks can be switched with relative ease and flexibility between departments. Hierarchies there may be, but open divergences are not supposed to be perceptible. This puts tremendous pressure on officials, especially when operating abroad, to seek to represent the government as a whole. It also makes them ill at ease when dealing with a government that is not unified.

The same point holds for the deeply engrained deference to the doctrine of ministerial responsibility. Officials are supposed to be the servants of their ministers; they can and do argue against policies they believe to be misguided, but once an issue is settled their professional task is to implement it as efficiently as possible, and with a real commitment to efficiency. Indeed, as recent episodes reveal – the Matrix Churchill case and the Pergau Dam affairs are both illustrative[1] – this loyalty to the preoccupations and preferences of ministers is sometimes pushed to extremes. It is also put under duress when ministers themselves are deviating from apparently agreed Cabinet compromises and may well lead officials into giving priority to the immediate preferences of ministers that may be at variance with longer-term 'national' interests.

Yet it is also supposed to be the case that officials can just as easily work for a minister or a government with a different policy from those that preceded. The hallmark of the good British official is supposed to be an ability to adapt with facility and enthusiasm to changes of policy, doctrine and personality. Still, very few officials in Britain are appointed to senior positions because of their explicit political affiliation. One qualification should, however, be added. The very long period in office of a Conservative Party marked by its crusading ambitions of policy radicalism has had a countervailing impact. It has become harder for officials dealing with the sharp end of policy to remain detached from the partisanship which has become a more pronounced feature of British government.

What then of the 'organizational culture' of Whitehall? It has traditionally been the case that the upper reaches of the civil service were marked by high morale, a strong sense of professionalism, a striking public service ethic and a commitment to the 'Crown' as the symbol of the durable interests of the state under the British constitution. These remain features of Whitehall, but are less strongly etched than they used to be. Over the past decade and a half far-reaching changes have been introduced, in particular to make the conduct of government more 'businesslike' – in both senses, more productive and more like a company – and to privatize erstwhile public functions and thus to redefine the role of the public service. The result has been to privilege managerial skills and aptitudes much more than before in the definition and implementation of policy and to place a greater weight on 'performance indicators'; these tend to be weighted more to the immediate than to the longer term. This leads to some tensions between the more traditional features of organizational culture and these new approaches. The shift in the definition of the public service is more marked in the UK than in other European countries, though not unlike some feature of the US administration.

These points provide part of the backcloth to the treatment of and responses to 'Europeanizing' influences on the public service. A thorough retrospective analysis of the past two decades would probably show that the weight of specific British traditions and recent innovations had been much greater in their overall impact than the pressures resulting from involvement in European integration. But an important exception should be added. There has none the less been an important effort to equip the public service to deal with European business effectively, but more as a set of tasks demanding efficiency than as a large-scale reorientation of approach.

STRENGTHS AND WEAKNESSES IN DEALING WITH EUROPEAN POLICY

Since British accession European policy has been orchestrated through tight co-ordination from the Cabinet Office and backed by remarkably effective permanent representation – 'UKRep' – in Brussels. In terms of the smooth and consistent management of business, the efficient transmission of communications and the preparedness for European meetings, British administration is second to none. Indeed, a 'peer review' would probably quite easily yield agreement on this point. If anything Whitehall is over-zealous in carrying out obligations that flow from Community rules, as a report for the Department of Trade and Industry concluded.[2] The European Secretariat in the Cabinet Office, though very sparsely staffed, manages an impressive process of cross-departmental consultations and briefings for EC negotiations, issuing much detailed guidance to all officials concerned with EC work.

The result is to leave little leeway to individual departments or officials to depart from agreed lines of reasoning. By the same token invasive influences from beyond the UK can also be contained and canalized within the system. So strength in preparing coherent bargaining positions and in building a united front is accompanied by the force of arguments derived from intra-UK considerations. To take a recent example, in preparing ministerial discussions on the thorny issue of qualified majority voting in the Council of the EU Whitehall conducted an identical exercise to that which was conducted at the time of the Single European Act negotiations, namely to ask individual departments systematically to assess the impact of different voting rules on particular policy positions favoured by the British government. In the case of the Single European Act it was rapidly concluded that on virtually every sensitive issue where qualified majority voting was proposed it would not cause any problems, in that blocking minorities could probably be established and that in some cases British interests would be enhanced by the ability to override what would otherwise be vetoes from one or two other member states. In the case of EFTA enlargement the same exercise concluded that a blocking minority of twenty-three was preferable on the issues believed to be the most sensitive. This could be clearly seen from explicit statements by ministers on, in particular, environmental and social issues. The review thus strongly reinforced a position that had been adopted originally for more conjunctural reasons of party politics and hardened the negotiating position of the government as a whole. Those areas of policy where the twenty-seven threshold might allow scope for EU policy changes, notably in steps to reform the common agricultural policy, were subordinated in the argument.

The strong system of co-ordination in London is buttressed by UKRep in Brussels. UKRep works as a tightly knit team, with officials drawn from a cross-section of Whitehall departments and very close liaison with London. It is well trusted by the policy-makers in the UK and has great weight in generating advice on tactical negotiating positions. Not much light can be seen between the positions expressed by UKRep-based staff and those pursued by officials travelling out from the UK for EC meetings. The diplomatic service manages UKRep, though home civil servants are recruited to the team. The European Union Department in the Foreign and Commonwealth Office provides the links with UKRep and with the Cabinet Office, as well as a substantial contribution to policy advice across the range of issues. Thus negotiating positions for EC meetings are rigorously prepared, though it is a real strength of the British system that negotiators are permitted tactical flexibility to a remarkable extent.

In all these important nodes of the network dealing with EU policies, as well as in the key positions within individual departments, can be found many of the most able of Whitehall officials. Indeed, an examination of career patterns rapidly reveals that a European *cadre* has developed over the past twenty years which now includes in senior positions officials who have spent most of their careers dealing with the EC. This reflects two factors. First, it has come to be recognized by the personnel planners that European work is sufficiently important and demanding to merit the attachment of particularly able people to European posts. Second, there has been self-selection by people who have taken to European work with flair and enthusiasm and worked hard to keep on the European recruitment track, not always easy in a public service where people move jobs quite frequently and where the virtues of the all-rounder as against the specialist remain highly esteemed. This European *cadre* brings considerable skill, experience and enthusiasm to the day-to-day conduct of EU work, features which equip the government to deploy talented staff in pursuit of its policies, as well as providing interlocutors elsewhere in the EU with impressive counterparts to represent the UK.

It should also be noted that training programmes for civil servants now include a wide range of European courses. Some are very specifically geared to the acquisition of particular skills and knowledge by young and mid-career staff. Others seek to add a European dimension to broader staff development programmes. The approach is by and large practical and functional. Material developed for use in these programmes, especially on negotiating techniques, has been 'exported' to the Ecole nationale d'administration and the European Institute of Public Administration.

Thus it is somewhat perplexing that the British system has taken so long to focus on the question of British staff for European institutions. Only when the low level of successful entrants to EC recruitment competitions combined with the dawning recognition that at the middle levels the British were 'underrepresented' were remedies sought. Four years ago the European Fast Stream was introduced, a separate stream of recruitment of young high-flyers to be given Whitehall posts and then groomed for EU competitions. It is too soon to see the results of this initiative, though it is interesting to note the popularity of the scheme among applicants to the British civil service and the results of the 1994/5 competitions were encouraging in producing more successful British candidates.

A further factor stems from the tradition of secrecy in Britain. The British have no freedom of information legislation; transparency and openness are not the habits of government. It is normal for government representatives to refuse to divulge information on issues being negotiated abroad either to Parliament or to the wider public. But it is also normal for government to plead the case for confidentiality across a wide range of government business. In the case of EU work this tendency towards ultra-discretion has been strongly reinforced by political controversies which have found both ministers and officials reluctant to expose their flank to domestic attacks. Moreover until quite recently ministers and officials have not been under any particular pressure from parliamentarians to be very forthcoming. Thus, for example, the various negotiating texts for Maastricht circulated outside government in the UK only in pirate versions, while being quite freely available in some other member states. Inexpensive copies of the final text were not easily available for purchase in the UK, contrary to the practice in many other member states. Hence there was profound irony in the British presidency's discovery of 'transparency' and 'openness' as virtues to be incorporated into the conclusions of the Edinburgh European Council of December 1992. This found the British pulled in opposite directions as the Council of Ministers and COREPER sought in 1993/4 to turn this commitment into operating practice in Brussels under pressure from, in particular, the *Guardian* newspaper.

THE IMPACT OF THATCHERISM

To these general attributes of European policy management has then to be added the impact of Thatcherism in terms of doctrine, strong reservations about European integration and an authoritarian policy style. The impact was reinforced by the long period of powerful single party government, until, that is, the election of 1992. It is on these grounds that a quite strong parallel can be drawn with the impact of Gaullism on France's European policy during the 1960s.

The long period of the Conservatives in office and the recurrent implausibility of an alternative government being formed have imprinted a particular set of lines of reasoning and methods of work on the policy process. Strong single party government under Mrs Thatcher, a Prime Minister who believed consensus and compromise to be signs of weakness, generated two effects. First, it induced a combative approach to policy development at home and abroad and, second, it discouraged dialogue on policy with those who had different views both inside and outside government.

In this context the doctrinal stance of missionary neo-liberalism had an effect which cannot be overstated. It led the government to introduce radical reforms across the range of government policies and to submit policy proposals to tough tests of congruence with the underlying doctrines. Market liberalization, deregulation, privatization, monetary and fiscal rectitude, labour market flexibility, retraction of social cushions, all became goals to be pursued forcefully at home and, if necessary, to provide the rationale for overturning long-established British legislation and practices. The discourse of politics was altered and so too was the discourse of policy-makers within the civil service. Access to influence and to positions of esteem came also to be easier for those groups and organizations that shared the same broad philosophy. Visibly the younger cohorts in the Conservative Party and in the civil service were socialized into taking these perspectives as their predominant frame of reference.

Logic and consistency led to the espousal of similar objectives at the European as well as the national level. Mrs Thatcher's government thus quite readily supported the 1992 programme, in part as an opportunity to proselytize in Europe. The resistance to the social chapter of Maastricht emerged from these strongly held beliefs and was one of the few European issues on which there has been agreement *throughout* an otherwise divided government and parliamentary party on European issues. It also clearly separated the Conservatives as a whole from most opposition parties and many non-governmental organizations, with the result that British resistance to European social policy proposals had to be seen as based on partisan preferences, although they were presented as the defence of the 'national interest'.

The reticence of Mrs Thatcher's government towards European integration as such and towards the reinforcement of the EC both politically and economically are well known. During her period in office the whole government machine was forced to follow her firm direction, though with the more pro-European ministers jibbing from time to time and many officials seeking opportunities to mitigate the harsher tones of her discourse. However, a nationalistic and 'sceptical' discourse did become the defining frame of reference within government and within the Conservative Party, especially for the younger age cohorts entering parliament. It also froze the evolution of attitudes within the civil service, which might under different ministerial direction have become more 'Community-minded'.

The Thatcher period also had an impact on the relative influence of different parts of the government machine. The powers of the Prime Minister were reinforced, the prestige of the Foreign Office diminished (too seduced by foreigners, in Mrs Thatcher's view), the weight of the Treasury grew and the policy scope of the Department of Trade and Industry (very relevant to EC work) was narrowed. The large majority in parliament from 1979 to 1992 seemed to make the wooing of backbencher support redundant, though there were repeated skirmishes with the more pro-European Conservative backbenchers.

Paradoxically it was disagreements on Europe, especially over economic and monetary union, that led to Mrs Thatcher's rejection by her own party in 1990. With the election of John Major as the new leader and Prime Minister it was widely expected that the subsequent administration would move to a more pro-European position, with a more emollient style and the unfreezing of restrictive positions that had separated the UK from other member states in European negotiations.

THE CONTROVERSIES OVER MAASTRICHT

The beginnings of the Maastricht negotiations had taken place with Mrs Thatcher still in office and set against the main thrust of what most other member states seemed to be set on pursuing to reinforce the EC. It led to British negotiating positions frequently setting for others in the EC the main blockages to be overcome, as a close reading of successive drafts of the texts reveals. The underlying British approach did not change as the negotiations progressed, though the tones of the discussion within the EC softened, helped by the relief of other governments and of the Commission at not having to do battle with Mrs Thatcher. But significantly in the UK no real attempt was made to alter the wider base from which policy was defined either within the government or in the party and parliament. Policy on EMU softened, with several leading ministers and outside business and financial groups keen to allow scope for the pound to be included inside

EMU, but policy on political union remained critical of 'federalizing' or 'centralizing' tendencies on the continent and the language remained that of national autonomy and intergovernmentalism to be protected. The government then sought to present the results of Maastricht as a triumph of British ideas about the future direction of the new Union.

It might have been expected that this would liberate the British from the weight of past disagreements on Europe, and certainly interlocutors elsewhere in the EU hoped thereafter to be able to work alongside British negotiators who would more often find themselves closer to the mainstream of debate and less doctrinally driven. Instead the British government, especially after the first Danish referendum of June 1992, found itself increasingly under pressure from an increasingly vocal group of twenty to thirty 'Euro-sceptics' on the Conservative backbenches and from an articulate group inside the Cabinet. The 1992 election had considerably reduced the governing majority to twenty-one members, a smaller group than the 'Euro-sceptics', and had produced a new intake of younger MPs ready to join some of the long-time opponents of EU developments if necessary to defeat their own government.

There followed the long anguish of the ratification of the Maastricht Treaty, the crisis in the exchange markets that led to the pound's withdrawal from the exchange-rate mechanism and the disappointments of the 1992 UK presidency of the Council. The weight of the 'Euro-sceptics' in defining the terms of the debate in the UK grew and the negativism of ministers' language on European issues became more marked. British officials could do little but respond to the constraints imposed by divisions within the government. Policy became locked into the survival of the government and the harsher arguments between different wings of the party and of the Cabinet.

Not much scope was to be found here for inventiveness by officials to soften the edges of policy. If anything a different and also costly tactic came to be deployed, namely efforts to shift attention from the big issues of European integration to smaller questions on which the British might be able to succeed in making the EC look more attractive. Much effort was for example put into lists of subsidiarity issues[3] where policy might be 'repatriated', into detailed criticisms of particular environmental and social legislation and into criticisms of poor financial control or over-zealous Brussels bureaucracy. To an extent this attempt to alter the terms of discussion backfired, however, in adding to the weight of the arguments of the 'Euro-sceptics' and the negative image of the EU within the UK.

TENSIONS UNDER THE MAJOR GOVERNMENT

By spring 1994 the Major government was suffering from an accumulation of problems: a weak Prime Minister, a tired Foreign Minister, a divided Cabinet, a fragile parliamentary majority and a group of Euro-sceptics who believed they were winning the argument. Disagreements on policy were evident on many other issues, but the running disagreement on Europe had become the most acute and in some ways the convenient scapegoat – open warfare on economic policy or the domestic social agenda would be harder to contain. Some in the Conservative Party also believed that a more overtly nationalist position would win or at least preserve rewards from the voters, a seductive argument in the face of the opinion polls and the European Parliament elections of June 1994. Over the short term this European neuralgia both made the Cabinet a fragile coalition and left its governing majority in parliament very exposed. It could not, for example, be taken for granted that the House of Commons would ratify an EFTA accession treaty which failed to buy off the 'Euro-sceptics'. The issues and images that thus predominated in the management of Britain's European policy were all sharply politicized and mostly defensive.

This left the public service caught by the consequences and able to respond only by being as effective as possible in containing the repercussions of intragovernmental dissension and fraught relations with EC partners. This produced four main effects for the public service. First, it forced officials to concentrate on 'fire-fighting', that is to say, concentrating on tactical positioning, since there was little opportunity for developing longer-term strategic policy. Second, it left the energy and excellence of British officials dealing with European issues to be channelled into negative rather than positive activities. Third, it exposed officials to continuous parliamentary pressure at home, forced to attempt to shore up ministers *vis-à-vis* parliamentary scrutiny which had been strengthened by the Euro-sceptics and the mood of public disquiet that had spread across the Community. Fourth, it pitted the traditions and norms of working for a unified government against the uncomfortable realities of coalition behaviour within the Cabinet and the governing party.

MOVING GOALPOSTS

Part of the problem for British policy has been that the European policy process has been so unstable or subject to so much flux. At each period of critical debate within the UK the government of the day has attempted to stabilize domestic policy around a compromise that rested on the assumption that the European process had reached a settled point. Each time the hard-won compromise has been threatened by a new debate elsewhere in Europe that has pressed the incumbent British government to enter the fray to defend that domestic compromise against European partners. The one exception was the Single European Act in which British policy had anticipated a change in European policy on the role of the market.

Barely was the Maastricht ratification out of the way when the preparations and pre-negotiations began for the 1996 intergovernmental conference. Simultaneously the British government faced two contending sets of pressure. The growing weariness of other EU partners fuelled a debate on 'multi-speed' versions of integration which would, among other things, provide a line of reasoning to exclude the British from some inner circles of European decision-making. Meanwhile at home the Euro-sceptics within the government and within the party rushed to pre-define the British negotiating position for the intergovernmental conference as one that must above all defend British sovereignty and resist supranationalism. In parallel they sought unconditional assurances that the Britsh would not accept a single currency. The result was to maintain a high degree of 'politicization' of policy that permeated also mamnagement of the day-to-day agenda of the EU.

CONCLUSIONS

This chapter has sought to explain the politics of Britain's European policy.[4] The recurrent polarization on core policy goals casts a long shadow over day-to-day issues and relationships. Though there are signs of a drawing back from maximalist integration elsewhere in the EU the British case has a clear specificity. What is particularly aggravating for Britain's partners is the effectiveness with which policy is projected so much of the time by rather cosmopolitan and highly capable officials.

The Gaullist parallel deserves a moment's reflection. France too went through a period of idiosyncratic nationalism, also during a period of distraction by other difficult domestic and external issues. French officials meticulously carried out European policy – it also took some time for them to adjust to a different European policy during the 1970s. But as French policy evolved so the public service was able to deploy its skills and strengths in pursuit of a different set of goals and with a more consensus-oriented style. In the UK, as long as the Conservatives stay in office, government policy on Europe is likely to retain the tensions of coalition or 'cohabitation' politics, implicitly at least. The tensions on this issue area are deeply rooted and have been much exacerbated over the past few years.

Two further factors need to be added to the balance sheet. One is the 'intervention' of the British parliament, where (as in many other national parliaments) parochial preoccupations so easily predominate. In a period in which real legislative power or policy control is hard to protect it is perhaps not surprising that some parliamentarians should seize what opportunities they can to exercise leverage over a vulnerable government. Intriguingly the combination of the European argument and other current episodes (the Matrix Churchill and Pergau Dam inquiries – one judicial, the other parliamentary) may produce a strengthening of mechanisms for the scrutiny of ministers on a wider basis.

A second factor to note is the absence of stable intellectual discourse in the UK on European issues. In most other EC countries there has (in the past at least) been an identifiable 'epistemic community' embracing intellectuals, political elites, economic elites and policy practitioners, not all-encompassing but including mainstream opinions. This 'epistemic community' has been largely supportive of European integration at crucial points in the past and through changes of government. No such epistemic community has ever existed in the UK. Or rather its British equivalent has been very much a minority view, although it has significantly been heavily represented in the civil and diplomatic services. Though the business and financial communities in the UK would probably rally by preference to a 'make the best of Europe' position they also lack the cementing political discourse that might help to consolidate the argument. Similarly the majority parliamentary opinion across political parties could be rallied to a more pro-European position, but again has lacked the defining vocabulary. So it may be here that the analyst needs to probe further for explanations of the paradoxes of Britain's European policy.

NOTES

1 The Matrix Churchill case concerned the aborted trial of two businessmen who were accused of selling arms equipment to Iraq before the Gulf War and who claimed government complicity in the sales, leading to a tribunal of inquiry. The Pergau Dam affair concerned the allegation that the government had given substantial development aid to Malaysia in return for guaranteed arms sales. In both cases officials were pulled between loyalty to Ministers and respect for proper procedures.

2 *Review of the Implementation and Enforcement of EC Law in the UK*, DTI, London, July 1993.

3 See, for example, the list agreed at the Franco-British bilateral summit of June 1993, some of which found its way into the conclusions of the Brussels European Council of December 1993.

4 For a range of accounts on current British policy see 'Europe before the IGC', special issue of *Political Quarterly*, January–March 1995, vol. 66, 1.

5 German administrative interaction and European union

The fusion of public policies

Wolfgang Wessels and Dietrich Rometsch

THE GROWTH OF THE EC/EU SYSTEM AND THE GROWTH OF NATIONAL ADMINISTRATIONS: CONTRADICTORY OR COMPLEMENTARY?

Benign neglect and no impact: the relations between national and European administrations

There is a broad consensus that public administrations are as much a 'product' as a 'characteristic feature' of what we call the 'state'.[1] In all phases of the state's formation[2] the changes in its characteristics are closely linked with respective developments in public administrations.[3] Given this salience, research into the role of public administration has been and is of considerable extent and density. Several works in the 1980s[4] have dismantled the Weberian model of bureaucracy,[5] stressing that 'bureaucracies are involved at every stage in public policy-making'[6] and the more 'co-operative' relations between politicians, interest groups and civil servants.[7]

This line of research has included studies comparing several nation states but has widely left out of the research focus all cross-border administrative relations. For a long time there was 'benign neglect' of transnational or international administrative activities. On the other hand works studying administrative relations within international or European organizations[8] describe and categorize the role and functions of international and national bureaucrats in the policy cycle (preparation, formulation and implementation of decisions) of these organizations.[9] Some look at the impact of national civil servants via permanent representation[10] or via specific functional roles such as presidencies.[11] They also include the role of bureaucrats and administrations in decision implementation.[12] The major focus is orientated to the 'autonomy',[13] the 'decision-making modalities'[14] or the capacity to 'integrate' national civil servants[15] into a new system 'transcending the existing nations'.[16] A fairly common view is that national bureaucrats are not developing into 'Trojan horses'[17] – destroying the walls of national sovereignty from within.[18] These findings stress that national administrations as such are not really affected by the trans-border activities of some perhaps marginalized civil servants. As no major impact has been observed, 'benign neglect' of these trans-border activities is a logical consequence. The last few years have seen the emergence of the research focus on *Verwaltungsverflechtung*[19] and on a 'multi-tiered system of governance'.[20] Both approaches are quite often disjointed.[21] There was and still is in many cases a hidden assumption that administrations remained entrenched in national decision-making and implementation – a focus which is no longer adequate for states, or at any rate not for those that are members of the European Union. This thesis of 'no impact' is increasingly questioned: the attention attracted by the multi-level interlocking of administrations in recent years points to the growing recognition that this is a crucial element for national and European public policies. The 'two-level game'[22] does not add up to zero, but between national and Community levels there is, at least to a certain degree, a positive sum game.

The fusion thesis: the 'Europeanization' and integration of public policies

The evolution of the European welfare state – the fundamentals

This chapter takes a view which is contrary to both the 'benign neglect' of the experts on national administrations and the 'no impact' conclusion of the works on international and European organizations. It contends that we may be witnessing in the administrative reality of the EU member states (at least) a significant trend towards a mutual *engrenage*, 'interlocking', *Verflechtung*.

When the European Community was established, the governments and administrations of member states sought to ensure a more effective public policy making which led them to transfer competences and 'pool sovereignty'.[23] The converse of these ambitions, however, was the loss of national autonomy that increased integration and entailed co-operation. As time has passed, this basic dilemma has grown: the greater the interdependence among European countries, the stronger the propensity to move to Community rather than stay with national policies. As interdependence rises, whether as a result of this kind of government policy or of market forces or of interest groups' behaviour, the impulse towards Community activity increases, as common or co-ordinated action seems to become more effective.

Since a state's own policies cope with and contribute to rising interdependence, the EU can be seen as both a product and a contributor to the shaping of the dynamics of the west European welfare and service states in situations of increasing interdependence. In addition, the decreasing stability of the specific security architecture of a global regime established by hegemonic powers as was the case during the East–West confrontation has opened the way to a 'new creativity' in national and international politics. Under such conditions the west European welfare states are involved in a 'process of Europeanization'[24] which is reorienting politics 'to the degree that EC political and economic dynamics become part of the organizational logic of national politics and policy-making'.[25]

The institutional evolution of the EC/EU is thus connected with the post-World War II history of west European states, which is characterized by a combination of participatory mass democracy, the capitalist market economy, and the development of a welfare and service state.[26] Politically, these changes are closely linked with trends toward extensive and intensive participation by interest groups[27] and a significant increase in the functions and number of bureaucracies.[28] The history of the nation state[29] has entered into a new phase, that of the 'co-operative state',[30] or the 'industrial state',[31] which all point to broader 'Europeanization'. This new European state is not a reborn version of those European nation states that died in the two world wars but a qualitatively new entity with some major new attributes. These changes in the nature of the state mean that substantial opposition to strong supranational European bodies does not only come from outdated elements of the traditional state in the defence of 'anachronistic sovereignty'.[32] Basic constraints and major dynamics of the evolution and performance of the EC/EU can also be explained by the principal structures and functions of this 'modern' west European state. The legitimacy and authority of national governments are preserved, but they are 'progressively permeated by environmental inputs which become, over time, internalized in politics and policy-making'.[33]

The dilemma of west European governments is that successful economic performance is a major prerequisite for the stability of these welfare and service states. Governments in power see their electoral fate as directly linked to an adequate performance by state services, which implies sufficient economic growth. To achieve this goal, west European economies have to be open to an international and European division of labour. With economic interpenetration, however, interdependencies increase and the (at least *de facto*) autonomy of national systems decreases. Looking for help outside Europe – as occurred during the 1960s and especially the 1970s – from international regimes that could solve or set rules for the management of the interdependent welfare states, becomes less and less useful. The capacity of the United States to guarantee appropriate regimes, capable of tackling the problems of modern welfare states, has been sharply reduced.[34] The uncertainties together with the demand for common European responses have thus grown constantly in recent decades.

The problem has become even greater for west European politicians in the last few years: rising expectations make the modern west European states more and more responsible for a performance that is less and less within the reach of their autonomous actions. The 'hard shell of the social state'[35] is broken by the very dynamics of its own internal logic. Thus, not only are *de facto* interdependencies important – this phenomenon always existed within the 50-called 'world economies'[36] – but the changed political sensibilities of Western democracies have accentuated the consequences of economic interpenetration. The EU as such has further increased this market-led interdependence by its own instruments; with the transfer of competences throughout the history of the EC/EU, the legal autonomy of political action by the nation states has decreased and the economic interpenetration has increased. These basic trends in western Europe have led to a 'core Europe'[37] which has progressively drawn other economies and societies and therefore governments to it.

This policy-led interdependence has even increased more in recent years, with direct consequences for major public policies and the national constitutional and institutional set-up. Member states have adapted their internal organization and procedures to the demands and new participation possibilities of the EU system. With the establishment of the internal market, and with the planned economic and monetary union (EMU), the dilemma will again become sharper.[38] The instruments in the hands of national governments or central banks will either be transferred to the European level and/or become even less effective than in the 1980s.

Facing this dilemma, governments realize that a doctrine of 'naive sovereignty', that is, keeping all policy instruments in their own jurisdiction, is mostly counterproductive: the real effect of their own instruments on the economic and political realities is getting more marginal or – as President Mitterrand learned in his first years in office from 1981 to 1983 – even negative. The EC/EU and especially the Council offer access and influence where decisions with real effects are made. Member governments move from the position of a *de facto* 'decision-maker'[39] to that of a 'co-decision-maker'.[40]

To sum up this argument, European integration is, contrary to some other statements, 'a thread woven into the fabric' of the European society.[41] The European Union and the Maastricht Treaty are based on more than just the 'political will' of heads of governments or merely 'formal integration'[42] based on binding treaty provisions (important as they may be). They are reactions to persistent fundamental patterns of west European political and social developments. These fundamentals have not basically changed but have acquired an additional dimension with the collapse of the Soviet Union and the process of democratization and liberalization in eastern Europe. Thus we do not need to revise this argument after '1989'.

Long-term trends in European integration – three indicators

One of the consequences of these fundamental dynamics is a long-term trend towards Europeanization and the integration of public policies.[43] This process of growth and differentiation can be measured by at least three indicators. The first is the scope enlargement of traditional and new public policies being pursued within the EU system; increasingly, the number of state-activity sectors dealt with at the European level is approaching the scope dealt with by western European states, at least after the ratification and full implementation of the Maastricht Treaty on European Union. There are very few subjects on the national agenda which are not also addressed – albeit with varying intensity – by the EU institutions. For an illustration see Table 5.1 in which the composition and the number of Council sessions are enumerated as an indicator of the extensity and intensity of areas dealing with public policies.

The second indicator concerns the competences of operating state instruments for public policies; they have increasingly been transferred upwards to the EC/EU level. This process has been brought about by comprehensive 'package deals'[44] such as the Single European Act[45] and the Maastricht Treaty on European Union,[46] but even more so by legal 'mutations'.[47] Thus, in contrast to international organizations, an increasing number of binding decisions are being taken in an increasing number of sectors of public policy. Figure 5.1 documents the quantitative relation between binding decisions of the EC/EU and the legislative work of the Bundesrat.[48] It shows – in a very rough comparison – that the number of legal acts of the Council has continuously grown, especially since the 1970s, whereas the number of binding decisions decided by the national parliaments has remained the same or has even become smaller in the same time period.

Third, perhaps the clearest indicator of a long-term integration trend in active public policies is to be found in the establishment and subsequent development of the EC/EU institutions and the increased differentiation of legislative procedures. An essential characteristic of this institutionaliz-ation is the all-embracing and highly differentiated participation of national

Table 5.1 Number of meetings of the Council of Ministers, by policy area, 1975, 1980 and 1990

Policy area	1975	1980	1990
Others	2	4	–
Agriculture	15	14	16
General affairs	16	13	13
Eco Fin	8	9	10
Internal market	–	–	7
Environment	2	2	5
Research	2	–	4
Industry	–	–	4
Traffic	2	2	4
Development	3	1	4
Social affairs	2	2	3
Fishery	–	7	3
Energy	2	2	3
Education	1	1	2
Telecommunication	–	–	2
Budget	2	3	2
Consumer	–	–	2
Health	–	–	2
Culture	–	–	2
Disaster prevention	–	–	1
Tourism	–	–	1
External trade	–	–	1
Total	57	60	91

Source: Twenty-third, twenty-eighth and thirty-eighth Annual Reports of the Council of Ministers

governments and administrations, which has grown considerably over the last forty years and has fuelled the tendency for considerable procedural differentiation. If, on the basis of the Maastricht Treaty, one combines the various Council voting modalities with the different forms of the participation by the European Parliament in the quasi-legislative decision-making, it is possible to count at least twenty-five distinct procedures for taking binding decisions within the EC/EU.

By participating in EU bodies and institutions, national civil servants gain 'access' to and 'influence'[49] over EC decision preparation, decision-making and implementation. This somewhat wearing process pays off for them by enlarging their administrative expertise, their factual knowledge and by increasing their weight inside their respective national networks. The same general cost–benefit calculation applies to Community officials, who gain 'access and influence' on 'national' policy domains by opening their segments of the policy cycles to their national colleagues – although

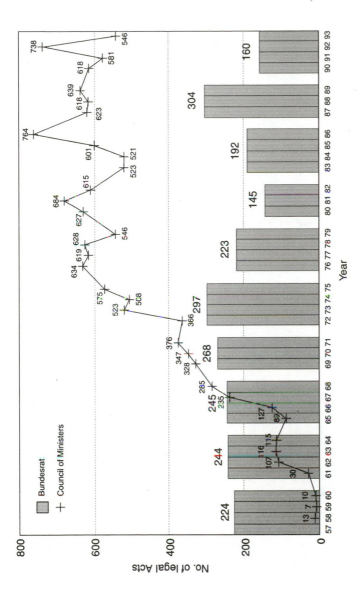

Figure 5.1 Comparison of the legislative 'output' of the Council of Ministers (per annum) and of the German Bundesrat (average per annum) during the legislative period: directives, regulations and decisions of the Council, and laws and ordinances (Rechtsverordnungen) co-decided by the Bundesrat

Source: Celex database and annual reports of the Commission (1991–3 only) for the Council, Bundesrat Handbook 1993/4 for the Bundesrat

traditional federalists and supranationalists would argue that this is an unacceptable loss of autonomy and independence on the part of the EC bureaucracy.[50] This kind of positive sum analysis by civil servants (*mutatis mutandis* by heads of state, ministers and interest groups, but not by national parliamentarians) creates major dynamics for integrating public policies. Such an evolution does not imply a 'transfer of loyalty'[51] by national officials to a new centre but reinforces trends towards a new system of shared government.

This stage in the evolution of the state is characterized by an increasing degree of co-operation, in vertical terms between different governmental levels, and in horizontal terms, among several groups of actors. The 'multi-level' interaction of civil servants of several national and international administrations thus supports trends towards specific forms of the 'sharing' or 'fusion' of powers between 'bureaucrats and politicians' which have also been identified by non-EU-related studies.[52]

The in-built dynamics of increasing multi-level participation by civil servants in EU public policy-making are thus closely linked with the evolution of the role and functions of states in western Europe. The fundamentals produce dynamic trends in administrative interaction. To understand this feature of public policies both sides of the coin have to be analyzed: not only the 'Brussels arena' (i.e. the EU level) but also the 'home game' (i.e. the national level).

THE GROWTH AND DIFFERENTIATION OF THE GERMAN ADMINISTRATION AND ITS IMPACT UPON THE EC/EU

Quantitative data on the involvement of German administrations: the increase in interaction

The German patterns of participation in the EU arena are certainly not typical but they illustrate the basic features of extensive and intensive Europeanization.

At first glance the picture of the administrative interaction between national and European level is – in the German case – rather complex, with many and different actors (see Fig. 5.2).[53] To this add the special roles played by two quite independent bodies, namely the Bundesbank (central bank) and the Bundesverfassungsgericht (German Constitutional Court), neither of which is directly involved in EU decision-making (with some exceptions in the case of the Bundesbank, see below). Nevertheless both have an important indirect influence on Germany's EU policy, as can be seen in connection with the ratification of the Maastricht Treaty and in connection with the Bundesbank's high interest rate policy and the

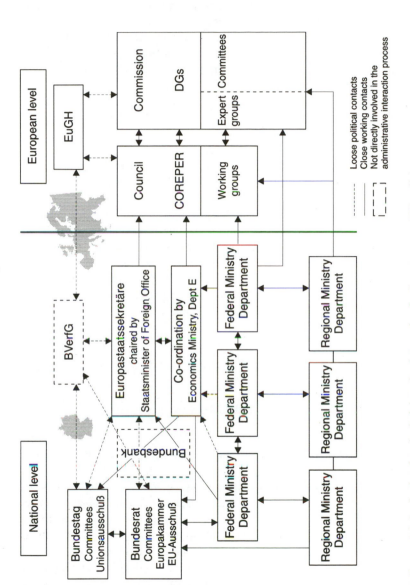

Figure 5.2 Institutional and administrative interaction in Germany over EU policies

debate about bringing in EMU. As a corollary of its federal structure there are different levels which intervene in the policy preparation, policy-making and implementation process. The policy-making power is distributed between the federal level, the *Länder* and the local level, all three of which dispose of specific rights under the constitution. The vertical division of power in the Federal Republic has led to a complex system of 'political interconnectedness' (*Politikverflechtung*)[54] in which there is no single decision-making centre but in one which different levels interact and participate on an equal footing in the cycle of making public policies.

At the ministerial level

Looking back over forty years of European integration with its three fundamental long-term trends, we can witness a parallel and in some ways proportional increase in the involvement of German administrations in the Community and EU affairs.[55] Whereas in the early 1960s it was mainly four Ministries that were shaping the Community policy cycle – the so-called 'four musketeers' in EC affairs i.e. the Foreign Office, the Economics Ministry, the Agriculture Ministry and the Finance Ministry – since the Single European Act and especially since the Maastricht Treaty on the European Union, we observe that practically every ministry is involved in Brussels, participating in the increasing number of Council meetings (see Table 5.1 above). With the exception of the Ministry of Defence, nearly all other ministries have 'their' Council session or even their various Council sessions in Brussels – the Economics Ministry is for example responsible for the internal market Council as well as for external trade policies and the session of the economic ministers. 'Technical' and 'sectoral' ministries like the social, family and environmental ministries are heavily involved, like more horizontally responsible ministries such as the Foreign Office and the Finance Ministry. Even those ministries which are traditionally oriented towards 'domestic' matters, such as the Ministry of Internal Affairs and the Ministry of Justice, are to an increasing extent – though still in somewhat different terms – involved in the Brussels business.

One indicator of this horizontal differentiation is the division of labour among the national ministries in times of an EC/EU presidency (see Table 5.2). A considerable number of ministries are involved: the Foreign Office and/or the Economics Ministry do not have a monopoly; the relative share of ministries outside, even beyond the 'four musketeers', has clearly increased between 1988 and 1994. In fact, during this period, concerning the presidency, their share has grown from 23 per cent to 30 per cent and in relation to the speaker of the German delegation their share increased from 35 per cent to 39 per cent in the same period.[56] Also the number of civil

Table 5.2 Division of labour among Presidents and representatives of the Federal Republic of Germany in the working groups of the Council during the German presidency, first half of 1988 and second half of 1994

Ministry	Presidency		Speaker of the German delegation	
	1988	*1994*	*1988*	*1994[a]*
Economics	29	23	48	49　(12)
Foreign Office	2	22[b]	1	22[b]
Agriculture	18	42	23	51　(23)
Finance	13	2	30	30　(1)
Justice	24	20[c]	25	22[c]　(10)
Labour	3	4	4	5　(6)
Transport	4	3	4	8
Youth, Family and Health	3	23[d]	13	28[d]　(7)
Interior	3	18[c]	3	21[c]　(13)
Permanent representation	91	96	26	30　(1)
Other	10	11	20	31　(12)
Total	202	264	197	297　(85)

Source: Wolfgang Wessels, *Die Öffnung des Staates. Modelle zwischenstaatlicher Verwaltungsstränge 1960–1990*, Bonn (forthcoming); concerning the *Länder* representatives only: Bundesrat, *Ausschuß für Fragen der Europäischen Union.*

Notes:
(a) Figures in parentheses show representatives of the German *Länder* in Council working groups in which they can generally participate (as of 2 January 1995).
(b) Because of the merger of the working groups (especially concerning the second pillar).
(c) Justice and Home Affairs has had working groups only since Maastricht.
(d) The Ministry of Youth, the Family and Health was split in 1994 into the Ministry of Health and the Ministry of Youth and the Family; for a better comparison the figures of the two Ministries have been added here.

servants in the permanent representation of the Federal Republic in Brussels indicates, in comparison to the other member states, intensive involvement by the German ministerial administration (see Table 5.3). In addition to this, the German permanent representation in Brussels is constituted mainly of civil servants from the Foreign Office and the Economics Ministry (approximately 50 per cent) but also from other ministries such as transport or science and research.[57]

If we want some kind of quantitative overview we may use two different methods to come up with an educated guess:[58] around 25 per cent of all Bonn-based federal civil servants who belong to the academically trained A-grade of civil servants are involved during their normal working activities in the affairs of the European Union. Another indicator is the differentiated division of labour within each ministry: over the years nearly all ministries have established a division (*Abteilung*) or subdivision (*Unterabteilung*) of

Table 5.3 Number of civil servants at the permanent representations to the EU (including B-level civil servants), 1960–95

Country	1960	1975	1985	1992	1995
Belgium	10	22	27	32	35
Denmark	–	22	29	35	37
Germany	19	39	40	46	59
France	10	24	28	40	46
Ireland	–	24	27	26	28
Italy	15	29	37	38	41
Luxembourg	2	5	4	6	7
Netherlands	14	23	24	28	36
United Kingdom	–	40	38	50	46
Total	70	228	254	301	335

Source: For 1960: M. Verally, P. Gerbert, J. Salmon, *Les Missions Permanentes auprès des Organisations Internationales*, vol. 1, Brussels, 1971, p. 583 ff.; for 1975, 1985, 1992 and 1995: *Yearbook of European Organizations*, Brussels, for the respective years.

international and European affairs.[59] There are *Europabeauftragte* in each ministry, i.e. higher civil servants who are responsible for overall information on EU affairs. The concrete responsibility is, however, located with the section (*Referat*) responsible for a certain sectoral or functional portfolio. Many ministries also have specialized units which monitor the policies of other ministries (so-called 'shadow units') and in this case especially the activities of these ministries in the EC/EU context. Some ministries also have specific horizontal responsibilities for EU matters, such as the Ministry of Finance. A civil servant from this ministry is present at virtually every Council session, but the Foreign Office too and the Ministry of Justice follow other activities closely; a more recent feature is the growing weight of the federal chancellery.

'Brussels' is thus not a low-key enterprise merely for some civil servants specializing in European affairs or certain marginalized experts or the province of only one level of the administrative hierarchy, but it is now woven into the daily routine of all levels of nearly all Bonn ministries. This increase in administrative involvement is not simply a consequence of an endogenous in-built bureaucratic expansion which Parkinson[60] or the economic theory of bureaucracies[61] would predict but reflects the increasing importance of EC/EU legislation to German public policies.

At the Land level

Given the quantitative and qualitative growth of EC/EU legislation, the *Länder* governments and their administrations have considerably increased their involvement in European affairs within the last seven years. The Single European Act and the law bringing about its ratification and even more the Maastricht Treaty on European Union and the consequent changes to the Basic Law (*Grundgesetz* or GG) – and here especially Article 23 of the Basic Law – as well as the subsequent laws enacting the rules,[62] have been pushed through by the *Länder* governments[63] and have led to extensive and intensive participation by *Länder* administrations in European affairs. In fact, in July 1995 there were 129 representatives of the *Länder* appointed to working groups of the Council and 232 to expert groups of the Commission.[64] *Länder* governments have opened offices in Brussels from the mid-1980s onwards[65] which are midway between a special lobby group and semi-state representation. Starting with one or two higher civil servants, some of them now have nearly all *Länder* ministries represented in Brussels and some have even moved the European Affairs units from the *Länder* capitals to Brussels.

In view of this internal structure most *Länder* governments have their own Minister of European Affairs (identical quite often with the Minister of Federal Affairs or Minister of Home Affairs, as in the case of Hessen) and some state chancelleries of the Prime Ministers of the *Länder* (such as in North Rhine-Westphalia, Bavaria and Hamburg) have special units responsible for co-ordinating *Länder* ministries in respect of EU affairs. With the new Article 146 TEU, Germany can now also be represented by ministers at the *Länder* level who are empowered to take decisions in the name of the Federal Republic as a whole. Until 1995 this has been the case in four Council sessions (education, culture, research, internal affairs). The *Länder* ministries have now become as experienced in EU affairs as their federal 'competitors' – with regard to the procedures and legal characteristics of EU affairs as much as in terms of the substance of policy. Their active participation in the newly established Committee of the Regions has further contributed to their expertise and to their direct involvement in the EU policy cycle in Brussels.

Procedural participation: the complexity of intra-German decision-making

The government/ministerial administration

Not only did the number of players increase at all administrative levels but also the procedure for reaching a German position in Brussels developed into a complex system involving of civil servants from different administrative units at several levels (see Fig. 5.2 above). On closer examination the analytical distinction between the horizontal dimension –

the federal level – and the vertical dimension of the involvement of the *Länder* and perhaps of the local authorities does not look very convincing. Since the Single European Act and even more since the Maastricht Treaty, the involvement of the *Länder* has been organized mainly via the Bundesrat, which in a constitutional perspective is a federal organ. Although according to Article 83 of the Basic Law the general rule is that the *Länder* are responsible for the administrative implementation of federal laws as well, the Bund in addition to this disposes of a special federal administration (*bundeseigene Verwaltung*, Article 87 of the Basic Law, such as the foreign service, the federal finance services, the German mail, the federal border guard, etc.); as a result the administrative interaction map is so complex – known by the term 'administrative federalism'[66] – that a simple and clear distinction between federal and *Länder* levels is no longer really adequate.

The policy cycle in Bonn has some persistent features. The instructions (*Weisungen*) on the position of the federal government are normally formulated in co-ordination sessions which take place at least once a week in the Economics Ministry, where Department E (for Europe) has the main responsibility for transmitting the instructions from Bonn to the permanent representation in Brussels and vice versa. These positions are normally based on a horizontal consensus-seeking among the ministries concerned, where the *Federführung*, i.e. the responsibility for steering the process, is located with the ministry responsible for the matter. In the event of conflicts arising among ministries the most important body is the Ausschuß der Europa-Staatssekretäre (Committee of State Secretaries with responsibility for European Affairs), which meets approximately once a month before the General Council. This body is chaired by the *Staatsminister* (Minister of State) in the Foreign Office (a junior minister who is also a member of the Bundestag). The secretariat of this committee is again the responsibility of Department E within the Economics Ministry. The Ausschuß der Europa-Staatssekretäre is composed of the 'four musketeers' who are mostly involved in EU business as well as by the permanent representative in Brussels and the state secretary responsible for Community affairs in the Federal Chancellor's office; state secretaries and higher civil servants from other ministries may join the meeting if business from their responsibilities is on the agenda.

As far as the irregular meetings of the European Delegates (*Europa-Beauftragte*, i.e. divisional heads or subdivisional heads) and the weekly meetings of the 'Tuesday Committee' (*Ressortleiter*, i.e. heads of section) are concerned, neither has the political authority to resolve inter-ministerial conflicts. The Tuesday Committee has the function of going through the agenda of COREPER to work out the instructions which are

Table 5.4 Inter-ministerial co-ordination committees in German EC policy-making

Committee	Date of creation	Function	Frequency of meetings and presidency
Cabinet Committee on European policy	1973	Important political matters; global strategy	One session in October 1973 and in the 1980s [CH]
State Secretaries' Committee (Europa-Staatssekretäre)	1963	Controversial political questions; preparation of political documents	Approximately every four weeks; during presidency more often [AA]
Europe Delegates (Europa-Beauftragte)	1971	Exchange of information	Approximately every four to six weeks [BMWi]
Tuesday Committee (heads of section)		Detailed technical matters	Weekly meetings

Note: CH Chancellor; AA Foreign Office; BMWi Economics Ministry.

then officially sent by the Economics Ministry to the permanent representative. In the session the principle of *Federführung*, may help to ensure a clear sharing of responsibilities, although this principle does not prevent conflicts arising between different ministries.

It is plain that in such large and heterogeneous groups it is difficult to co-ordinate the divergent views and to develop a common and comprehensive strategy with regard to Brussels. Too many actors and issues are involved on a non-regular basis to make it easy to formulate a coherent overall approach. Thus very often the co-ordination gets stuck in the 'morass of technical details' and ministerial self-interest prevails. This may explain why the German position in Brussels is often based on individual ministries and why, even in the permanent representation, civil servants often show a higher degree of loyalty to their home ministry than to a coherent European policy of the Federal Republic.

The rather byzantine division of labour and responsibilities between the Economics Ministry and the Foreign Office goes back to an agreement in 1958 between the then Ministers Brentano and Erhard which reflected the balance of power at the time between the rather weak Foreign Office and the strong Economics Ministry.[67] This sharing of responsibilities does not imply, however, that the two ministers are the 'masters of the game' in Bonn. Apart from sarcastic remarks by representatives of other ministries ('Let them get on with co-ordinating each other and we'll do our European business as we would like to do it anyway'), each ministry is careful to retain its area of competence and is normally quite successful in doing so.

Some ministries, as for example the Ministry of Agriculture, also have 'their' own direct channels to their Council and COREPER sessions. Thus the lack of effective co-ordination of European policy may give rise to a situation where the Agriculture Ministry is asking Brussels for more money for its farmers while the Ministry of Finance at the same time is reminding its European partners that the EC has to reduce its expenditure. And this 'polyphony'[68] may become yet more complicated if the *Länder* are representing Germany in the Council and they bring up their specific positions on an issue.

As a consequence of the unitary institutional structure of the EU (Article C TEU) and the key role of COREPER for all three pillars (Article 151 TEU), the battle to steer the internal preparation has been relaunched. In May 1993 the Foreign Office established a new division of European affairs (the Europaabteilung) which brings together into one unit the European economic section and the EC section, hitherto separate. But even this limited rearrangement soon ran into problems with the political division of the Foreign Office, which still hosts the 'European correspondent' responsible for CFSP matters. In clear difference from the French system of the Secrétariat Général du Comité Interministériel and the British European Section of the Cabinet Office there is no specialized independent agency set up to run and organize the positions for Brussels.

The highest level of conflict resolution among federal ministries is supposed to be the Europa-Kabinett, a special committee of the government, which met once in 1973 and at the beginning of Kohl's chancellorship. The reason for this is that EC/EU affairs have become so important that they are almost permanently on the agenda of the Cabinet. Chancellor Kohl in particular prefers to overcome differences between ministries in small personal meetings and not in quasi-official sessions of the Cabinet. This enables the Chancellor to keep EC policy-making 'under control' and to develop its own style of a kind of 'permanent leadership' in European affairs.

The Länder and the Bundesrat

In addition to these inter-ministerial co-ordination processes, we have to look from the perspective of the growing involvement of the *Länder*. Right from the beginning of EC history civil servants of *Länder* ministries, when competent, have been involved informally in the preparation of EC business. However, with the Single European Act, the ratification of the Maastricht Treaty on European Union and the amendment of the Basic Law, their role in decision preparation and decision-making has been considerably extended. To this add their specific competences in the field of the third pillar – the police are mainly under *Länder* competence as well as some provisions concerning asylum seekers and foreign residents; however, the CFSP is excluded from *Länder* involvement.

The participation of the *Länder* and their 'sphere of influence' – the Bundesrat – includes a set of rights and competences which are differentiated according to the constitutional provisions relating to the *Länder*. Since Maastricht, the representatives of the *Länder* governments are fully informed about almost every step in Community deliberations via the official minutes of each meeting. According to Article 23 § 5 the federal government has to give 'due consideration' (*maßgeblich zu berücksichtigen*) to the opinion of the Bundesrat in the negotiations in Brussels in case the legislative powers of the *Länder* are 'essentially . . . affected' (*Wenn im Schwerpunkt Gesetzgebungsbefugnisse der Länder . . . betroffen sind*). According to Article 23 § 6 the Bund even has to hand over the representation of German interests in the Council to a minister of the *Länder* whenever matters which are the exclusive legislative competence of the *Länder* are being debated.[69]

Should the government and the Bundesrat fail to reach a common position concerning affairs on which the *Länder* have exclusive competence (such as education and culture, but others too), the Bundesrat can impose its view by a two-thirds majority against the Bund.[70] This provision is not applicable in cases where the Bund is financially involved and must be interpreted in accordance with the constitutional principle of 'federal loyalty' (*Bundestreue*, Article 37 GG). This principle is reaffirmed in other words in § 5 of the implementation law of March 1993, stating that 'the responsibility of the federal level for the German state as such'[71] has to be respected by the *Länder*. The in-built tension in these provisions cannot be overlooked and may give rise to future legal disputes between Bund and *Länder* in EU affairs.

To secure a prompt and efficient reaction to deliberations in Brussels the Bundesrat created in 1988 a Europakammer, i.e. a kind of 'mini-Bundesrat' for European affairs, with the power to take decisions for the Bundesrat as a whole. Since Maastricht and the subsequent constitutional changes the Europakammer is now explicitly mentioned in Article 52 § 3a of the Basic Law. Since its creation the Europakammer has convened seven times; its latest meeting concerned the Commission's White Paper on 'growth, competitiveness and employment'. Moreover the newly established Conference of the European affairs ministers of the *Länder* (*Europaministerkonferenz*) in October 1992 is an additional instrument for the *Länder* to closely follow EU affairs, to co-ordinate their views and to exert influence on the decision-making process in the Council.[72] In this context Article 23 of the Basic Law can be called a 'vertical instrument' with regard to the Bund for better information and participation in EC matters whereas the *Europaministerkonferenz* is essentially a 'horizontal instrument' for better co-ordination among the *Länder*.

This involvement of the *Länder* is a rather complex affair which – at least since the Single European Act – has, surprisingly, worked quite efficiently and without major problems. There have been two or three problematic cases so far, one of which – the so-called 'television directive' – was brought before the jurisdiction the Bundesverfassungsgericht for a decision. In the preliminary ruling of April 1989 the federal level won this case, since the general external interest of the Bund seemed to prevail over *Länder* interests. However, in its decision of 22 March 1995 the Bundesverfassungsgericht repeated this point, but added that in spite of its central role the Bund had violated the principle of 'federal loyalty', since it had not sufficiently taken into account one major point of the *Länder*'s concerns in the negotiations over the 'television directive' in Brusssels.

The search for a broad multi-level consensus is a basic principle and pattern for the making of many public policies in the Federal Republic of Germany. We do not expect constant constitutional battles in the future – though legal disputes will certainly increase – but that the capacity of the German politico-administrative system to act and react to Brussels will be of a sufficient degree of efficiency to increase the chances of effective implementation as well (see below).

The Bundestag

So far the Bundestag has complained quite often and quite bitterly that it has been more or less excluded from the preparation for and making of decisions in Brussels.[73] A major problem, however, was that the Bundestag itself was not able to organize its internal procedures in order to arrive at an official position in reasonable time. In some cases the Bundestag approved a statement on what it took to be a proposal by the Commission which in fact had already been published as a legal Act in the Official Journal of the EC.[74] The Bundestag has tried various ways to organize itself with respect to the EC; in order to deal with European affairs it established a 'commission' (1983), a 'subcommittee' of the Foreign Affairs Committee (1987) and the 'EC Committee' in 1991.[75] With the amendment of the *Grundgesetz* – here Article 45 – and the implementation law of 12 March 1993[76] the Bundestag also established a new Ausschuß für Angelegenheiten der Europäischen Union (Committee on European Union Affairs, or Unionsausschuß for short) which can – but not always – take decisions for the Bundestag as a whole. Furthermore, according to the new Article 23 § 2 of the Basic Law the Bundestag will be informed at all stages 'comprehensively' and 'as quickly as possible' of the activities of all bodies of the European Union.[77] The position of the Bundestag is supposed to serve as 'basic platform' for the negotiations of the federal government in Brussels. According to Article 23 § 3 of the Basic Law, the government must empower the Bundestag to vote on a resolution 'before' a decision is taken in the Council. The government has agreed to 'base' (*zugrunde legen*) the negotiations in Brussels on the Bundestag's opinion.[78] No evaluation of the concrete application of these provisions has yet been attempted, however, it is expected that the impact of the Bundestag especially in the preparatory phase of the EC/EU decision-making process will have been improved. The new Unions-ausschuß convened for the first time in December 1994 and is composed of thirty-nine regular members and eleven associated members of the European Parliament. What is new about the Unionsausschuß is that the plenary of the Bundestag *can* authorize it to assume the rights of the Bundestag as a whole with regard to the government in European affairs. The idea is that the Bundestag should be enabled to react quickly to changes in the legislative drafts coming from Brussels, thus being a 'competitor' to the Europakammer of the Bundesrat. As of December 1994 it is not yet clear what will be the specific competences of the Unionsausschuß, especially in relation to the existing specialist committees of the Bundestag (*Fachausschüsse*), like those on agriculture and foreign affairs, and under which conditions it would get what kind of – general or partial – authorization of the rights of the Bundestag.[79] This last point is important, since a *general* delegation of the rights of the Bundestag to the Unionsausschuß as mentioned in Article 23 GG would make it a quite powerful body. In December 1994 an amendment to § 93 of the rules of procedure of the Bundestag was approved, including the introduction of a new § 93a on the Ausschuß für Angelegenheiten der Europäischen Union. According to these new provisions the Unions-ausschuß has in principle – if the Bundestag does not decide otherwise – the main responsibility (*Federführung*) concerning the treatment of EU documents and it can invite to its deliberations in addition to the eleven associated German MEPs further German members of the European Parliament. It is questionable whether the Unionsausschuß and the other committees of the Bundestag have achieved a workable *modus vivendi* in EC/EU affairs, as it is difficult for parliamentarians to adapt their working methods to the Brussels speed and style; thus many EU issues will not be perceived as politically relevant.

There are also in-built conflicts between the Bundestag and the Bundesrat about sensitive issues which rank high on the government/opposition agenda and which are primarily of a political nature.[80] Again the general assumption is that, although the complexity has increased, the procedures as such will work on the basis of 'federal loyalty' and 'consensus' and will not create permanent and major structural problems for the position of the federal government in the Council. However, the Bonn set-up must at least try to make itself 'fit' for the demands and challenges of the EU policy styles. Much, of course, will also depend on the state of the parties within the Bundestag and the Bundesrat and the general attitude of public opinion with regard to the European integration process.

The implementation of EC legislation in the Federal Republic: not an easy task

In general terms the German political system contains a basic dilemma with regard to the implementation of EC legislation: there is a vertical division of power between the federal level, the *Länder* level and the local level (*Bund – Länder – Gemeinden*) in which the Bund clearly dominates the decision preparation and making segments of the policy cycle because of its broad competences and its responsibility for the state as a whole; this gives rise to a tendency to centralization which affects EC/EU matters in particular and which the Bundesverfassungsgericht acknowledged in its decision on the 'television directive'. In contrast to its power the Bund heavily depends on the *Länder*, and also the *Gemeinden*, concerning the implementation of legal acts. Any decision taken at the federal level is useless if the other levels – especially the regional and local administrations – do not fully and correctly implement them. A case study of the application of the EC social regulations in the transport sector has shown that at the end truck drivers are controlled by the police, who act under the direction of the *Länder* and who report offences to the competent town clerk's office (i.e. the *Gemeinde* level). The local level is responsible for the subsequent proceedings both to the commercial inspectorate of the *Länder* (the Gewerbeaufsichtsamt) and the Federal Agency for Long Distance Haulage (Bundesanstalt für Güterfernverkehr).[81] Thus, although at a later stage federal agencies and ministries come in, there is no denying that the federal level depends on the co-operation of the local and regional authorities, which in turn assigns to the latter attributes an important 'administrative power'.[82]

Concerning implementation the Basic Law contains specific provisions under which the *Länder* execute federal laws either as 'own affairs' (Article 84 GG) or 'by order of the Bund' (Article 85 GG, *Bundesauftragsverwaltung*). In political practice these provisions developed into a system of centralized decision-making (upstream) and decentralized implementation (downstream) which was – as mentioned above – not completely unfavourable to the *Länder*, since they gained access to and influence in Bonn. To this observation add the provisions on the so-called 'mixed tasks' (*Gemeinschaftsaufgaben*, Article 91b) which were introduced into the Basic Law in the late 1960s and which had a similar effect. The closer co-operation of Bund and *Länder* and the overlapping of competences led to a system in which both levels join in both, in the upward as in the downward stream; this pattern becomes more and more dominant in the EC/EU framework. Some see, however, the Bund as exerting a certain leadership in this two-way policy stream, especially in the preparation and making of public policies.

Local administrations are also considerably concerned with EU affairs as they have to implement EC decisions and as their own policies have to stick to EC rules.[83] In spite of being the object of EC policies they are considerably less involved in the preparation and making of those policies. Though they also have some kind of external representation through certain specialized administrative units such as port authorities, or trade fair agencies, they have not yet developed any kind of organizational set-up comparable to that of the Bund or the *Länder*. They are represented in Brussels by some small offices of associations of local authorities such as Eurocommunal[84] or the Council of Local Authorities and Regions in Europe. After a considerable political battle they gained three seats in the new Committee of the Regions. The struggle over their role in EU affairs reflects a basic issue: are the local authorities a third or – with the EU – even a fourth level of the state[85] or even a sort of 'co-state'[86] or, on the other hand, just a service organization for implementing the policies decided upon elsewhere by EU, federal and *Länder* officials.[87]

The Basic Law states (Article 28 § 2 GG) that in local affairs the *Gemeinden* dispose of a so-called 'administrative autonomy' which is applicable 'within the framework of the law'. This last phrase gave the Bund the right to intervene in local activities and, in political practice, to make use of local government as a kind of 'indirect state administration'. Equally, however, the local level could enlarge the sphere of its influence beyond strictly local matters and today plays an important role as a body of implementation and of (local) integration. The provisions mentioned also apply in principle to the implementation of EC legislative Acts which – after they have been incorporated (as in the case of EC directives) into the German legal order – have to be fully applied and executed by the responsible authorities.[88]

The specific problem of Community law in this context is twofold: first, it only rarely takes account of regional and local peculiarities – not to mention the specific administrative conditions and traditions of the regions and local communities – which does not make its full application any easier. Second, the farther away a decision is taken (i.e. in Brussels or Strasbourg) and the less the local and regional levels are involved in the decision-making process – or even more are unable to fully follow and understand this process – the more difficult it becomes to get the full support which is necessary for the correct application of an EC rule.

One way to check whether legislative Acts having their origin in Brussels are correctly and fully implemented in the Federal Republic of Germany is to look at the infringement proceedings (Article 169 of the EEC Treaty) the European Commission has initiated against it. In 75 per cent of cases the infringement proceeding is used by the Commission against poor or incomplete incorporation of EC directives into national law.

It seems that although there has been an increase in the total number of infringement proceedings in the Community, the number of infringement proceedings against the Federal Republic has declined slightly. This observation is especially true concerning the first phase of the infringement proceeding, i.e. the phase of setting a final deadline for incorporation. In fact the number of the German infringement proceedings in relation to the total number of infringement proceedings in the Community has fallen from approximately 10 per cent in 1988 to 8 per cent in 1992. However, concerning the fourth phase, i.e. the rulings of the Court of Justice, the record is worse: Article 169 rulings against Germany have risen from three in 1988 (5.3 per cent) to six in 1992 (12 per cent) yet the total number of infringement decisions in the Community has fallen from fifty-six to fifty.[89] However, in spite of this deterioration the German record is still quite good when compared with that of other member states: the figures in the 'List of Sinners' (see Fig. 5.3) for the period 1980–93 indicate that Germany is among the countries with the lowest number of infringement rulings from the European Court of Justice.

If one looks more closely at the German case there are three policy fields in which most of the infringement proceedings were initiated against the Federal Republic: the internal market, agriculture and environment/ nuclear safety. In fact those three policy fields together make up about 70–80 per cent of all infringement proceedings against Germany (calculated on the basis of the figures of the first phase concerning the letter setting a deadline). Compared with the number of *decisions* of the European Court against Germany, nearly all of them have also been in the above-mentioned fields. In total there were twenty-one decisions by the Court between 1988 and 1992, eight of which were in the field of the environment.

The reason for the relatively high number of infringement proceedings

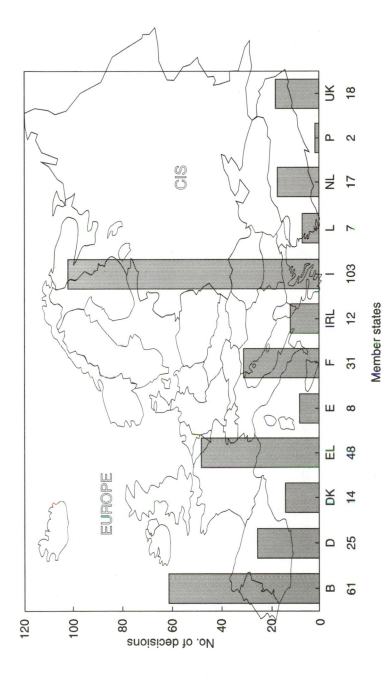

Figure 5.3 The 'List of Sinners': Article 169 decisions of the European Court against EC member states, 1980–93

Source: Fifth and eleventh annual reports of the Commission to the European Parliament on monitoring the application of Community law

in the environmental field[90] may be that in this field very often competences of the *Länder* are involved, which could explain the difficulties of incorporating – or even unwillingness to incorporate – a directive. This reluctance is quite understandable in the case of the directives on ground water[91] and on surface water,[92] in which the *Länder* are asked to meet certain technical standards which would involve considerable investment in order to reach the water quality required by the EC. Concerning both directives Germany has been condemned by the European Court of Justice and the procedure according to Article 171 of the EEC Treaty has been invoked, according to which Germany may have to pay a fine.[93] A similar issue concerns the Court's decisions on the protection of wild birds, where Germany has passed the requisite national law but it has not been correctly applied by some of the *Länder* governments. Compared with the number of Court rulings (by 31 December 1993) which are not complied with in other member states, Germany has rather a bad record, ranking ninth among the twelve; only France, Italy and Belgium are worse.[94] This is in contrast to the 'List of Sinners', where Germany was better placed. It seems that, once a ruling has been made, Germany has problems in complying with it. The above-mentioned cases are not very problematic. What both of them have in common is that the *Länder* and/or the Bundesrat are involved. A preliminary conclusion therefore could be that the complex internal decision-making process in Germany and the distribution of competences between the Bund and the *Länder* contribute to a lack of conformity with EC legislation and Court rulings. To qualify this, one has to add that in the past there have been other cases – such as the 'purity of German beer', the tax problem of so-called 'butter trips' and the question of substitutes for milk – which were less a problem of *Länder* involvement than of national traditions and of consumer protection. Thus, it seems – and in this respect further empirical studies are needed – that a mixture of structural, i.e. linked with the complex politico-administrative German system, and policy reasons, i.e. linked with the specific substance of an issue, are responsible for some of the problems Germany has in its efforts to implement EC legislation and to comply with rulings by the European Court of Justice.

In general, however, the complex multi-level administration fulfils *grosso modo* the standards for effective implementation of EC legislation. The involvement of those implementing EC decisions upstream improves the capacity to fulfil their obligations downstream.

EVALUATION

The impact on German and European administrations

The image portrayed when looking at these individual detailed pictures is a trend towards a complex 'multi-level' administrative system. German civil servants at all levels have pushed and have been pulled into a growing EU system. In functional terms, i.e. in describing who is participating in decision preparation, decision-making and decision implementation, it is clear that national civil servants from all levels are now part of the EU administration; a strictly legal definition of the EU's bureaucracy which takes into account only civil servants who are employed under the statute for EU personnel is thus of only limited use.[95]

For many German civil servants this 'multi-level game' is an addition to the game which they use to play inside the Federal Republic. Experience of 'co-operative federalism'[96] or of *Politikverflechtung*[97] creates a certain administrative culture[98] which is open to a flexible and collegial way of co-operating with civil servants from other administrative systems with whom there are no hierarchical relations. For civil servants coming from all federal levels, an additional level to work on is of course also an enormous challenge, although it does not constitute a completely new situation. The internal pre-negotiations may even increase the strength and the weight of the position of German representatives in the EU Council and the Council's working groups.[99]

Of course this kind of experience does not imply that Brussels is an easy game for German civil servants. They are confronted with partly different administrative cultures and of course also with highly qualified and partly politically better supported administrations. Complaints are constant from the inside as well as outside,[100] that the German internal way of preparing EC/EU decisions is too slow, too incoherent and does not get enough political support in the event of conflict. Other national administrations like those of France and Britain are taken as positive models compared with which the German set-up – even before Maastricht induced changes – is supposed to be less competitive.[101] Irrespective of the claim, not addressed here, that those systems function better,[102] the overall record of maintaining the German position in Brussels does not seem to be too negative – especially when taking into account the complexity of the federal system but also a certain passive, reactive position of humility which was part of the post-war attitude and strategy of German politicians and administrations in all Western and international organizations.[103]

The decentralization and fragmentation of German decision-making in

EU affairs reflect clearly the constitutional provisions and – partly also – political circumstances: as for the Basic Law, ministers are responsible for their own area (*Ressortzuständigkeit*) and the *Länder*'s administrations are mostly responsible for the implementation of EC decisions. The specific political situation in Germany is that German governments are coalition governments in which important portfolios are held by heads of important coalition parties or at least leading figures in those parties. This explains also the amount of effort that is put into the horizontal co-ordination work.

The strong specialization and decentralization in favour of several levels might lead to sectorization and fragmentation of positions. However, there is a clear trade-off between the positive and negative sides of specialization and decentralization: if a specific ministry deals with detailed matters in closed policy networks, the civil servants turn into experts, knowing the relevant policy matter and knowing also the relevant partners within the specific policy networks, which are quite often reinforced by relevant lobby groups at the national and European level as well as increasingly by parliamentary committees. With Maastricht the trend towards 'un système en réseau' has been reinforced.[104] The evolution we are approaching is commonly referred to in the United States as the 'Iron Triangle'. The lack of broader and overall political co-ordination by generalists is more than compensated for by this kind of expertise.

In cases not uncommon to the European Union, in which political problems are solved by package deals,[105] this specialization reduces the capacity of the Federal Republic to pursue a comprehensive and coherent position. Germany's EU activities are characterized by weak horizontal and vertical co-ordination power leading to 'bureaucratized policy-making' without strong political impetus. However, this does not prevent Germany from successfully mobilizing all national actors in the case of major initiatives. In such cases a special effort of political leadership is needed, not least because of the weakness of hierarchical centralization in European affairs. So, although perhaps not as easily applied and employed as in other member states, leadership is a resource which is available – depending on the circumstances – to the German system of dealing within the EU. The Chancellor and in certain cases the Foreign Minister too are able to mobilize support for vital decisions in EC/EU matters. Schmidt with the European Monetary System, Kohl with the Single European Act and the Delors packages, as well as the Maastricht Treaty on European Union, give clear examples of this kind of leadership, which implied, however, that there were internal side payments to opponents of these policies, especially to the monetary establishment and to the *Länder* governments.

This complex machinery is of course also a problem for partners inside the EU, who are quite often confronted with the cacophony of several and quite often divergent positions coming from the Federal Republic of Germany which are difficult to rely on and to relate to a coherent position which is calculable.

Europeanization and integration: extending, not reversing, integration trends

One of its most astonishing features is that the German administrative and political system has not basically changed, given the dramatic increase in Community and EU affairs. No 'European ministry' or 'European unit' has been established, centralizing the different activities. With a certain time lag the *Länder* governments as well as the Bundestag have moved to become 'co-players' within their respective competences. Thus, they just perhaps re-establish the original intra-German equilibrium which was characteristic of the German constitution but which has now become an even more complex way of mutual interaction and control. The different levels of administration have had to adapt to a new situation to make themselves 'fit' to participate adequately in the 'multi-level European game'. Hence the result we observe in the early 1990 is that no administrative level or unit is really replaced by or substituted for others but that they are all involved in an ever increasing complexity of administrative networks based on interactions within and across the German border. This reinforces the trends which were already developing before the creation of the EC and continued parallel to it within the Federal Republic, which was called *Politikverflechtung*,[106] *der unitarische Bundesstaat* (the unitary federal state)[107] or *der verkappte Einheitsstaat* (the disguised unitary state).[108] A trend which can also be characterized as a 'fusion' of state instruments at different levels for managing public policies, an argument with which we return to some of the considerations raised at the beginning of this chapter.

Administrative fusion: modernization or weakening of policy-making?

The working hypothesis of this chapter was to explain that the evolution of the German administration follows fundamental trends of the EU, mixing and merging national and EU administrations in a system of mutual *engrenage*. These patterns of administrative and political interaction document a trend according which member states are 'pooling' their sovereignties[109] and mingling them with competences of the EU into a system to which the notion of a 'fusioned federal state' (*fusionierter*

Föderalstaat) can be applied.[110] The more intensive the forms and the stronger the impact of the common public policies the more extensive and intensive are the organizational devices for access and influence which national officials and politicians preserve for themselves.

To characterize this phenomenon as 'administrative fusion' evokes a major desideratum for further debate: it concerns the yardstick by which to evaluate these trends. The process identified in the evolution of western European states may be seen as a 'modern' way to tackle problems in an interdependent society and world. The return to the complexity of a new 'middle age'[111] is evaluated as a positive evolution which makes a state and its administrations 'fit' for the complexity of the modern world. The administrative interactions increase the mutual calculability and the confidence in the actions of partners. Civil servants develop norms and rules of working together, reducing the fear of being exploited by co-players.[112] The stability of interaction systems and the overall productivity of decisions are enhanced. All actors concerned are participating in a pluralistic and 'consociative' way.[113]

From an alternative perspective this process of 'administrative fusion' creates considerable problems. The administrative and political 'labyrinth' changes the established and accepted ways and capacities to tackle political problems in democracies. By its complex procedures it reduces efficiency when measured by the time needed to reach a decision and by the quality of the output: national governments and administrations are moving into 'joint decision traps', achieving only sub-optimal outputs;[114] by shifting the major parts of the *de facto* decision-making to anonymous bodies, it diffuses responsibilities and reduces transparency; traditional democratic and parliamentary norms are eroded and governments become less accountable for decisions affecting the citizens by whom they are elected. For the normal citizen the 'state' becomes less and less a clear object of 'identification'.[115] National politicians still offer a certain degree of legitimacy, but the mechanism (or assumption) behind this notion is no longer valid: in such an 'interlocked system' politicians cannot be responsive or responsible to their electorate. 'Fusion' means 'diffusion of responsibility and accountability'[116] and undermines the very basis of Western democracies without replacing them with a real EU democracy. This perspective warns against a 'legitimacy gap' which gets wider and wider within the process of fusion and which in the run-up to the 1996 intergovernmental conference seems to get additional dimensions. On this view the European Parliament is not (yet) an equivalent replacement for this growing deficit.[117] Needed therefore are certain basic rights for national parliaments.[118]

Our view is that the administrative fusion which we believe we have identified in the multi-level EU areas of Brussels and Bonn is not constituted by developments and tendencies which are out of date in comparison with the other 'normal' developments of public policies in western Europe but that they are significant indicators of as well as factors in modern west European states moving towards a new state-like system. The criticism deriving from the standards and criteria used for the (classical) constitutional and nation state of the nineteenth century and the beginning of the twentieth are consequently not wrong but they may be outdated, given the development towards interdependent welfare states in western Europe. This kind of analysis does not, however, imply that we can be content with what we are observing. Principles and standards like transparency, responsibility, efficiency, participation, effectiveness have to be clearly taken into account to shape a new reality: a step forward, not backward, has to be taken.

ACKNOWLEDGEMENTS

See for some earlier excerpts of this chapter Wolfgang Wessels, 'Adminstrative interaction', in William Wallace (ed.), *The Dynamics of European Integration*, London, Pinter Publishers, 1990, pp. 229–41; Wolfgang Wessels, 'The EC Council: the Community's Decision-making Center', in Robert Keohane and Stanley Hoffmann (eds), *The New European Community: Decision-making and Institutional Change*, Boulder, San Francisco and Oxford, Westview Press, 1991, pp. 133–54.

NOTES

1 See e.g. Gabriel A. Almond and G. Bingham Powell, *Comparative Politics: a Developmental Approach*, Boston, Little Brown, 1966, p. 35; Ernst Forsthoff, *Der Staat der Industriegesellschaft, dargestellt am Beispiel der Bundesrepublik Deutschland*, Munich, C. H. Beck, 1971, pp. 11 *et seq.*; Charles Tilly, 'Reflections on the History of European State-making, in Charles Tilly (ed.), *The Formation of Nation states in Western Europe*, Princeton, Princeton University Press, 1975, pp. 31 *et seq.*; Renate Mayntz, *Soziologie der öffentlichen Verwaltung*, Heidelberg and Karlsruhe, C. F. Müller, 1985, pp. 12 *et seq.*; Gérard Timsit, 'L'Administration', in Madeleine Grawitz and Jean Leca, *Traité de science politique*, Paris, PUF, 1985, vol. 2, p. 446.

2 See especially Stein Rokkan, 'Dimensions of State Formation and Nation Building: a Possible Paradigm for Research on Variations within Europe', in Charles Tilly (ed.), *The Formation of National States*, pp. 571 *et seq.*

3 See among others Charles Debbasch, *Science administrative, administration publique*, Paris, Dalloz, 1980, pp. 1–7; Thomas Ellwein, 'Geschichte der öffentlichen Verwaltung', in Klaus König *et al.* (eds), *Öffentliche Verwaltung in der Bundesrepublik Deutschland*, Baden-Baden, Nomos, 1981, p. 49; Jost

Delbrück, 'Internationale und nationale Verwaltung, inhaltliche und institutionelle Aspekte', in Kurt G. A. Jeserich *et al.* (eds), *Deutsche Verwaltungsgeschichte. Die Bundesrepublik Deutschland,* Stuttgart, Deutsche Verlagsanstalt, 1987, vol. V, p. 398; Jacques Ziller, *Administrations comparées. Les systèmes politico-administratifs de l'Europe des Douze,* Paris, Montchrestien, 1993, pp. 11–13; Spyros A. Pappas (ed.), *National Administrative Procedures for the Preparation and Implementation of Community Decisions,* Maastricht, European Institute of Public Administration, 1995.

4 See especially Joel D. Aberbach *et al., Bureaucrats and Politicians in Western Democracies,* Cambridge and London, Harvard University Press, 1981; Renate Mayntz, 'German Federal Bureaucrats: a Functional Elite between Politics and Administration', in Ezra N. Suleiman (ed.), *Bureaucrats and Policy Making: a Comparative Overview,* New York and London, Holmes & Meier, 1984, pp. 174–205; Gérard Timsit, 'L'Administration', pp. 446–51; Jacques Ziller, *Administrations comparées.*

5 See Max Weber, 'Bureaucracy', in H. H. Gerth and C. Wright Mills (eds), *From Max Weber: Essays in Sociology,* New York, Oxford University Press, 1958, pp. 196–244 (in German: Max Weber, *Wirtschaft und Gesellschaft, Grundriß der verstehenden Soziologie,* 4th edition, Tübingen: Mohr, 1956, originally 1922).

6 Yves Mény, *Government and Politics in Western Europe: Britain, France, Italy, West Germany,* Oxford, Oxford University Press, 1990, p. 240.

7 See especially Joachim Jens Hesse, 'Aufgaben einer Staatslehre heute', in Thomas Ellwein *et al.* (eds), *Jahrbuch zur Staats- und Verwaltungswissenschaft,* Baden-Baden, Nomos, 1987, vol. 1, pp. 55–87, at pp. 75 *et seq.*; Wolfgang Wessels, *Alternative Strategies for Institutional Reforms,* European University Institute Working Paper, No. 85/184, Florence, 1985, p. 58; Sabine Pag, 'The Relations between the Commission and National Bureaucracies', in Sabino Cassese *et al., The European Administration,* International Institute of Administrative Sciences and European Institute of Public Administration, Maastricht, 1987, pp. 446 *et seq.*

8 See especially Robert W. Cox *et al., The Anatomy of Influence: Decision-making in International Organizations,* New Haven, 1973; Reinhard Lohrmann, 'Multinationale Entscheidungsprozesse in der Verwaltung der Europäischen Gemeinschaften', in *Regionale Verflechtung der Bundesrepublik Deutschland. Empirische Analysen und theoretische Probleme,* Schriften des Forschungsinstituts der deutschen Gesellschaft für auswärtige Politik, Munich and Vienna, Oldenbourg, 1973, pp. 193–212; Theodor Holtz, 'Die europäischen Behörden und die nationalen Bürokratien. Probleme der Zusammenarbeit und der Personalstruktur', in *Regionale Verflechtung in der Bundesrepublik Deutschland,* 1973, pp. 213–29; Helmut Schmitt von Sydow, 'Die Zusammenarbeit nationaler und europäischer Beamter in den Ausschüssen der Kommission', *Europarecht,* 1974, vol. 9, pp. 62–71; Harold K. Jacobson, *Networks of Interdependence: International Organizations and the Global Political System,* New York, Alfred A. Knopf, 1984; Giuseppe Ciavarini Azzi, 'Les Experts nationaux: Chevaux de Troie ou partenaires indispensables?', in Joseph Jamar and Wolfgang Wessels (eds), *Community Bureaucracies at the Crossroads,* Bruges, de Tempel, 1985, pp. 99–104; Sabino Cassese, 'Theoretical Sketch of the Co-operative and Multidimensional Nature of the Community Bureaucracy', in ibid., pp. 39–46; Wolfgang Wessels, 'Community

Bureaucracy in a Changing Environment: Criticism, Trends, Questions', in ibid., pp. 8–36.

9 See Wolfgang Wessels, *Die Öffnung des Staates. Modelle zwischenstaatlicher Verwaltungsstränge 1960–90* (forthcoming).

10 See especially Gerda Zellentin, *Les Missions permanentes auprès des organisations internationales: conclusions théoriques*, Brussels, Bruylant, 1976; Fiona Hayes-Renshaw, 'The Role of the Committee of Permanent Representatives in the Decision-making Process of the European Community', Ph.D. thesis, London School of Economics and Political Science, London, 1990.

11 See especially Geoffrey Edwards and Helen Wallace, *The Council of Ministers of the European Community and the President-in-Office*, Federal Trust Paper, London, 1977; Colm O. Nuallain (ed.), *The Presidency of the European Council of Ministers: Impacts and Implications for National Governments*, London, Croom Helm, 1985; Axel Vornbäumen, *Dynamik in der Zwangsjacke. Die Präsidentschaft im Ministerrat der Europäischen Gemeinschaft als Führungsinstrument*, Bonn, Europa Union, 1985.

12 Heinrich Siedentopf and Jacques Ziller (eds), *Making European Policies Work: the Implementation of Community Legislation in the Member States*, London, Sage, 1988.

13 See Gerda Zellentin, *Les Missions permanentes*, pp. 125 *et seq.*

14 See Harold K. Jacobson, 1984, *Networks of Interdependence*.

15 See e.g. Theodor Holtz, 'Die europäischen Behörden'; Wolfgang Wessels, 'Community Bureaucracy in a Changing Environment'.

16 See Ernst B. Haas, *The Uniting of Europe: Political, Social and Economic Forces 1950–1957*, Stanford, Stanford University Press, 1968, p. 9.

17 See for this term Giuseppe Ciavarini Azzi, 'Les Experts nationaux', p. 99.

18 See especially Gerda Zellentin, *Les Missions permanentes*.

19 See Fritz W. Scharpf, 'The Joint Decision Trap: Lessons form German Federalism and European Integration', *Public Administration*, autumn 1988, vol. 66, pp. 239–78; Fritz W. Scharpf, *Mehrebenenpolitik im vollendeten Binnenmarkt*, Max-Planck-Institut für Gesellschaftsforschung, paper No. 4, Cologne, October 1994.

20 See Simon Bulmer, 'The Governance of the European Union: a New Institutionalist Approach', *Journal of Public Policy*, 1994, vol. 13, 4, pp. 351–80, at p. 355.

21 Even with works like those of Debbasch, Gabriel and Powell, and Ziller, who stress the EU dimension, one gets the impression that the EU dimension is always added but not really integrated.

22 See for this term Robert D. Putnam and Nicholas Bayne, *Hanging Together: the Seven-power Summits*, Royal Institute of International Affairs, London, Heinemann, 1984, pp. 4 *et seq.*

23 See Robert O. Keohane and Stanley Hoffmann, 'Institutional Change in Europe in the 1980s', in Keohane and Hoffmann (eds), *The New European Community*, p. 7.

24 See Dietrich Rometsch and Wolfgang Wessels, *The European Union and Member States: Towards Institutional Fusion?*, Manchester, Manchester University Press (forthcoming).

25 See Robert Ladrech, 'Europeanization of Domestic Politics and Institutions: the Case of France', *Journal of Common Market Studies*, 1994, vol. 1, pp. 69–88, at p. 69.

26 See Peter Flora, 'On the History and Current Problems of the Welfare State', in
    J. N. Eisenstadt and Ora Ahimeir (eds), *The Welfare State and its Aftermath*,
    London, Barnes & Noble, 1985.
27 See Gerhard Lehmbruch and Philippe C. Schmitter (eds), *Patterns of
    Corporatist Policy-making*, Beverly Hills, Sage, 1982; Yves Mény, *Government
    and Politics in Western Europe*, pp. 100–28.
28 See Gérard Timsit, *Théorie de l'administration*, Paris, Economica, 1986;
    Renate Mayntz, *Soziologie der öffentlichen Verwaltung*; Yves Mény, *Govern-
    ment and Politics*, pp. 238–95.
29 See Stein Rokkan, 'Dimensions of State Formation'.
30 See Joachim Jens Hesse, 'Aufgaben einer Staatslehre heute'.
31 See Ernst Forsthoff, *Der Staat der Industriegesellschaft*.
32 See for the term Ernst-Otto Czempiel (ed.), 'Die anachronistische Souver-
    änität', *Politische Vierteljahresschrift*, 1969, special edition, Werdenkler
    Verlag, Cologne, 304pp.
33 See Robert Ladrech, 'Europeanization of Domestic Politics and Institutions', p. 70.
34 See Robert O. Keohane, *After Hegemony: Co-operation and Discord in the
    World Political Economy*, Princeton, Princeton University Press, 1984; Paul
    Kennedy, *The Rise and Fall of the Great Powers: Economic Change and
    Military Conflict from 1500 to 2000*, London, Unwin Hyman, 1988.
35 See Karl Kaiser, 'Interdependence and Autonomy: Britain and the Federal
    Republic in their Multinational Environment', in Karl Kaiser and Roger
    Morgan (eds), *Britain and West Germany: Changing Societies and the Future
    of Foreign Policy*, London, Oxford University Press, 1971, pp. 17–40, at p. 35.
36 See Fernand Braudel, *Sozialgeschichte des 15.–18. Jahrhunderts*, vol. 3:
    Aufbruch zur Weltwirtschaft, Munich, Kindler, 1986.
37 See William Wallace, *The Transformation of Western Europe*, London, Pinter
    Publishers, 1990, pp. 93 *et seq.*; this term is here not used like the concept of
    'Kerneuropa' (core Europe) which according to the so-called Schäuble and
    Lamers paper meant five or six countries 'oriented to greater integration and
    closer co-operation' and which would constitute 'a strong centre, to counteract
    the centrifugal forces generated by constant enlargement'; see CDU/CSU-
    Fraktion des Deutschen Bundestages, *Reflections on European Policy*, 1
    September 1994, p. 7.
38 See, for example, the debate about the 'magic triangle' of fixed exchange rate,
    national autonomy in monetary policies, and the free movement of capital; see
    for this the report to the European Commission by Tommaso Padoa Schioppa
    et al., *Efficiency, Stability and Equity: a Strategy for the Evolution of the
    Economic System of the European Community*, Brussels, EC, 1987.
39 See Robert D. Putnam and Nicholas Bayne, *Hanging Together*.
40 See Wolfgang Wessels, *Die Öffnung des Staates*.
41 See Alan S. Milward, *The Reconstruction of Western Europe, 1945–1951*,
    London, Methuen, 1984, p. 493: 'the process of integration is neither a thread
    woven into the fabric of Europe's political destiny nor one woven into the
    destiny of all highly developed capitalist nation states'.
42 See William Wallace, *The Transformation*, 1990, p. 54.
43 See Wolfgang Wessels, 'Maastricht: Ergebnisse, Bewertungen und Langzeit-
    trends', *Integration*, 1992, vol. 1, pp. 2–16, at pp. 2–4.
44 See Helen Wallace, 'Making Multilateral Negotiations Work', in William
    Wallace, *The Dynamics of European integration*, pp. 223–6.

45 See Andrew Moravcsik, 'Negotiating the Single European Act', in Robert Keohane and Stanley Hoffmann (eds), *The New European Community*, pp. 41–84.

46 See Wolfgang Wessels, 'Maastricht'.

47 See Joseph Weiler, 'The Transformation of Europe', *Yale Law Journal*, 1991, vol. 200, 8, p. 2431.

48 The Bundesrat has been chosen since its legislative work also includes decisions on executive law (so-called 'ordinances' or *Rechtsverordnungen* decided by the government) and is thus more comparable with the work of the Council than that of the Bundestag would be.

49 See, for these terms, Glenn H. Snyder and Paul Diesing, *Conflict among Nations: Bargaining, Decision-making and System Structure in International Crises*, Princeton, Princeton University Press, 1977.

50 See e.g. the lively debate on the so-called 'comitology'; see Gérard Deprez and Edouard Poullet, 'The Place of the Commission within the Institutional System', in Christoph Sasse *et al.*, *Decision-making in the European Communities*, New York, Praeger, 1977, pp. 127–240.

51 See for this kind and definition of integration the early neo-functionalist Ernst B. Haas, *The Uniting of Europe*, pp. 4–29 and 512–27.

52 See Guy Peters, *The Politics of Bureaucracy*, London, Longman, 1978; Aberbach *et al.*, *Bureaucrats and Politicians;* Renate Mayntz, *Soziologie der öffentlichen Verwaltung*; Gérard Timsit, 'L'Administration'.

53 We have purposely arranged the institutional set-up in a horizontal perspective and have not used a pyramid with the EU as the hierarchical top, as that gives a distorted signal; see also Ziller, *Administrations comparées*, pp. 475–6.

54 See Fritz W. Scharpf, 'The Joint Decision Trap'; see also Joachim Jens Hesse (ed.), *Politikverflechtung im föderativen Staat. Studien zum Planungs- und Finanzierungsverbund zwischen Bund, Ländern und Gemeinden*, Baden-Baden, Nomos, 1978.

55 See generally Christoph Sasse *et al.*, *Decision-making in the European Communities*; Elfriede Regelsberger and Wolfgang Wessels, 'Entscheidungs-prozesse Bonner Europapolitik. Verwalten statt gestalten?', in Rudolf Hrbek and Wolfgang Wessels (eds), *EG-Mitgliedschaft: ein vitales Interesse der Bundesrepublik Deutschland?*, Bonn, Europa Union, 1984, pp. 469–99; Dietrich Rometsch, 'The Federal Republic of Germany', in Dietrich Rometsch and Wolfgang Wessels (eds), *The European Union and Member States*.

56 Figures calculated on the basis of Table 5.2; as a matter of methodological caution: the ministerial origin of the civil servants from the permanent representation could not be identified and has not been included in this calculation.

57 See Hans-Christian Röhl, 'Die Beteiligung der Bundesrepublik Deutschland an der Rechtsetzung im Ministerrat der Europäischen Union. Die Rolle des Ausschußes der Ständigen Vertreter (COREPER) und der Ständigen Vertre-tung', *Europarecht*, 1994, vol. 4, pp. 409–44, at pp. 431–2.

58 One method is based on a set of interviews within each federal Ministry in the middle of the 1980s and in 1994. The other one is based on a calculation of the approximately 1,150 'committees' in Brussels in 1994, i.e. the study and expert groups of the Commission (600), the Council and Council working groups (270) and the implementation committees of the Commission (280) which are all composed of national civil servants being active in Brussels. (See on these

figures generally Wolfgang Wessels, 'Verwaltung im EG-Mehrebenensystem. Auf dem Weg zur Megabürokratie?', in Markus Jachtenfuchs and Beate Kohler-Koch (eds), *Europäische Integration*, Opladen, Leske & Budrich/UTB (forthcoming). We assume that there is one civil servant per committee, which takes into account that many of the committees are served by two or three German civil servants and that some civil servants are serving two or three committees. In 1990 there were approximately 4,700 higher civil servants in Bonn, which means that 25 per cent are necessary to have a German representative in each of the committees in Brussels.

59 See on the organization of EC policy-making in the federal government for more details Simon Bulmer, *The Domestic Structure of European Community Policy-making in West Germany*, New York and London, Garland Publishing, 1986, pp. 45 *et seq.*

60 See C. Northcote, *Parkinson's Law, or, The Pursuit of Progress*, London, J. Miora, 1958.

61 See Anthony Downs, *Inside Bureaucracy*, Boston, Little Brown, 1967; Roland Vaubel, 'Von der normativen zu einer positiven Theorie der internationalen Organisation', in *Probleme und Perspektiven der weltwirtschaftlichen Entwicklung*, Schriften des Vereins für Sozialpolitik, 1985, vol. 148, pp. 412 *et seq.*; see also Roland Vaubel, 'A Public Choice Approach to International Organization', *Public Choice*, 1986, vol. 59, pp. 39–57.

62 See Thomas Läufer (ed.), *Europäische Gemeinschaft – Europäische Union. Die Vertragstexte von Maastricht mit den deutschen Begleitgesetzen*, Bonn, 1993, pp. 273 *et seq.*

63 See Charlie Jeffery, *The Länder strike back: Structures and Procedures of European Integration. Policy-making in the German Federal System*, Discussion paper in Federal Studies, No. FS94/4, University of Leicester, September 1994.

64 See Bundesrat, Ausschuß für Fragen der Europäischen Union, Gremien des Rates und der Kommission zu denen der Bundesrat Ländervertreter benannt hat (Committee for questions on the European Union, bodies of the Council and the Commission to which the Bundesrat has assigned representatives of the *Länder*), unpublished document, Bonn, July 1995.

65 Hamburg and Schleswig-Holstein have a common 'Hanse Office'; since 1990 the five new *Länder* have also started to establish their respective *Länder* offices in Brussels; see for the more recent development: Charlie Jeffery and Roland Sturm (eds), *Federalism, Unification and European Integration*, London, Frank Cass, 1993; Rudolf Hrbek and Sabine Weyand, *Betrifft: Das Europa der Regionen. Fakten, Probleme, Perspektiven*, Munich, Beck, 1994.

66 See Joachim Jens Hesse and Thomas Ellwein, *Das Regierungssystem der Bundesrepublik Deutschland*, Opladen, Westdeutscher Verlag, 1992, 7th edition, vol. 1, p. 88.

67 See Sasse *et al.*, *Decision-making in the European Communities*, p. 11.

68 See Simon Bulmer, *The Domestic Structure of EC Policy-making*, p. 87.

69 See an unofficial translation of Article 23 of the Basic Law in Spyros A. Pappas, *National Administrative Procedures*, p. 158.

70 See § 5 of the Law on the Co-operation of Bund and *Länder* in Affairs of the European Union, 12 March 1993, printed in Läufer, *Europäische Gemeinschaft*, pp. 280 *et seq.*

71 See ibid.

72 Florian Gerster, 'Die Europaministerkonferenz der deutschen Länder. Aufgaben – Themen – Selbstverständnis', *Integration*, 1993, vol. 2, pp. 61–7.

73 See e.g. Carl-Christoph Schweizer, *Die nationalen Parlamente in der Gemeinschaft – ihr schwindender Einfluß in Bonn und Westminster auf die Europagesetzgebung*, Bonn, 1978; Alwin Brück, 'Europäische Integration und Entmachtung des Deutschen Bundestages. Ein Unterausschuß ist nicht genug', *Zeitschrift für Parlamentsfragen*, 1988, vol. 2, pp. 220–4; Renate Hellwig (ed.), *Der Deutsche Bundestag und Europa*, Bonn, Aktuell, 1993.

74 Between July 1980 and July 1986 2,506 bills were transferred to the Bundestag, out of which 256 (i.e. 10 per cent) have been dealt with in plenary on the proposal of the committee which was responsible. Of those 256 bills 167 have already been published in the Official Journal when the Bundestag was passing a resolution on them; see Klaus Hänsch, 'Europäische Integration und parlamentarische Demokratie', *Europa-Archiv*, 1986, vol. 7, pp. 191–200, at p. 197.

75 See Eberhard Schoof, *Stichwort EG-ausschuß. Der Deutsche Bundestag und die Europäische Gemeinschaft*, Bonn, Deutscher Bundestag, 1993.

76 See Thomas Läufer, *Europäische Gemeinschaft*, pp. 278–9.

77 See for the translation of Article 23 GG Spyros A. Pappas, *National Administrative Procedures*, p. 158.

78 See § 5 of the Law on Co-operation between the Federal Government and the German Bundestag in Affairs of the European Union, printed in Thomas Läufer, *Europäische Gemeinschaft*, p. 279.

79 See Sven Hölscheidt and Thomas Schotten, 'Der Unionsausschuß des Deutschen Bundestages – Gestaltungsprobleme', *Integration*, 1994, vol. 4, pp. 230–3.

80 See Renate Hellwig, *Der Deutsche Bundestag und Europa*.

81 See Sabine Pag and Wolfgang Wessels, 'Federal Republic of Germany', in Heinrich Siedentopf and Jacques Ziller (eds), *Making European Policies Work*, National Reports, London, Sage, 1988, vol. II, pp. 165–229, at pp. 204–7.

82 See Joachim Jens Hesse and Thomas Ellwein, *Das Regierungssystem der Bundesrepublik Deutschland*, p. 88.

83 See e.g. G. Seele, *Der Kreis aus europäischer Sicht. Die übergemeindlichen Kommunalverwaltungen im Spiegel der nationalstaatlichen Verwaltungsstrukturen und der europäischen Gemeinschaftspolitik*, Colgne, 1991; Joachim Jens Hesse, *Analyses of Twenty Western Industrialised Countries: Local Government and Urban Affairs in International Perspective*, Baden-Baden, Nomos, 1991, pp. 353–85.

84 This is the Brussels office of German Communal Self-autonomy (Europabüro der deutschen kommunalen Selbstverwaltung) which represents the Deutsche Städtetag (German Association of Cities), the Deutsche Städte- und Gemeindebund (German Association of Cities and Communes) and the Landkreistag (Association of German Counties).

85 In the sense of contributing to a 'policy of local proximity', see Joachim Jens Hesse and Thomas Ellwein, *Das Regierungssystem*, pp. 58–77, at p. 75.

86 In the sense of the 'principle of universality' established by the Prussian High Administrative Court 100 years ago, according to which the local communities have all-encompassing (natural) competences which exclude an enumeration of (only) some specific tasks and functions, ibid., pp. 66–7.

87 See R. A. W. Rhodes, *European Policy-making, Implementation and Subcentral*

Governments: a Survey, Maastricht, 1986; J. Biancarelli, 'La Communauté et les Collectivités locales', *Revue française d'administration publique*, 1988, pp. 557–71; Christian Engel and Joseph Van Ginderachter, *Trends in Regional and Local Government in the European Community*, Louvain, Acco, 1993.

88 See for more details Rudolf Streinz and Matthias Pechstein, 'The case of Germany', in Spyros A. Pappas, *National Administrative Procedures*, pp. 133–59.

89 See Tenth Report of the Commission to the European Parliament on Monitoring the Application of Community Law 1992, Com (93) 320, 28 April 1993.

90 There were eight new environmental directives, not taken into account in this calculation, for which the incorporation deadline had already elapsed and which were not (yet) incorporated into national law; see ibid., p. 111.

91 See directive 80/68/EEC on ground water.

92 See directive 75/440/EEC on surface water.

93 See decision of 28 February 1991, case C-131/88 and decision of 17 October 1991, case C-58/89.

94 See Eleventh Annual Report of the Commission to the European Parliament on Monitoring the Application of Community Law 1993, *OJ* C 154, 6 June 1994, Annexe V, p. 169.

95 See Wolfgang Wessels, 'Community Bureaucracy in a Changing Environment', pp. 11 *et seq.*; see also Wolfgang Wessels, 'Administrative interaction', pp. 236–7.

96 See Joachim Jens Hesse and Thomas Ellwein, *Das Regierungssystem*, pp. 86–90.

97 See especially Fritz W. Scharpf, 'The Joint Decision Trap'.

98 See Wolfgang Wessels, 'Community Bureaucracy', pp. 19 *et seq.*

99 There is the joke saying that if you and your position survive the confrontation with sixteen *Länder* governments you will be well qualified to live up to the challenges of defending your position against fourteen other national positions.

100 See e.g. Michel Butler, *Europe: More than a Continent*, London, Heinemann, 1986, pp. 131–2.

101 See Simon Bulmer, *The Domestic Structure of EC Policy-making*, pp. 376 *et seq.*; Elfriede Regelsberger and Wolfgang Wessels, 'Entscheidungsprozesse Bonner Europapolitik', pp. 469–99.

102 See for France: Christian Lequesne, *Paris–Bruxelles: comment se fait la politique européenne de la France*, Paris, Presses de la FNSP, 1993; Kenneth Armstrong and Simon Bulmer, 'United Kingdom', in Dietrich Rometsch and Wolfgang Wessels, *The European Union and Member States*.

103 For the 1950s and 1960s the general attitude was put into a joke by a former state secretary in the Foreign Office: 'Our European partners do not want to be led by the Germans – not even straight into paradise.'

104 See Jean-Louis Quermonne, 'Trois lectures de Maastricht. Essai d'analyse comparative', *Revue française de science politique*, October 1992, vol. 42, 5, pp. 802–18.

105 See e.g. Helen Wallace, 'Making Multilateral Negotiations Work', pp. 213–28; Wolfgang Wessels, 'The European Council: a Denaturing of the Community or Indispensable Decision-making Body?', in Jean-Marc Hoscheit and Wolfgang Wessels (eds), *The European Council 1974–1986: Evaluation and Prospects*, Maastricht, EIPA, 1988, pp. 7–33.

106 See F. W. Scharpf, B. Reissert, and F. Schnabel (eds), *Politikverflechtung*, Kronberg, Scriptor, 1976.

107 See Konrad Hesse, *Der unitarische Bundesstaat*, Karlsruhe, C. F. Müller, 1962.

108 See Heidrun Abromeit, *Der verkappte Einheitsstaat*, Opladen, Leske & Budrich, 1992.

109 See Robert Keohane and Stanley Hoffmann, *The New European Community*, p. 7; the Bundesverfassungsgericht has repeated the sense of that notion in its rulings on the Maastricht treaty, using the term of *Staatenverbund* ('association of states' or *groupement d'Etats*) when describing the current state of development of the EU.

110 Wolfgang Wessels, 'Staat und (westeuropäische) Integration. Die Fusionsthese', in Michael Kreile (ed.), 'Die Integration Europas', *Politische Vierteljahresschrift*, 1992, vol. 23, pp. 36–61, at p. 40.

111 See David Held, *Political Theory Today*, Cambridge, Polity, 1991; Fritz W. Scharpf, 'Die Handlungsfähigkeit des Staates am Ende des zwanzigsten Jahrhunderts', *Politische Vierteljahresschrift*, 1991, vol. 32, pp. 621–34.

112 See, for theories of co-operation in situations of interdependence, Robert O. Keohane, *After Hegemony*.

113 See Heinrich Schneider, *Rückblick für die Zukunft. Konzeptionelle Weichenstellung für die Europäische Einigung*, Bonn, Europa Union, 1986, p. 97.

114 See Fritz W. Scharpf, 'The Joint Decision Trap'.

115 See Jost Delbrück, 'Internationale and nationale Verwaltung'.

116 See Fritz W. Scharpf, 'The Joint Decision Trap', p. 270.

117 See Eberhard Grabitz *et al.*, *Direktwahl und Demokratisierung. Eine Funktionenbilanz des Europäischen Parlaments nach der ersten Wahlperiode*, Bonn, Europa Union, 1988. In its ruling on the Maastricht Treaty of 12 October 1993 the Bundesverfassungsgericht attributed to the European Parliament only a 'supportive function' concerning the legitimacy gap in the EU.

118 In this sense also the Bundesverfassungsgericht in its Maastricht ruling of October 1993.

6 French central government and the European political system

Change and adaptation since the Single Act

Christian Lequesne

For the last forty years France has both contributed to the emergence of a new political system and, at the same time, had to adapt to it. This novel phenomenon can be seen from the changes that have taken place within the French political and administrative system and which intensified following the publication of the Commission's White Paper on the Completion of the Internal Market and the signature of the Single European Act. In fact, from the mid-1980s onwards, there has been an acceleration in the process of the European construction in France, which paradoxically was not fully acknowledged by the French people until February 1992 with the signing of the Treaty on European Union.

This chapter analyses some of the changes and adaptations that have been imposed by the creation of the Community on French central government since the signing of the Single European Act. To that end, three arguments will be explored. They will focus first upon the attitude of the higher echelons of public administration. Second, the paper will explore the challenge to the traditional model of intra-administrative co-operation that this process represents. And finally, the evolution of various forms of mediation that now exist between administration and interest groups.

THE HIGHER ECHELONS OF THE CIVIL SERVICE IN FRANCE AND EUROPE

Without ever having conducted any empirical investigation into this subject, analysts have generally tended to consider the attitudes of the top ranks of the French civil service as proof, until the mid-1980s, at least, of a general climate of mistrust towards the European construction at that level. Thus, for Antoine Winckler, this mistrust could not merely be explained by a 'resentment of method' of the Monnet/Schuman project, nor 'with the imposition of a shadow hierarchy, operating behind the normal negotiating channels'.[1] Rather, its origins lay in the ideological impossibility of admitting that an external entity – i.e. the European Community – could challenge the fundamental principles of the Jacobean state (in particular, sovereignty) and in some instances claim to be superior to it.[2] Indeed, Winckler went on to conclude, 'It is not surprising then, . . . that for a long time the [French] State only wanted to see [European construction] as a "foreign affair"'. Given this background, much effort was invested in reassuring the French civil service that everything was 'normal', i.e. negotiations went on between countries, civil servants defined their 'national' stances, and, thus, reached compromises with other sovereign states.[3]

In France there has traditionally been a close relationship between the widely accepted ideology of sovereignty and the reticence of the higher echelons of the civil service, which constitute central government,[4] in accepting the process of the European construction, yet the surveys we conducted between 1986 and 1993 lead us to suggest a more complex reality.[5] Generally speaking, the majority of high-ranking French civil servants do not seem to perceive the European construction as a great danger and therefore one which must be opposed. Even though this does not prevent fairly regular outbursts of hostility, Europe is viewed primarily as an exogenous constraint which encourages the state to fulfil its duties more efficiently.[6]

One of the factors which explains this attitude is the manner in which high-ranking civil servants participate in the process of the European construction. Wolfgang Wessels, for example, has shown that the European construction has led to a system of political 'interpenetration', as he calls it, or even the 'fusion' of elites, a phenomenon characterized by the 'pooling' and 'mixing' of national and Community competences which results in actors at both levels permanently having to lead a double life.[7] This model, which is sometimes attributed to a process of 'co-operative federalism',[8] helps to explain why the development of Europe has not necessarily led, as a corollary, to the weakening of western Europe's nation states as a result of a parallel realist zero-sum game. The transfer of power from the national level to the Community level has, in fact, been compensated by the increased participation of national actors in the decision-making process in Brussels. Nevertheless, as Wessels has pointed out, there are 'winners' and 'losers' in such a political system. The former managed to insert themselves into the policy networks and, therefore, carried out, as it were, the 'mixing' and 'pooling'. They were generally ministers, 'central' civil servants and interest groups, as opposed to members of parliament or political parties, whose 'patterns of cross-border activities have not developed resources and comparable structures'.[9]

In France, high-ranking civil servants of central government are actors who enjoy regular access – if not in terms of influence, then at least in terms of information – to the various committees of the Commission and the Council of the European Union, and who establish informal relations with the Commission, and with other national administrations as well as with specific interest groups. To the extent that a fusion between political agendas at national and Community level is growing, individuals are able to occupy and mobilize the process of exchange. However, this is not a wholly consistent pattern. High-ranking civil servants are not, themselves, a perfectly homogenous group, for among them there are also 'winners' and 'losers', at least in terms of the benefits and losses which the European construction brings to their departments or 'corps', and/or individually to their respective careers.

Second, there is a tendency among high-ranking civil servants from central government to consider the process of the European construction purely from a narrow personal perspective. An explanation for this phenomenon can be found in the evolution of the French politico-economic debate which took place from the 1980s onward. Following the change of economic policy since March 1983, the Single European Act and the '1992 programme' led to a broadening of the debate over the modernization of state and society by market forces that had been initiated by the Socialists.[10] The higher echelons of the civil service, which effectively form the central government, were 'impregnated' by this liberal discourse. In the surveys we conducted between 1986 and 1993 the internal market was clearly seen as a means of 'cleaning up' and 'rationalizing' outdated domestic public policies and of offering France 'better conditions' in the context of the internationalization of economies. For example, one civil servant was delighted that his ministry could finally introduce common and commercial law reforms by invoking Community obligations which, otherwise, he would not have been able to do. This explains the improved application of Community policies from 1989, which was reinforced by the removal of the Conseil d'Etat's resistance to the primacy of Community law.[11] It also explains why high-ranking civil servants were so insistent on adapting on their own to the process of European construction, a quite definitive mix of fear and will. Since the entry into force of the Single European Act, on 1 July 1987, the various reports that have been compiled by the government and civil service have proved to be revealing. For instance, a diplomat remarked in 1989:

> Our country, as a founder member of the European Community, has not yet conceived a suitable global and systematic plan for the training of the civil servants who take part directly in the negotiation and the implementation of Community legislation, [adding that] the relative modesty of our efforts in this field is clearly shown in comparison with

the achievements of our principal partners who were latecomers to the Community – notably, the United Kingdom and Spain.[12]

The argument is always presented in the same manner, starting first with self-criticism – the poor preparation of the French administration for the process of the European construction – and then concluding that the need to adapt to this new 'norm' has become a condition for survival in the European context, for the process leads to greater competition between the national administrations of the various member states. However, the quest to adapt is strongly checked by the weight of both the *acquis* and naturally long-standing habits. Indeed, all effective change which has taken place within the central administration has been the result of a continuing interaction between various internal contradictory forces over the years. For example, it was not until 1990 within the administration itself, that the Ecole Nationale d'Administration began to offer high-ranking civil servants a more serious education in Community affairs.

INTRA-ADMINISTRATIVE CO-ORDINATION: CHALLENGING THE HIERARCHICAL MODEL

Refuting what he considered to be an 'error . . . on the part of Jacobins and jurists', Lucien Nizard observed in 1973 that the state machinery was not an 'enormous Leviathan-like computer capable of producing aims which are compatible with each other, whilst at the same time respecting a strict hierarchy, and moreover, one that is capable of pursuing its goals effectively through totally coherent practice'.[13] There have been numerous studies in Europe which clearly indicate that the state has become a very complex and segmented entity, and, moreover, that it no longer enjoys the prerogative of being the sole 'organizer' of 'social driving forces'.[14] National administrations must now be studied with a view to understanding how they relate to their social environment. Furthermore, the phenomenon of administrative co-ordination can no longer be explained simply by undertaking research into the equilibrium that may or may not exist between the various administrative actors. Specific forms of intra-administrative co-ordination, which seek to preserve the coherence of decision-making within the state apparatus, can be identified.[15] In France this intra-administrative co-ordination takes place within a one-sided hierarchical mechanism – a legacy of the Jacobin state – which was considerably reinforced under the Fifth Republic by inter-ministerial co-ordination (*interministériel*).[16]

L'interministériel normally takes the form of (1) meetings (inter-ministerial committees, etc.), (2) organs of state (the General Secretariat of

Government, etc.) and (3) procedures (the preparation of drafts, arbitration, etc.) which are overseen by the Prime Minister's office, as well as that of the President of the Republic, with the overriding goal of ordering different public policies.[17] The French administration has projected this hierarchical structure of intra-administrative co-ordination on to the area of Community policies. Since the creation of the ECSC, the position of Ministers who are concerned with negotiations within the Council of Ministers and the European Council has been subject to a 'filter', i.e. a special unit that is linked directly with the Prime Minister, known as the SGCI.[18] Indeed, from 1986 the SGCI was also entrusted with the task of co-ordinating Community policy implementation at domestic level.[19] When the disputes between the various administrations cannot be solved at SGCI level, inter-ministerial meetings (at the ministerial Cabinet level) and, in some cases, ministerial meetings (for example, on the GATT dossier in 1993) are held at Matignon. The Prime Minister's Cabinet (given that the general secretary of the SGCI often has an advisory capacity therein), or sometimes the Prime Minister himself, has the task therefore of arbitrating, i.e. settling disputes between divergent opinions between the bureaucracy. This power can be challenged only by the intervention of the President of the Republic. This occurred on several occasions owing to the uncertainties that existed during the first period of 'cohabitation' between May 1986 and May 1988.[20]

As long as there was only a limited range of policies on the Community's agenda – customs union, energy policy, competition policy, agricultural policy, commercial policy, social policy – and the Council of Ministers of the Community remained the dominant nexus in a decision-making process that was 'ruled' by the principle of unanimity,[21] the hierarchical approach to co-ordination enabled the goal of coherence to be achieved. However, the progressive enlargement of the Community's agenda, allied to institutional reforms, which was formally brought about by the Single European Act and the Maastricht Treaty of European Union, revealed its limits. In fact, these developments marked the emergence of a decision-making process which attached greater importance to policy networks that were more or less established and formalized.[22] It also permitted civil servants to operate more flexibly within a sphere that became increasingly difficult to control hierarchically. Thus, when the Prime Minister's circular of 21 March 1994 established that contacts between French administrative representatives and the Commission services had to be prepared in concert with the SGCI, it became effectively impossible for the latter to co-ordinate the day-to-day interaction between national civil servants and Commission officials and representatives of interest groups. This was particulary the case with the problem of exploring sector by sector the 'intellectual and normative frameworks'[23] which determined the orientation of Community policies.[24] Furthermore, the SGCI cannot undertake a co-ordinating role in all the relations that take place between civil servants (for example, those from the Ministry of Industry or from the Ministry of the Environment) and members of the European Parliament, who, since the Single European Act, have become increasingly 'useful' mediators as a result of their increased involvement in the EC decision-making process. It would be equally impossible to install systematic inter-ministerial control of all the direct channels which exist between local political and administrative actors (who have gained power by virtue of the process of decentralization), representatives of local economic interests, local government and Commission officials, whenever a matter involves the definition or the implementation of Community policies such as those in the economic and social spheres or the environment.

In fact, European construction tends to replace intra-administrative co-ordination, based upon hierarchy, with an alternative form which tends to be based more on negotiating networks. Each department, each ministerial Cabinet or civil servant increasingly influences a stage in Community policy-making, the interests of these sectoral networks being 'knitted' with those of elected politicians (at local, national or European level), civil servants (whether of the Commission, other member states or local government) and representatives of interest groups. Whilst meetings at SGCI and Matignon remain committed to maintaining a centralized process of decision-making from top to bottom,[25] 'Matignon decisions' have increasingly become the product of micro-level negotiations which have occurred in many different political and administrative structures, and which, in consequence, are very difficult to identify.

This leads to two further considerations. First, as Yves Mény has shown,[26] the implementation of Community policies by national bureaucracies or others actors[27] gives them many opportunities to adjust or manipulate the Brussels decisions. Second, the co-existence of the traditional French policy style[28] (*style décisionnel*) – centralized and hierarchical – and the new way of negotiating and lobbying at the Community level (networks) has become a source of potential conflict or, at least confusion.[29]

NEW FORMS OF MEDIATION BETWEEN THE ADMINISTRATION AND INTEREST GROUPS

The neo-corporatist analytical framework has never found favour in France, in so far as institutionalized macro-negotiating between the state and large social organizations has been unable to establish itself.[30] E. Suleiman, and above all B. Jobert and P. Muller, have, nevertheless, stressed that the existence of a *sectoral corporatist* form of mediation between administrations and interest groups has traditionally guaranteed the cohesion of public action.[31] This form of mediation was considered 'ill-suited from the moment that the given problems need to be dealt with from a perspective which no longer fits preconceived models',[32] and, as a result, it has been challenged by the process of the European construction – perhaps even more so since the launching of the internal market.

First, in a way reminiscent of David Spence's comments on the United Kingdom, the French central government (departments, ministerial Cabinets, Matignon, the permanent representation in Brussels) remains the prime target of French interest groups, whether at the formulation stage or during the implementation of Community policies.[33] Mediation between the various administrations and interest groups is organized on a *sectorial* basis. Initiatives are normally taken either by an interest group or by a ministry which is in search of a prop to enable it to assert its interests in relation to a particular subject that is under discussion at inter-ministerial level (the reason, hence, why it is so important to 'control' positions of responsibility within the SGCI and the permanent representation) or at Community level (hence the importance of 'keeping ties' within the Commission). For example, in February 1990 an adviser from the Ministry of Overseas *Départements* and Territories (Ministère des DOM-TOM) declared that between 1988 and 1989 he had increased the number of meetings with various professional organizations in the overseas *départements*. This was in order to listen to misgivings over a modification of their commercial and fiscal status by the internal market, as well as to gain their support for compensatory measures within the SGCI, Matignon and the Commission.[34] It would be easy to come to the conclusion that he was implementing a corporate model which is often described as 'typically French' in the scholarly literature,[35] and which is normally the result of an administration or state 'corps' taking control of the implementation of a public policy. However, such a method remains inappropriate in any discussion of Community policies – especially given that the European construction has created a system of pluralist representation which allows interest groups to employ several parallel channels in securing their objectives, somewhere between pressure and mediation (Commission, European Parliament, European professional federations, etc.).[36] In retrospect, pluralism encourages competition between, as well as diversification of, interests which make it difficult for a French administration (or one of its *corps*) to control the formulation or the implementation of a policy in symbiosis. A process that has traditionally been known in France as the *professions*. In their study of the 1992 reform of the common agricultural policy François-Gilles le Theule and David Litvan illustrated that the system of pluralist representation of interests at Community level was a factor which contributed to the incapacity of the Ministry of Agriculture and the French agricultural trade unions to conceive a common stance towards the Commission and other member states.[37] Similar conclusions could also be drawn, in the French case, from the policy that was adopted towards imports of Japanese cars (1991) or the 1993 reform of the common fisheries policy.

Second, because the European construction follows objectives within specific frameworks in order to stimulate its development ('the 1992 objective' being the most obvious example), actors are obliged to give greater weight to time scales in the preparation of their agendas. This explains the importance of *expertise*, which, within the Community arena, is rarely monopolized by a sole actor. On the contrary, there is often confrontation between various sources of expertise which function side by side, but often with little co-operation from the Commission, the committees of the European Parliament, the socio-professional organizations, and the national administrations. Indeed, after having focused on the SGCI for a long time, expertise on the European construction within the French central government fragmented as the debate on the internal market got under way. Furthermore, one of the institutional outcomes of this evolution has been the increased use of mediating apparatus in disputes between the public and private sectors. This has usually served the purpose of 'prioritizing' elements in order to make reflection on the future of Community policies more efficient through the production of written reports. Moreover, such an approach has brought together members of administrations, locally elected representatives, managers, bankers, trade unionists, academics, or even representatives of non-governmental associations. For example, we may cite the Commission de réflexion économique pour la préparation de l'échéance 1992, chaired from 1987–8 onwards by Marcel Boiteux, honorary chairman of EDF; or again the *groupes d'études et de mobilisation* set up in September 1988 by Edith Cresson, Minister of European Affairs, and renewed from 1991–2 during her term at Matignon. Indeed, two further comments need to be made at this juncture. First, there are no grounds for concluding that the decisions taken by various French administrations with regard to the 1992 deadline were inspired by their interaction with social actors. Being associated with the administration does not necessarily mean exercising an influence upon it. Second, the association of social actors with the management of the internal market project was not carried out in the same way as for the more political project on European Union.

Are universal suffrage and parliamentarism the only means of legitimation and democratic control of the EU political system, or do others exist? In an essay which appeared in 1992 Laurent Cohen Tanugi submitted the thesis that *law* is an essential element of democratic regulation within the European Union.[38] What then is the importance of interest groups? Some Scandinavian authors have no hesitation in considering them as key players in the democratic game of the EU political system, where the principle of the functional representation of interests has tended to gradually replace the principle of parliamentary representation.[39] From this perspective, one can better comprehend the logic that lies behind the desire of all national parliaments to exert greater control over the formation and implementation of Community policies. The French parliament has not been inactive in this area, having adopted new procedures (Loi Josselin, 10 May 1990; new article 88.4 under the constitutional revision of 25 June 1992), which, from now on, will oblige the central administration (the SGCI and SGG, through the Conseil d'Etat) to inform the lower House (Assemblée nationale) and the upper House (Sénat) of any proposals made by the Commission at the earliest possible stage. This new process of information transfer should not be considered solely as a response to the preponderance of executive power or to the institutional activism of the European Parliament. In the same way that the right of the two Houses to vote on resolutions on Commission proposals which contain provisions of a legislative nature is also respected. They reflect a fundamental fear of marginalization of the French parliament which, faced with the increasingly decisive role which interest groups are playing in the political system of the European Union, is, indeed, potent.

NOTES

1 Winckler Antoine, 'La France, état et société face à l'Europe', introductory report to the Second Round Table syposium organized by the Mouvement européen, 6 February 1993, published, p. 6.
2 In a study paper published in 1985, Vlad Constantinesco took a similar position, establishing a correlation between 'la conception diffuse [de la souveraineté] qui imprègne le fonctionnaire [français] et la réticence de l'administration "à accepter ou à subir des contrôles émanant de l'extérieur [la Communauté européenne]"'. See 'France: synthèse nationale', in Giuseppe Ciavarini Azzi (ed.), *L'Application du droit communautaire par les Etats membres*, Maastricht, IEAP, 1985, pp. 55–6.
3 Antoine Winckler, 'La France', p. 8.
4 Political scientists and sociologists (J.-L. Bodiguel, G. Grémion, M.-C. Kessler, J.-L. Quermonne, E. Suleiman) have demonstrated how difficult it is to give a precise definition of a French high-ranking civil servant. In this survey the quality attributed to high-ranking civil servants simply refers to the criterion of

having been prepared in a state school, *grande école de l'Etat* (ENA or state engineering school: Ecole Polytechnique, ENGREF, etc.).

5 See Christian Lequesne, *Paris–Bruxelles: comment se fait la politique européenne de la France*, Paris, Presses de la FNSP, 1993.

6 Our arguments thus corroborate the results of a survey conducted by Luc Rouban among 501 civil servants from external and central administrative departments. Cf. his work *Le Pouvoir anonyme: les mutations de l'Etat à la française*, Paris, Presses de la FNSP, pp. 90–108.

7 Cf. Wolfgang Wessels, 'Administrative interaction', in William Wallace (ed.), *The Dynamics of European Integration*, London, Pinter, 1990, pp. 229–41; and also 'Staat und westeuropäische Integration. Die Fusionsthese', in Michael Kreile (ed.), *Die Integration Europas*, Opladen, Westdeutscher Verlag, 1992, pp. 36–61.

8 Wolfgang Wessels, *Alternative Strategies for Institutional Reform*, Working Paper 85/184, Florence, European Institute, 1984, p. 58; and 'Administrative interaction', p. 238.

9 Wolfgang Wessels, 'Administrative interaction', p. 235.

10 Elie Cohen, 'Représentation de l'adversaire et politique économique. Nationalisation, politique industrielle et Acte unique européen', *Revue française de science politique*, October 1993, vol. 43, 5, p. 802.

11 Cf. decisions *Alitalia, Nicolo, Boisdet, Philip Morris France*.

12 Alexandre Carnelutti, 'La formation des agents de l'Etat aux affaires européennes', *Revue française d'administration publique*, July–September 1989, vol. 51, p. 510. In the same vein, see also Josseline de Clausade, *L'Adaptation de l'administration française à l'Europe*, Paris, La Documentation Française, 1991, or the *Rapport Public 1992 of the Conseil d'Etat*, Paris, La Documentation Française, 1993.

13 Lucien Nizard, 'Administration et société: planification et régulations bureaucratiques', *Revue française de science politique*, 1973, vol. 23, 1, p. 213.

14 'Régulations sociales et régulation politique: les systèmes d'échanges politiques en mutation', working paper by the working group RESOPOLIS, CERAT/IEP, Grenoble, 1994, unpublished paper, p. 1.

15 Gérard Timsit, 'Le concept de coordination administrative', *Bulletin de l'IIAP*, October–December 1975, vol. 36, p. 128.

16 Cf. Bruno Jobert and Pierre Muller, *L'Etat en action*, Paris, PUF, 1987, p. 211.

17 Jacques Fournier, *Le Travail gouvernemental*, Paris, Presses de la FNSP, 1987.

18 Secrétariat général du comité interministériel pour les questions de coopération économique, set up in 1948 with a view to co-ordinating the French position in relation to the OEEC (now OECD).

19 Cf. circular of 5 May 1986 (not published in the Official Journal) and circular of 25 January 1990 (*OJ* 1 February 1990).

20 Christian Lequesne, *Paris–Bruxelles*.

21 Cf. Philip Budden and Burt L. Monroe, 'Decision-making in the EC Council of Ministers', statement presented to the ECSA Congress, Washington, 26–9 May 1993, unpublished paper.

22 Pierre Muller, 'La mutation de politiques publiques européennes', *Pouvoirs*, 1994, vol. 69, p. 73.

23 Ibid., p. 67.

24 On exchanges between administrators of the French Minister of Agriculture and those of the Commission Directorate General of Agriculture (DG VI)

during the last reform of the CAP, see François-Gilles Le Theule and David Litvan, 'La réforme de la PAC: analyse d'une négociation communautaire', *Revue française de science politique*, October 1993, vol. 43, 5, p. 771.

25 Alain Claisse would speak of 'the administration as the forum for ideological coherency' (*Les implications régionales de l'intégration économique régionale: l'exemple de la CEE. Approche comparative*, Acts of Madrid Symposium, Brussels, IISA, 1991, p. 163).

26 Cf. his chapter on France in Jacques Ziller and Heinrich Siedentopf (eds), *L'Europe des administrations*, Brussels and London, Bruylant and Sage, 1988, vol. 2, pp. 277–373.

27 What is referred to in Christian Lequesne, *Paris–Bruxelles*, as formal execution.

28 On the notion of 'policy style', see Jeremy Richardson (ed.), *Policy Styles in Western Europe*, London, Allen & Unwin, 1982.

29 Cf. Pascal Lamy, 'Choses vues en Europe', *Esprit*, October 1991, pp. 67–81; and also Hervé Dumez and Alain Jeunemaître, 'La France, l'Europe et la concurrence; enseignements de l'affaire A.T.R./De Havilland', *Commentaire*, spring 1992, vol. 57, pp. 109–10.

30 Cf. Andrew Cox and Jack Hayward, 'The Inapplicability of the Corporatist Model in Britain and France', *International Political Science Review*, 1983, vol. 4, 2, pp. 217–40; and also Bruno Jobert and Pierre Muller, *L'Etat en action*, p. 172.

31 Ezra Suleiman, *Les hauts fonctionnaires et la politique*, Paris, Le Seuil, 1976, pp. 202–13; Bruno Jobert and Pierre Muller, *L'Etat en action*, pp. 171–206.

32 Bruno Jobert and Pierre Muller, *L'Etat en action*, p. 205.

33 David Spence, 'The Role of the National Civil Service in European Lobbying: the British Case', in Sonia Mazey and Jeremy Richardson (eds), *Lobbying in the European Community*, Oxford, Oxford University Press, 1993.

34 Interview.

35 Cf. Jack Hayward, 'Mobilising Private Interests in the Service of Public Ambitions: the Salient Element in the Dual French Policy Style?', in Jeremy Richardson (ed.), *Policy Styles in Western Europe*, p. 117; or again, Peter A. Hall, 'Pluralism and Pressure Politics in France', in Jeremy Richardson (ed.), *Pressure Groups*, Oxford, Oxford University Press, 1993, p. 172.

36 Cf. Wolfgang Streeck and Philippe C. Schmitter, 'From National Corporatism to Transitional Pluralism: Organized Interests in the Single European Market', *Politics and Society*, 1991, vol. 19, 2, pp. 133–64.

37 François-Gilles Le Theule and David Litvan, 'La réforme de la PAC'.

38 *L'Europe en danger*, Paris, Fayard, 1992 (particularly chapter III).

39 Cf. Svein S. Andersen and Tom R. Burns, 'The European Community and the End of Parliamentary Democracy: Continuing Discourse on Post-parliamentary Politics', communication presented at the thirty-first congress of the Institut International de Sociologie, Paris, 21–5 May 1993, unpublished paper; also Janne Haaland Matlary, 'Quis Custodiet Custodes? The European Commission's Policy-making Role and the Problem of Democratic Legitimacy', communication presented to the ECSA Congress, 26–9 May 1993, unpublished paper.

Part III

The European impact on domestic policies

7   Which social policy for Europe?

Giandomenico Majone

The question appearing in the title of this chapter can, and should, be analyzed at two different levels. At the positive level, the problem is to determine the range of options open to the European Union, given the constraints set by the available resources and by the political will of the member states. At the normative level, putting feasibility issues aside, we must examine the desirability of a European social policy modelled along the lines of the historical evolution of national policies. Since our conclusion is that a European welfare state, now or in the foreseeable future, is neither possible nor desirable, we must also face a third question concerning the role which the Union can/should play in the social field.

The need to separate conceptually these various issues is demonstrated by the recent Green Paper of the European Commission *European Social Policy – Options for the Union.*[1] The paper takes as its working definition of social policy 'the full range of policies in the social sphere, including labour market policies', but does not address quality-of-life issues such as risk, consumer safety, the environment, or the protection of diffuse interests and non-commodity values.

Such a definition – too broad and at the same time too narrow – is understandable in historical and institutional terms. It is inspired by traditional conceptions of social policy and follows the formal competences of the Directorate General responsible for drafting the document; it also reflects certain conceptual ambiguities already present in the Treaty of Rome. The result, however, is a seriously incomplete representation of European achievements in the social field, and a failure to provide clear indications about likely future developments. Greater analytical precision is needed.

FROM SOCIAL POLICY TO SOCIAL REGULATION

As noted above, there is considerable ambiguity about the meaning and scope of a European social policy in the Treaty of Rome itself.[2] The section on social policy – Title III of Part Three of the Treaty – enumerates a number of 'social fields' (employment; labour law and working conditions; vocational training; social security; health and safety at work; collective bargaining and the right of association) where member states should co-operate closely (Article 118, EEC). In the following article, member states are urged to 'maintain the application of the principle that men and women should receive equal pay for equal work'. The same Title III also establishes the European Social Fund with the goal of improving employment opportunities and facilitating the geographical and occupational mobility of workers.

What is arguably the most significant social policy provision in the Treaty – the social security regime for migrant workers – appears not in the section on social policy but in the one on the free movement of persons, services and capital (Title III of Part Two, Article 51, EEC). Finally, one of the objectives of the common agricultural policy is, according to Article 39(b), 'to ensure a fair standard of living for the agricultural community, in particular by increasing the individual earnings of persons engaged in agriculture'.

Thus, to the framers of the Treaty 'social policy' included not only social security and interpersonal distribution of income, at least for certain groups of workers, but also interregional redistribution, elements of industrial and labour market policy (vocational training, measures to improve labour mobility) and social regulation (primarily occupational health and safety, and equal treatment for men and women).

However, the enumeration of matters relating to the social field in Article 118 and the limited role given to the EC Commission in Title III – to promote co-ordination of national policies, to undertake studies, deliver opinions and arrange consultations – indicate that the social policy domain, with the exceptions noted above, was originally considered to be outside the supranational competence of the institutions of the Community.[3] In fact, Commission activity in the area of social policy and social regulation was quite modest between 1958 and the end of the 1970s, with one notable exception: environmental policy. The terms 'environment' or 'environmental protection' do not even appear in the Treaty of Rome. Despite the lack of an explicit legal basis, a Community environmental policy has been growing vigorously, if not harmoniously or systematically, since 1967. The significance of this development will become clear as we proceed with our argument.

The Single European Act assigns a number of new competences to the Community in the social field. The main lines of development of Community activities in this field are beginning to emerge clearly: they are regional development (new Title V, Economic and Social Cohesion), and social regulation (Article 100A, Article 118A, and the new Title VII, Environment). As noted above, prior to this the social policy belonged to the competence of the member states, with the power of initiative of the Commission essentially limited to promoting intergovernmental collaboration. In particular, Article 118 of the Rome Treaty did not give the Community the power to regulate in the field of occupational health and safety. Hence the first directives in this area had to be based on Article 100 (which deals with the approximation of laws directly affecting the functioning of the common market) and thus needed unanimity in the Council of Ministers. Under the new Article 118A directives in the field of occupational health and safety can be adopted by the Council by qualified majority and without the need to prove that they are requisite to the completion of the internal market.

To complete this picture of significant progress in social regulation at Community level, one should also make mention of Article 100 A (3), which states that the Commission will start from a high level of protection in matters relating to health, safety, and environmental and consumer protection. This implies that the reference to minimum requirements in Article 118A ('the Council . . . shall adopt, by means of directives, minimum requirements for gradual implementation, having regard to the conditions and technical rules obtaining in each of the Member States') does not mean that Community health and safety standards should reflect the lowest level prevailing in the member states. Rather, Community standards represent a lower threshold for national regulators, who are free to maintain or adopt standards incorporating higher levels of safety.

The increasing importance of social regulation is also revealed by the action programme implementing the Community Social Charter adopted by the member states, with the exception of the United Kingdom, on 9 December 1989. Of the twenty directives/regulations listed in the programme, ten are in the area of occupational health and safety, three deal with improvements in living and working conditions, and three with equal treatment for men and women, disabled persons, and the protection of children.[4]

The Treaty of Maastricht continues this trend. It contains a new section on consumer protection (Title XVIII); it introduces significant innovations in the area of occupational health and safety; it introduces qualified majority voting for most environmental protection measures. It even adds transport safety to the regulatory tasks of the Community (Article 75,

1(C)). But the Treaty is silent about most areas of traditional social policy. Moreover, the creation of the Cohesion Fund has subtly modified the nature of Community 'social' spending. 'Whereas hitherto the purpose of structural spending was to assist particular regions or sectors of the economy, the new fund was directed at specific countries for environmental projects or ones relating to trans-European networks, with no restriction on where the expenditure should go.'[5]

Why have European policy-makers consistently favoured social regulation over social policy? To answer this question we must first understand what makes social regulation different from traditional social policy. Then we have to explain why regulation has become such an important part of EC policy-making; this will be done in the following section.

A useful analytical distinction between social policy and social regulation can be drawn using the language of welfare economics. A fundamental theorem of welfare economics states that, under certain conditions, competitive markets lead to an efficient ('Pareto-optimal') allocation of resources. Recent research has identified a number of situations in which this theorem does not hold. Such situations are referred to as 'market failures' and provide a set of rationales for government intervention, acceptable also to economic liberals. The major types of market failure are:

1 Failure of competition.
2 Public goods.
3 Externalities.
4 Incomplete markets.
5 Information failures.
6 Unemployment, inflation and disequilibrium.

Two further rationales for government intervention not related to market failure are:

7 Redistribution.
8 Merit goods.

These eight reasons for public intervention fall into three groups which correspond to the three fiscal functions of government in the sense of Musgrave: the allocation function (1 to 5), the stabilization function (6) and the distribution function (7 and 8). Thus an analytical distinction between social regulation and social policy can be drawn on the basis of the rationales for government intervention. The purpose of social regulation (health and safety, the environment, consumer protection) is to solve problems created by specific types of market failure – especially public goods, negative externalities and information failures. Air and water pollution are prime examples of externalities, while a number of regulatory activities in the fields of safety and consumer protection are motivated by imperfect information and the belief that the market, by itself, will supply too little information.

If there are no market failures the economy is Pareto-efficient and there is no economic justification for government intervention. But the fact that the economy is Pareto-efficient says nothing about the distribution of income. A very unequal distribution of income may be unacceptable to a majority of citizens, and that will legitimize government intervention on political and moral grounds, even at some loss of economic efficiency.

The second argument for government intervention in a Pareto-efficient economy arises from concern that individuals may not act in their own best interest. Goods that the government compels individuals to consume, like elementary education and low-cost housing for the poor (instead of giving cash grants), are called merit goods. Of course, the paternalistic argument is plausible only if one assumes that government knows what is in the best interest of individuals better than they themselves do.

Now, while 'social policy' is not a technical term with an exact and uniform meaning, there is general agreement that its central core consists of social insurance, public assistance, the health and welfare services, and housing policy. Hence social policy is primarily concerned with interpersonal redistribution of income and with the provision of 'merit goods', while social regulation, like economic regulation, addresses problems arising from various types of market failure.

Analytically distinct, social policy and social regulation are historically and institutionally related; they belong to the same 'policy space' – a policy space being a set of policies that are so interconnected that it is impossible to make useful descriptive or analytical statements about one of the policies without taking the other elements of the set into consideration.[6] The most interesting aspect of a policy space is how its internal structure changes in time. As the number and importance of some elements grow relative to the size of the space (as determined by the amount of financial and political resources devoted to it), individual policies increasingly compete with each other for public support. Some policies may become so important that they form a distinct sub-space within the original space. This is how social regulation has evolved within the social policy space – a development most students of social policy have failed to notice because of their fixation on particular programmes and institutional arrangements. In thinking about the future shape of a European 'social state', it is important to pay attention to the dynamics of the entire social policy space, including social regulation, and also to the specificity of European policy-making.

THE EUROPEAN COMMUNITY AS A REGULATORY STATE

The Treaty of Maastricht has established the European Union (EU), but the supranational core of the new construction remains the European Community (EC). The other two 'pillars' of the Union – foreign and security policy as well as justice and internal affairs – are, for the time being, strictly intergovernmental arrangements. Now, if one examines the policies of the EC in the light of the traditional economic functions of the state – allocation, stabilization, redistribution – one is struck by the fact that only the allocative (regulatory) function is well developed, whereas macro-economic stabilization and income redistribution remain largely the responsibility of the member states.

The immediate reason for this asymmetrical development is, of course, the very small size of the Community budget. This budget represents less than 1.3 per cent of the gross domestic product (GDP) of the Union and less than 4 per cent of the central government spending of the member states. Given such limited resources, only regulatory policies aimed at increasing allocative efficiency could be developed at the European level. In fact an important characteristic of regulatory policy-making is the limited influence of budgetary limitations on the activities of regulators. The size of non-regulatory, direct-expenditure programmes is constrained by budgetary allocations and, ultimately, by the size of government tax revenues.

In contrast, the real costs of most regulatory programmes are borne directly by the firms and individuals who have to comply with them. Compared with these costs, the resources needed to produce the regulations are trivial. This structural difference between regulatory policies and policies involving the direct expenditure of public funds is particularly important for the analysis of Community policy-making, since not only the economic, but also the political and administrative, costs of enforcing EC regulations are borne by the member states. The financial resources of the Community go, for the most part, to the common agricultural policy and to a handful of distributive programmes. The remaining resources are insufficient to support large-scale initiatives in counter-cyclical spending or in traditional social policy. Hence the only way for the EC Commission to increase its role and competences was to expand the scope of its regulatory activities.[7]

At the same time, member states have been willing to surrender important regulatory powers to the Commission, despite their strenuous defence of the principle of national sovereignty in fields such as foreign affairs, taxation, defence and social policy. This is because problems of 'international regulatory failure' severely limit the usefulness of purely intergovernmental arrangements in the regulatory field. For example, where pollution has international effects and fines impose significant costs on firms that compete internationally, national regulators may be unwilling to prosecute violators as rigorously if they determine the level of enforcement unilaterally rather than under supranational supervision. Hence the transfer of regulatory powers to the Commission makes stringent regulation more credible in the eyes of the firms themselves and of governments inside and outside the EU.

Also, because the Commission is involved in the regulation of a large number of firms throughout the Union, it has much more to gain by being tough in any individual case than a national regulator: weak credibility would destroy its credibility in the eyes of more firms. Thus it may be more willing to enforce sanctions than a member state would be.[8] Even more important is the fact that the Commission is a non-majoritarian institution.[9] Not being directly responsible to voters or to elected politicians, the Commission can take decisions which national governments and regulators would find politically too costly. For example, it has consistently taken a stricter pro-competition stance than national regulators such as the British Monopolies and Mergers Commission, the German Bundeskartellamt, or the French Conseil de la Concurrence.

In short, the low credibility of intergovernmental agreements explains the willingness of member states to delegate important regulatory powers to the European level. Thus, the combination of several factors – budget constraints, the desire of the Commission to increase its competences and the willingness of national governments to delegate regulatory powers, among others – explains the development of the Community as a 'regulatory state'. In the remainder of the chapter I shall explore the implications of this development for Europe's 'social dimension'.

EFFICIENCY AND REDISTRIBUTION IN THE REGULATORY STATE

To accept the logic of the regulatory state is not to deny the importance of the other functions of government, including redistribution. This logic suggests only that different functions ought to be assigned to different branches or levels of government, each operating in relative autonomy according to its own principles. In particular, programmes of economic and social regulation should be designed to correct specific cases of market failure as efficiently as possible, not to support other policy objectives. There is a good deal of evidence, in Europe and elsewhere, that the improper use of regulatory instruments usually leads to unsatisfactory results.

To take some examples from EC policy-making, the common agricultural policy, which relies heavily on price regulation, effects a considerable transfer of money from consumers and taxpayers to farmers, and in that sense it may be considered part of a 'welfare state for farmers'. However, the CAP represents not only an inefficient but also a perverse type of redistributive social policy, since it favours the well-to-do farmers of northern and central Europe rather than the poor hill farmers of the south. Only if the current system of price support is transformed into a direct income grant will agricultural policy become a true social policy, though limited to a particular occupational group.

Another interesting example is EC regional policy. Demands for regional redistribution within the EC have become pressing in recent years,[10] leading to a doubling in the expenditure of the structural funds by 1993. The recent reforms of structural policy have created new possibilities for EC decision-makers to deal directly with political actors in individual regions. Proponents of a 'Europe of the regions' are eager to exploit these possibilities to implement their vision of a new European order in which increasing centralization of decision-making in Brussels is counterbalanced by the emergence of powerful regional institutions directly linked with the centre.

Despite these interesting political perspectives, regional redistribution must be considered an inefficient instrument of social policy. In their enthusiasm for 'social cohesion' some EC policy-makers seem to forget that there is an important distinction between reducing inequality among individuals and reducing disparities across regions. The problems of targeting regions to achieve a better individual state of distribution are well known.[11] Since most regions contain a mix of poor and rich individuals, a programme aimed at redistributing resources to a region whose average income is low may simply result in a lowering of the tax rate. The main beneficiaries of the programme will thus be rich individuals in poor regions – a phenomenon well known in the Italian Mezzogiorno and which may be replicated in other regions of the Union as a result of the increases in the regional funds.

On the other hand, in a federal or quasi-federal system it is politically difficult to aim redistribution directly at individuals. Even in the United States, where the federal government pays three-quarters of the cost of welfare assistance, the states set the benefit levels. States differ in their assessment of what a family needs to meet a reasonable standard of living, and in the percentage of that standard they are willing to pay to help a family meet its needs. States also differ in the requirements an applicant must satisfy in order to be eligible for welfare assistance. As a consequence of these differences, the level of welfare assistance among the American states varies widely, more so than interstate disparities in wage rates or the cost of living.[12] Similarly in Europe, the governments of the countries of the southern periphery, foremost among them Spain, advocate non-individualized transfers of Community funds.

In fact, at both the Maastricht and the Edinburgh summits, Spain demanded that the newly established Cohesion Fund should be directed to member states, not to poor regions within member states, as was the previous practice in structural spending. In this way Spain succeeded in cutting out two of the three most populous poorer regions in the Union, the Mezzogiorno and eastern Germany, which are in relatively wealthy member states, and in claiming for itself 55 per cent of the Fund.[13]

Spain's demand, though clearly self-serving, carries to its logical conclusion the philosophy of structural spending and regional integration in the EC. From the start, regional subventions were viewed less as redistributive measures than as side payments to obtain unanimous approval of efficiency-enhancing reforms of the Community system. Thus, the Regional Fund was established in 1975 in the wake of the first enlargement of the Community. Both the United Kingdom and Ireland had serious regional problems that led them to side with Italy in its long-standing demand for a Community regional policy. Similarly, the introduction of the Integrated Mediterranean Programmes in 1984 for Greece, southern Italy and parts of southern France was a side payment to offset the increased competition in Mediterranean agricultural products that was bound to result from the enlargement of the Community to include Spain and Portugal.

Also the doubling of the structural funds decided in 1987 was a payment to the poorer member states in return for their assent to the package of liberalizing measures required for the completion of the internal market. As Yves Mény pointed out some time ago, EC regional policy has always been tightly controlled by the national governments. Hence the fact that the Cohesion Fund – the side payment for acceptance of monetary union – is directed at specific countries for projects relating to the environment and to trans-European networks, with no restriction on where the expenditure should go, is merely explicit recognition of what was already happening in practice.

These developments show how implausible is the thesis, advanced by some scholars as well as by members of the Commission and of the European Parliament, that the growth of the structural funds is a result of changing conceptions of fairness and social justice. It has been argued that underlying the concern for regional inequality is the realization that, if the Community is to gain the loyalty of individual citizens, it must provide for the expression of basic moral concerns for justice and equality that have formerly been confined to nation states.[14]

The notion of a European welfare state, somehow emerging as a 'transnational synthesis' of national welfare systems, has been advocated on similar grounds. Historically, social policy has made an essential contribution to the process of nation-building in nineteenth-century Europe by bridging the gap between state and society. National insurance, social security, public education, socialized medicine were, and to a large extent remain, powerful symbols of national solidarity. It is argued that a supranational welfare state would provide an equally strong demonstration of Europe-wide solidarity.[15]

However, such analogies are seriously misleading. The very success of the national welfare state sets limits to an expanded social policy competence of the Community. Given the progressive loss of control over economic policy, social policy is one of the few remaining bulwarks of national sovereignty, and for this reason alone national governments will do their best to protect it. It is also possible that the development of welfare-state institutions at the European level, instead of generating a sense of supranational solidarity, would reinforce popular dislike of centralization, bureaucratization and technocratic management.

On the other hand, the advocates of a larger role for the Community in interregional redistribution run the risk of committing the 'ecological fallacy' which consists in deducing properties of individuals from properties of groups of individuals. Strictly speaking, only individuals, not regions, are rich or poor. As explained above, because even 'poor' regions contain a mix of poor and rich individuals, programmes aimed at regional redistribution may not in fact improve the interpersonal distribution of income, but may actually benefit rich individuals most. Also, if the EC budget were reformed to become deliberately redistributive, it would be impossible to avoid a difficult trade-off between interregional transfers and the fiscal autonomy of the member states, as well as politically divisive debates about domestic choices that led to regional underdevelopment in the first place.

SUBSIDIARITY AND SOCIAL WELFARE

The preceding analysis leads to the conclusion that a clearer allocation of functions between the Union and its member states is the only way of resolving the 'big trade-off' between efficiency and a more equal distribution of income and wealth that has confronted every democracy since the dawn of industrialization. The Commmunity has not the financial, political, or institutional resources to play a significant role in the redistribution of income or in the provision of merit goods. In fact, there is a striking difference between the scale and scope of national welfare policies and the modest role of (traditional) social policy in the process of European integration.

As I have attempted to show, redistributive programmes at the Community level are generally ineffective if judged by criteria of social welfare such as the redistribution of resources in favour of the poorest members of society. Such programmes must be evaluated by other criteria: political, as in the case of the common agricultural policy, or economic – the social security regime for migrant workers, for example. Since the mid-1970s the structural funds have been consistently used as side payments to facilitate acceptance of efficiency-enhancing reforms by all member states: successive enlargements of the Community, the completion of the internal market, monetary union.

A larger redistributive role is not only unfeasible because of the financial and political constraints noted previously, but also undesirable at the present stage of development of the European polity. The delicate value judgements about the appropriate balance of efficiency and equity, which social policies express, can be made legitimately only within fairly homogeneous communities. It is difficult to see how politically acceptable levels of income redistribution and of provision of merit goods can be determined centrally in a community of nations whose stages of economic development and political and legal traditions are still so different. At the same time, because historical and linguistic barriers reduce the mobility of European society, the case for centralizing income redistribution is less compelling in the EU than in the nation state or in a mature federal system like the United States.

This does not mean that the process of European integration should be driven only by economic considerations. It is certainly true that the creation of a common market is not a goal capable of eliciting the loyalty and attachment of the people of Europe to their supranational institutions. A social dimension is also needed, but one must be clear about the meaning of this ambiguous expression. Nowadays, quality of life depends at least as much on social regulatory intervention as on traditional instruments of social policy. National social policies are the outcome of the struggles of the past over the division of the domestic product. But, even at the national level, traditional cleavages along class or party lines are becoming less significant than new 'transversal' divisions over cultural diversity, public participation, the environment, or the risks of modern technology.

It is a fact of great significance that for many of these issues the national dimension is essentially irrelevant: solutions must be found either at the local or at the supranational, even global, level. There is, in other words, a natural division of labour between sub-national, national, European and international institutions. The nature of the problem, rather than ideological preconceptions or historical analogies, should determine the level at which solutions are to be sought. This is precisely what subsidiarity means or ought to mean.

As we have seen, each successive revision of the Treaty of Rome has expanded and strengthened the competences of the Community in social regulation. Hundreds of directives have been approved in the areas of environmental and consumer protection, product safety, the safety of food and medical drugs, health and safety in the workplace, equal rights for men and women. Even more important than the quantitative expansion of Community regulation has been its qualitative deepening. For example, most social regulatory measures no longer have to be justified exclusively in terms of the free movement of goods or the completion of the internal market.

Perhaps the most surprising qualitative change – surprising because it so clearly contradicts the received view of EC policy-making – is the innovative character of some Community policies. It used to be said that EC regulations, in order to be accepted by the member states, had to represent a kind of lowest common denominator solution. The fact that national interests are strongly represented at each stage of European policy-making seemed to preclude the possibility of innovation, while giving a bargaining advantage to those member states which oppose high levels of protection. Hence the widespread fear that a larger role of the Community in social regulation would open the door to social dumping.

In reality, among recent and even older directives one can find several striking examples of regulatory innovation.[16] Thus, in the field of environmental protection the 1976 PCB directive (76/769/EEC) had no parallel in existing member state regulations, while the directive on sulphur dioxide limit values (80/779/EEC) established, on a Community-wide basis, ambient air quality standards which most member states did not previously employ as a control strategy.[17]

The framework directive on health and safety at work (89/391/EEC) goes beyond the regulatory philosophy and practice even of the most advanced member states, such as Germany.[18] Among the notable features of the directive are its scope (it applies to all sectors of activity, both public and private, including service, educational, cultural and leisure activities), the obligations it imposes on employers concerning the development of a coherent overall prevention policy, the adaptation of work to the individual and worker information, and the emphasis on the participation and training of workers.

Equally innovative are the Machinery Directive (89/392/EEC) and, in a more limited sphere, Directive 90/270 on health and safety in work with display screen equipment. Both directives rely on the concept of the 'working environment', and consider psychological factors like stress and fatigue important elements to be considered in a modern regulatory approach. It is difficult to find equally advanced principles in the legislation of any major industrialized country, inside or outside the EU.

In many areas of social regulation, notably the environment, risk management, food and drugs, and consumer safety, the United States has played a pioneering role, providing methods and techniques which European regulators used extensively in the 1960s and 1970s. A possible explanation of US leadership in these domains is that because America was a 'welfare laggard' compared with Europe, it devoted to social regulation the financial and political resources which in Europe were absorbed by the growing needs of the welfare state. A similar argument could explain why, in today's Europe, policy innovation in regulatory matters comes increasingly from the Community.

NOTES

1 Commission of the European Communities, 'European Social Policy – Options for the Union', 1993, *COM (93) 551 final*.
2 Giandomenico Majone, 'The European Community between Social Policy and Social Regulation', *Journal of Common Market Studies*, 1993, vol. 31, 2, 153–70.
3 Eliane Vogel-Polski and J. Vogel, *L'Europe sociale 1993: illusion, alibi ou réalité*, Brussels, Editions de l'Université de Bruxelles, 1991.
4 Commission of the European Communities, 'Action programme relating to the implementation of the Community Charter of Basic Social Rights for Workers', 1989, *COM (89) 568 final*.
5 Michael Shackleton, 'The Community Budget after Maastricht', in Alan W. Cafruny and Glenda G. Rosenthal (eds), *The State of the European Community*, Harlow, Longman, 1993, vol. 2, pp. 373–90, at p. 385.
6 Giandomenico Majone, *Evidence, Argument and Persuasion in the Policy Process*, New Haven, Yale University Press, 1989, pp. 158–61.
7 Giandomenico Majone, 'Market Integration and Regulation: Europe after 1992', *Metroeconomica*, 1992, vol. 43, 1–2, 131–56; and 'Regulatory Federalism in the European Community', *Government and Policy*, 1992, vol. 10, pp. 299–316.
8 Kristos Gatsios and Paul Seabright, 'Regulation in the European Community', *Oxford Review of Economic Policy*, 1989, vol. 5, 2, pp. 37–60.
9 Giandomenico Majone, 'The Rise of the Regulatory State in Europe', *West European Politics*, 1994, vol. 17, 3, pp. 77–101.
10 Gary Marks, 'Structural Policy in the European Community', in A. Sbragia (ed.), *Europolitics*, Washington, DC, Brookings Institution, 1992, pp. 191–224; Harvey Armstrong, 'Community Regional Policy', in Juliet Lodge (ed.), *The European Community and the Challenge of the Future*, New York, St Martin's Press, 1989, pp. 167–85; Helen Wallace, 'Distributional Politics: Dividing up the Community Cake', in Helen Wallace, William Wallace and Carole Webb

(eds), *Policy-making in the European Community*, 2nd edition, Chichester, Wiley, 1983, pp. 81–113.

11 Richard A. Musgrave and P. B. Musgrave, *Public Finance in Theory and Practice*, New York, McGraw-Hill, 1973.

12 Paul E. Peterson and M. C. Rom, *Welfare Magnets*, Washington, DC, Brookings Institution, 1990.

13 Gary Marks, 'Structural Policy and Multilevel Governance in the EC', in Alan W. Cafruny and Glenda G. Rosenthal, *The State of the European Community*, pp. 391–410.

14 Gary Marks, 'Structural Policy in the European Community', p. 206.

15 Wolfgang Streeck, 'La dimensione sociale del mercato unico europeo', *Stato e Mercato*, 1990, vol. 28, pp. 29–68; Claus Offe, 'Europäische Dimensionen der Sozial Politik', Bremen, Centre for Social Policy Research, unpublished paper, 1990; Stephan Leibfried, 'Europe's Could-be Social State', Bremen, Centre for Social Policy Research, 1991.

16 Majone, 'The European Community between Social Policy and Social Regulation'.

17 Eckhart Rehbinder and R. Stewart, *Environmental Protection Policy*, Berlin and New York, De Gruyter, 1985, pp. 213–14.

18 Kerstin Feldhoff, *Grundzüge des Europäischen Arbeitsumweltrechts*, Bochum, Ruhr Universität, 1992.

8 Europe between market and power: industrial policies

Specialization, technology, competition and foreign trade

Elie Cohen

Ten years ago we were about to take a decisive leap forward:[1] the Single European Act. Predictions had already been made as to the costs of failing to Europeanize, about the effects of neo-protectionism, and about falling behind Japan industrially. Yet this leap had become caught up in a quarrel over initial questions (enlargement, completion, extension of powers) in the on-going conflict over the fair financial repayment claimed by Mrs Thatcher, and the extent to which systematic closures in unprofitable sectors with no future, however small they might be, had to be programmed. The analysis had also been based on the assumption of Europe's impotence and fragmentation against the background of planetary domination established by Russians and Americans.[2] The strategic initiative launched by President Reagan, known as 'star wars', had revealed the potential cost of European division in the sector of high technology. Thus, President Mitterrand came up with the civil alternative to the threat to the defence industries, known as Eureka. For his part, Etienne Davignon had instigated the creation of a lobby for the major industrial undertakings with the aim of obliging Europe to take charge of its problems in industry: competitiveness, research and development, fragmentation of the Community market, regulatory obstacles, etc. The road had therefore been mapped out for a European revival, which required two approaches: a voluntarist one, promoting the setting up of a basis for European industrial co-operation in the high-tech sectors, these being, Esprit, Eureka, Brite, Race, Euram; the other, institutional, promoting the creation of a real single market, with its famous directives leading to the creation of a complete European internal market.

Here I would like to point to the fact that there is a strong asymmetry between policies brought about by market forces, such as competition policy, foreign trade policy, on the one hand, and voluntarist industrial policies, on the other. The first ones, which require a strong political input at the outset, subsequently fall under semi-automatic pilotage, whereas voluntarist industrial and technological policies, which equally need continuous attention, are likely to be challenged at each and every turning point, and, in the long run, have every chance of falling by the wayside. On this basis, one can therefore conclude that market policies have succeeded comparatively well against voluntarist policies of industrial specialization.

DYNAMICS OF UNEQUAL INTENSITY

The European Act incorporated a two-tier approach, each of equal importance: the programme for the 'four' freedoms (free movement of persons, goods, capital and services), and accompanying policies (monetary, fiscal, research and development, environment and economic and social cohesion, etc.). It is probable that there were several interpretations of the compromise, and equally probable that certain states would undergo hardship in the name of internal imperatives; nevertheless, the two-tier structure of the Single European Act remained. Moreover, there was a certain logic behind the dismantling of all internal barriers as a way of spurring European undertakings into international competition, at the same time allowing the undertakings to catch up where they lagged behind in the new technology sectors, through the deployment of voluntarist policies of specialization, through research and development, even through procurement policies. This was the post-war strategy in France,[3] also that of Japan until recently.

Directive after directive was adopted with the seal of the Single European Act, the 1993 objective, the no-tariff obstacles to trade were removed, although mention must be made of the areas of taxation on savings and consumption, technological co-operation, social matters, where Europe has not advanced at the same rate. One can certainly interpret the Maastricht Treaty as the voluntarist political arm of the Single European Act, since it contains the definition of monetary union, organizes the convergence of macro-economic policies, and opens new areas of competence to the Commission as well as providing the platform for intergovernmental co-operation. However, on the one hand, the convergence policies concern the structural adjustment much sought by the IMF, and not a catching-up strategy, and, on the other, a disequilibrium between market policies and policies for industry[4] became more and more obvious. Note must be taken of this.

Market policies

By market policies I mean the programme of the four freedoms, and particularly, foreign trade policy, competition policy, state aid and mergers policy.

I will not go into detail about the four freedoms here. Suffice it to say how much its success has been exemplary, and how much the twelve states have given proof of their zeal in the adoption of the directives in domestic law. The incessant quarrels over the purity of beer, over the right to call heated milk products 'yoghurt', over the reusable packing of mineral water . . . all of which became obsolete from one day to another by the establishing of a general principle according to which what is deemed 'good' for one of the Twelve *ipso facto* becomes so for the others,[5] except where proof can be established of the existence of a danger to public health which would therefore justify a minimal degree of harmonization. The dispute over harmonization which either had to precede or follow liberalization, and which kept European bureaucrats and lobbies going for around ten years, thus ceased for lack of adherents. Other reforms, which challenged national regulatory traditions, specific organizational methods, even national styles of regulation have achieved their aims. The adoption of the Cooke rationale has opened the way to an amazing business in relation to the recapitalization of banks, the deregulation of air transport has started, the Commission has begun to take an interest in mergers, state monopolies, financial services, etc. Even in public procurement, where the stakes were higher, owing to the degree of connivance between local political powers, contracting undertakings and national political parties, the rule of silence has been broken and cases have been brought before the Luxembourg Court.[6]

There are two areas, however, where a country like France should have *a priori* made a stance and where *de facto* it behaved like a model pupil: in the areas of competition policy and financing the public sector. France has always inscribed its competition policy within the framework of its industrial policy, where it has not only favoured mergers, promoting national winners, but where it has also contributed to the organization of cartels. The European Commission, on the contrary, has given immediate priority to competition policy for obvious reasons of transparency in the nascent internal market, which led to its prohibition of abuse of a dominant position, exclusive markets and price discrimination. In competition policy, where consumers' interests were permanently threatened by the market power of oligopolistic firms, the former took precedence. Yet whereas all European legislation envisaged a form of political or administrative power to intervene in respect of competition, what makes competition policy frighteningly efficient is the omnipotence of DG IV, and this for three reasons:

1   In the treatment of cases, as is shown by Dumez and Jeunemaître,[7] the only basis for determination is competition criteria, without any industrial policy dimension or the interests of the European producer to poison this reasoning.[8]

2   DG IV is vested with special powers, since it has the sovereign decision whether to bring an action, and to be involved in both the examination and the sanctioning stages.

3   The threat of transfer to the Court of Justice further reinforces the position of the Commission. Competition policy has thus been transformed into an arm against national settlements and the Commission has made the law the vector for the opening of markets.

From that moment on, one should not be surprised that this desired policy 'marches on', at the same time unleashing the passions of those who see their industrial intervention machine being challenged. In at least two situations the Commission has been able to prove its formidable efficiency device, since, in the De Havilland case, it was able to forbid a further acquisition by a Franco-Italian consortium in the aerospace sector, and it has relied on general provisions on competition policy to force the opening of the market in an exclusive sector, for example Telecom.[9]

In order to gain a better understanding of market policies, especially as regards normative expansionism, it is worth taking note of state aid policy and the Community's treatment of a 'public service'. On the one hand, public service[10] undertakings are obliged to limit their public service missions to a strict minimum, whilst, on the other, national undertakings, falling under the category of competition sector in difficulty, can only get out of their difficulties by privatization. This is how, starting with the imprecisely phrased provisions of the Treaty of Rome, intended for a quite different purpose, normative expansionism has arrived at a new treaty. By following this line of reasoning, I wonder whether this is a question of the Commission's power strategy, or rather a technique accepted by national governments, since this allows the treatment of not easily solvable national issues as technical problems.

1   Article 222: neutrality of the Treaty as to forms of ownership. Article 222 of the Treaty of Rome stipulates that the Community is neutral with regard to forms of ownership. States may nationalize, privatize, or have at their disposal a large or a small public sector, and the Community refuses to interfere with financial structures of national capitalism. At least this was so until the end of the 1980s.

2   Articles 85-6: the opening of markets and competition is the basis of the European construction. Article 85 forbids arrangements, cartels and

other measures (price fixing, exclusive outlets, etc.) which have the effect of limiting competition. Article 86 condemns the abuse of a dominant position and any discriminatory clauses, especially nationality. Of course, from the common market to the single internal market, the opening objective is fundamental. To recall this periodically, when there is a question of evidence, amounts to intimidation. Invoking, for example, the first provisions of the Maastricht Treaty, which portrays a broader perspective for European citizens, is therefore bad taste. Article 2 of the Treaty on European Union provides:

> The Community shall have as its task, . . . sustainable and non-inflationary growth respecting the environment, a high degree of convergence of economic performance, a high level of employment and of social protection, the raising of the standard of living and the quality of life, and economic and social cohesion and solidarity among Member States.

3   Article 90-1 foresees the application of the general provisions of the Treaty to public undertakings. Public undertakings, like private undertakings, can be subject to Community enquiries if they are suspected of abuse of a dominant position. A logical consequence of my second point is that the Commission, in its quest to rid the Community of dominant positions, cannot be opposed by the company's status as a public undertaking. There is one limitation to this, however, which concerns state monopolies, or rather undertakings with exclusive rights, which gives rise to my fourth point.

4   Article 90-2 limits the effects of Article 90-1 for reasons of general economic interest. The Treaty recognizes exclusive rights and monopolies when there is a public service and an economic interest. The Treaty draftsmen could not foresee that one day a postal service would be a competitive commercial activity and that the subtleties of the ONP would have taken such great care in affirming states prerogatives in relation to monopolies of public services. Yet the absence of any notion of public interest – or public service, for that matter – would lead to the opening up of an incredible perspective for the proponents of free market policies.

5   Article 90-3 invests the Commission with the role of ensuring the application of Article 90: in the absence of a clear definition of general public interest, it has fallen to the Court to exercise its jurisdiction, relying upon the general objectives of the Community . . . which are the achievement of the single market, the free circulation of goods, services and capital. This closes the loophole and public service is now under close observation.

6   Any shareholder has the right to invest in an undertaking and make a loss, except where the shareholder enjoys exclusive rights, because that

would impede competition. The neutrality as to forms of ownership is attenuated here in relation to the manifest inequality of the position of a public undertaking. A private undertaking can make a loss without the fact requiring regulatory intervention, since it will be sanctioned by the market to curtail any dysfunction. Everyone knows, however, that a private undertaking can cause considerable harm before disappearing. There are no such freedoms for a public undertaking granted exclusive rights, the actions of which are immediately subject to scrutiny.

7   It is necessary and legitimate to consider the extent to which aid can be concealed in relation to an increase of capital by state undertakings. As a corollary of point 6, a donation of capital to a state company cannot be considered as a classical increase in capital despite the principle of neutrality. But what should the state as shareholder do in this case?

8   The state has to behave as a classical shareholder seeking normal profitability from invested capital. At the end of these processes, the only thing left for the public undertaking is to become the clone of a private undertaking.

9   The state company is condemned to disappear. Briefly stated, a public service first has to mutate into a universal service, then into a delegated service, and finally into a marketable service. This is the fate of all public service undertakings: deregulation leads to privatization which reduces the public service to a suitable size. These were also the terms accepted by the French government when it negotiated plans for the recapitalization of state-owned companies like Bull, Renault or Air France.

This legal mechanism is extraordinarily powerful, since it is nourished by its own internal logic, by market economy principles, the decentralized initiative of economic agents, even the masked political will of national governments. This amazing excrescence grew from a few provisions of the Treaty of Rome which had fallen into oblivion. In order to defeat its logic it would be necessary to arouse a strong and unanimous political will. This objective cannot possibly be achieved within the framework of the Council, or more generally, under intergovernmental forums.

To draw conclusions on the relative success is not to discount the negotiation of sanctions and arrangements sought in order to favour the necessary transition in sectors in difficulty. Rather it is simply to observe that in the sector of market policies the Commission, nominated by governments, has today its own authority and visible results. The more political will is lacking or weak, or the more political consent is implicit, the more the above described process is likely to produce mechanical effects. In practice numerous compromises are possible, but they depend on the internal power structures of the Commission, appreciation of the context by commissioners and their directorates, and, more generally, national public opinion.

Policies for the promotion of an industrial base

By the promotion of an industrial base I mean the whole gamut of research and development policies, the most important European projects, and, more generally, all policies aiming at sectoral intervention to promote a competitive European industrial base.[11] I immediately exclude policies based on 'fair returns' such as Airbus and Ariane, in which the Community has never taken much interest. In the case of Airbus, states used aggressive strategies to obtain financing through a system of reimbursable advances,[12] protectionism, and commercial promotion of national aeronautical industries, with the stated aim of breaking Boeing's hegemony not by market techniques but by political will.[13]

Why can one speak of the relative failure of policies to promote a European industrial base?[14] As for market policies, I take as examples two memorable projects, the Esprit programme and the HDTV project.

From the moment the First Esprit Programme was launched, following the work of the Davignon–Guilenhamar group, the dominant position was that Europe should bring itself into line with the body of developed countries in the sphere of information technology. In two sectors in particular the risk was considered to be extremely high: computers and electronic components. Ten years later the accounts are mediocre, with the trade balance for the information technology sector taking the following form. Europe buys from the United States three times as much as it sells, it buys from Japan fourteen times as much as it sells, it buys from the 'four dragons' ten times as much as it sells, and exports exceed imports only in relation to developing countries and eastern Europe. Intra-Community exports, which form the European domestic market, are six times higher than total exports to the United States, Japan and the 'four dragons' together. Worse still, far from making up for its laxity, Europe has stood by and passively watched the resistible rise of Japan, the return to power of the United States, and the explosion of Korean growth.[15] During the whole of this period the Twelve, victims of the successive stages of rebuilding, have almost left the world stage of information technology. If this policy can be described as a relative failure, it is only because, in as much as the effort of R&D did not lay the foundations for the building of the industry as was expected, it still aided the emergence of a European technological environment. Co-operation has actually been thrashed out between small and large undertakings from different European countries, research networks have been formed, institutions have opened their doors, progress has been made in basic technological research, commercial outlets have been found on occasion, thanks to the contributions of Esprit (DCM by Bull, CD-I by Philips, flat planel displays),[16] but the general decline of the sector has not been stopped, technology has been sought from abroad and alliances obey a completely different logic (the take-over of ITT Europe, the bankruptcy of Nixdorf, the take-over by GEC of Plessey, then the take-over of GPT by Siemens; ICL was finally taken over by Fujitsu).

There are numerous reasons for this relative failure. They relate to the Community's idiosyncratic stance: the obsession with competition, which puts pre-competitive research on a pedestal, which is interspersed with financial incentives and egalitarian ideology, whilst showing open hostility to all forms of policies promoting national leaders without making the means available to promote European champions, a dramatic lack of means and inability to react. In this period the sector has undergone very rapid change, a very volatile evolution, since the components industries have been exposed to a cycle of particularly accentuated stages. The rapidity of bringing products to market and the shortening of the period of the development of a product as well as its life span equally have created additional constraints which European industrialists have not been able to overcome. If one adds to these additional factors the traditional rivalry between Siemens and GEC, between Thomson and Philips, despite their common weaknesses and the absence of any significant trump cards, then one must necessarily observe that Europe is not going to bridge that gap. From that moment, only forging alliances with Japanese or American undertakings has allowed European undertakings to survive on a world scale under the banner of restructuring, but in an *ad hoc* way.

The battle for European high definition television (HDTV) is a case in point. What was required was to give the electronics consumer a breath of fresh air, to end once and for all the plurality of broadcasting norms in Europe (Secam, varieties of Pal), to offer cinema at home, to inject dynamism into the culture industries, to block the irresistible advance of the Japanese in components, whether electronics for general consumption or specialized purposes, and to find a way of making original creations in European languages. One can understand why France and Germany make this the symbol of European industrial, political and cultural recovery.

This desire for reconquest led to the installation between 1985 and 1990 of a master policy for advanced television. Europe has thus given itself a universal channel. It has succeeded in unseating the Japanese in the normative battle (Muse was not adopted at Dubrovnik), and has managed to achieve co-operation between industrialists (Bosch, Philips, Thomson) within the framework of the Eureka 1995 project, and has even decided to make a progressive and compatible standard for direct satellite broadcasting compulsory (D2Mac, HDMac analogue, then numerical) and to make funds available for the production and promotion of programmes. At Albertville demonstrations of HDMac were possible, notwithstanding the fact that D2Mac-Europcrypt was used as a back-up system for the fee-paying Nordic channels.

However, in the final analysis, its failure is a foregone conclusion, due to the Community having slyly abandoned all its initial objectives. First, it refused to extend to telecom satellites the obligation to broadcast in accordance with the D2Mac/HDMac norms, thus succumbing to the arguments of the satellite broadcasters (Murdoch, Canal+ and Astra from Luxembourg). This was followed by its refusal to go through with the commitments which it had solemnly made in connection with aid to broadcasting and programmes. The United Kingdom was opposed on the basis of its interests concerned with contributions to Europe, the doctrine of *laissez-faire* and the American numeric norm. Brussels finally buried HDMac completely, rallying to an 'all numeric' solution. This abandonment has been justified by the need to preserve what it could. The foreseeable result of so many abandonments has been the recent decision by Philips and Thomson to stop their development on HDMac and to work in the framework of the American Alliance towards an American norm which will be applied on a worldwide scale.[17]

However, there is no need to succeed as long as you persevere, it would seem in the Commission's case, which, by launching the idea of a trans-European infrastructure in transport, telecom and energy, intends to bring Keynesian therapies back into fashion in its drive to revive the European construction. Yet these joint projects give rise to three problems which lead one to doubt their ability to succeed.

1   There is no agreement between the Twelve on the opportunities for large-scale investment in infrastructures, and particularly in relation to the raising of the necessary funds through borrowing. Germany, for example, in principle supports the project, but censures it in practice by evoking its budget deficits.

2   If a joint project is going to have the effect of constituting a base on which industry can build, there is an opportunity to organize a European supply side policy. Such an idea is diametrically opposed to the economic philosophy of free market states, such as the United Kingdom and Holland and, by derivation, the Commission.

3   In the name of competition the Community is in the process of dismantling national monopolies, especially in telecommunications, but one cannot have information superhighways without involving powerful actors. As was the case with HDTV yesterday, tomorrow information superhighways will provide the pretext for distributing the odd R&D

subsidy, which will undoubtedly contribute to intensifying the European debate over the way out of the crisis.[18]

EXPLANATIONS OF THE IMBALANCE BETWEEN MARKET POLICIES AND DEVELOPMENT

If one accepts these assertions in their entirety, one question springs to mind: why is there unequal performance between, on the one hand, the relative success of market policies, and, on the other, the relative failure of voluntarist policies promoting the European industrial base? Three answers are usually advanced. In the first, it is taken for granted that the European construction is principally, if not exclusively, oriented towards the institution of a domestic European market. From that moment on, common policies, especially in relation to R&D, are at worst considered a waste of resources, at best the price one has to pay for consenting to what is essential, i.e. market policies. In the second, the answer advanced is one of a chronological typology, in that Europe would have come to the industrial question later; in the meantime, it was necessary to wait for the Maastricht treaty to devote some space to it. From then on, again, industrial policy and more generally neo-mercantilist policies would be part of Europe in the forthcoming decade in the same way that customs policy was to Europe in the first decade of the EEC. Finally, in the last response, pure rationality is evoked as a way of lending force to the argument that the imbalance between the European public policies is the desired product of nations with the framework of intergovernmental decision-making, whereas the 'spill over' theories and the 'Delors effect' are nothing but tedious explanations. Let's now consider each answer in more detail.

The genetic model

According to this thesis, legal experts, liberal economists, as well as English political economists, believe that the European construction was first of all a legal and economic construction. They recall that, beyond the rhetoric, the Treaty of Rome built a customs union between the Six, and gave powers to Community organs to bring about a real internal market between the Six founding nations. Since, elsewhere, in the framework of GATT, the progressive removal of the common external tariff was foreseen, one could legitimately believe that the true nature of the European construction was that it was to be based on a free exchange area, with the common agricultural policy being nothing more than the price to be paid for French archaism. The relative success of market policies intervening in the context of an amplified tendency towards the withdrawal of state involvement (deregulation, privatization, liberalization), the neo-classical inspiration of the authors of reports leading to the White Paper, the failure of Keynesian therapies revealed by stagflation, were all factors leading to the creation of an intellectual environment which was favourable to proponents of the neo-liberal school – the latter basing the European revival on market liberalization. This is a very convincing argument, where one could only expect that the customs union, even with its new name, the internal market, would be a driving force in the industrial specialization of the Twelve. However, it is only partially correct to say that the true objective of the European construction was the bringing into effect of common customs services in creating the common market, leading to the institution of a vast domestic market. As everyone knows, the Treaty of Rome was adopted subsequent to the ECSC Treaty, and the reason for its coming into existence lay in the political treatment of the Ruhr question; further, that it took effect after the failure of the CED. Moreover, it is sufficient to compare the EEC with EFTA to be convinced that the Europe of the Six was at the very outset a political construction. The model must therefore be corrected, by pointing out that the basic strength of the common market derives from the fact that the possibility of mutation was written into its genetic code.[19] The imbalance in the development of Community policies, and the anticipation of a federal Europe, have always been driving forces in the concrete functioning of Europe. Thus, it is legitimate to question the unequal success rates of the two policies, to try to become more aware of them, and, at the same time, to ask the question of what would be the outcome of a possible breakdown in the Community project in its global construction.

The gradualist model

Advocates of the gradualist model hold that industry will be to Europe in the 1990s what competition was in the 1960s and 1980s, that is, the driving force of integration. According to Lester Thurow,[20] owing to its economic power, the efficiency of its vocational training policies, and the social cohesion which it has been able to forge, something which the United States has not been able to do, Europe is in a position to dictate the new terms of international trade. The achievements of Europe in joint programmes such as Airbus, Ariane, etc., will serve as a basis for co-operation on a larger scale, again through successful integration and the European Union programme. To European officials Article 130 of the Maastricht Treaty heralds a new era of Community intervention, since, for the first time, the ground policies for industrial policy have been explicitly recognized by the European construction.[21] It is difficult to sustain this thesis, however. Suffice it here to present three arguments to this effect, the first relating to political procedure, the second substantive, and the third concerning administrative sociology. In order to take action in the sphere of industrial policy, unanimity among the Twelve is required, thus it is necessary to have the unanimous will of nations to initiate any one such action, which is the case with neither competition policy nor foreign trade. Further, when one reads the work of Martin Bangeman,[22] which is representative of commissioners collectively, it can be seen that what he refers to as industrial policy is in fact horizontal policies for competition (R&D, vocational training, competition, the internal market). On the contrary, what is referred to as French industrial policy is denounced for its position in promoting national champions. Finally, the fragmentation of Community administrative machinery and the absence of an integrationist platform prevent an industrial policy from being carried through, as was decided and illustrated only too well in the HDTV case. L. Cartelier[23] does not share our criticisms and falls into the category of proponents of the gradualist model. Her arguments can be summarized as follows. Industrial policy has long been illegitimate because it has lacked theoretical foundation. In the works of J. Brander, B. Spencer[24] and R. Krugman,[25] challenging the optimal characteristic of general free-exchange markets, and equating the role of states with that of private companies in oligopolistic markets, the context has changed. Here, states' industrial policies are seen as an element of 'competitive advantage among nations'.[26] Thus, according to Cartelier, it is essential for Europe to intervene in the sphere of industrial policy, which it has begun to do. This thesis does not stand up to analysis for the above-mentioned reasons, but equally for three others:

1   It is not enough to establish the functional necessity of a policy in order for it to be brought about; the political climate must also be right.

2   R. Krugman himself, in presenting these arguments, and even in his bold assertion in recognition of the utility of public intervention, saw only macro-economic policies as competitive, and not sectoral policies.[27]

3   The recent statements of the Commission as to the necessity of creating a policy for the information technology sector are without doubt a major leap forward, as were the identical statements made by Viscount Davignon thirteen years earlier. In the intervening period whole industries in this sector have disappeared.

The model of intergovernmental compromise

To the third school of thought, the Single European Act, and European public policies more generally, can be seen essentially as conforming to a compromise between nations. There is logic for the autonomy of the Community, its power being strictly circumscribed by the Council. This thesis was developed during a debate between experts on the European Community from Boston and California. The Moravcsik[28]–Zynsman[29] debate juxtaposes two streams of thought from the liberal school of international relations, the neo-functionalists who advocate the idea of a 'spill over' and of the *sui generis* character of the Commission, and the neo-liberalists, for whom the pure intergovernmentalist logic dictates the development of Community spirit. The neo-liberal school sees the Single European Act as a compromise between states, to be explained by the pure logic of national interests (Moravcsik), whilst for neo-functionalists the Community dynamics are to be understood as a double phenomenon: one mechanical – the imbalances in the construction require continuous progress – the other, more institutional, tends to see the increasing role of the Community machinery as the architect of acceptable political solutions. Both approaches have their merits, the Commission has its own role, there is undoubtedly the dynamics of law, the unbalanced and provisional character of each compromise justifies its being superseded. Moreover, the role of states in each step forward is decisive, and still today states maintain their sovereignty even if they have delegated competence. One begins to encounter difficulties with this approach, however, when one analyses the stages of progress reached and the breakdowns as well as the unequal results of policies desired by governments themselves and introduced by the very same bureaucratic institutions.[30]

PUBLIC POLICY DECISION-MAKING IN EUROPE

It is not possible to understand the consequences of the way the Community functions without simultaneously taking into account the effects of the different dynamics in force, their distinctive interpretations and the responses they evoke from the national and supranational players.[31] A complicated game can thus be set up within the triangle of the Community institutions and the national political-administrative systems. The breakdown of the Community machine makes sense the moment one is able to identify the complete group of actors and decision-makers and the way they interacted – in sum, the moment one reconstitutes the array of forces at play and the meaning behind them, and places them in the proper context in time. In pointing to the relative progress and relative failure of Community policies in the industrial sphere, I will try to develop an axiom for public policy decision-making in Europe and give some explanations for the relative failure and success of industrial policies. In fact, it is a question of using well researched policies as the basis for analysis of processes of decision-making as well as those of the internal regulation of the Community system. In relation to the other arguments advanced, my position consists in departing from the European process of public policy-making to disentangle the logic of structuring and change from the Community system. From this point of view, one can argue that intergovernmental decision-making is decisive at any stage of the Community's development. Yet the fact remains that states, which differ in terms of their institutions and internal political equilibrium, choose to converge at a given moment which is affected by the action of national and European elites and the mediation capacity of the Commission.

1 A European public policy has more chance of succeeding if it relies upon automatic regulation processes (market dynamics, legal dynamics). This automatic policy, even if it may sometimes surprise the national political authorities, is nevertheless founded on an initial political will. Thus, if the political initiative takes priority in terms of market policies, its administrative activation by the Community apparatus establishes and fixes a doctrine and a method which are legitimated by the case law of the European Court of Justice. In signing the Treaty of Rome, then the Single European Act, French heads of government could not possibly have imagined that they would be condemning their state sector to programmed extinction, or that they would be favouring the importation of foreign cars at the expense of nationally produced cars, still less that free market policies would be axiomatic for all their national policies, and certainly not that they would be subordinating the international expansion of their companies to Community legal imperatives – yet the treaties, once signed, required all these elements. The question why governments, having discovered its legal dynamics, allowed its perpetuation is a completely different matter.

2 The stages of Community progress correspond to periods of prosperity. Progress is therefore financed by the appropriation of a growth surplus. During a crisis period national interests take over as a matter of course. Any public policy going against the legal-economic dynamics, which moreover has been decided in the name of Community cohesion, is valid only in the context which gave rise to its existence. In the name of higher political imperatives one can consent to significant redistribution obligations in favour of poor regions; in the name of Community cohesion, one can even give huge funds to the least developed countries, which are more likely than others to suffer from monetary restrictions, yet these obligations cannot be left to the self-regulatory effects of free market policies: they require budgetary supervision, they are exposed to criticism from all sides, they depend on the macro-economic situation, and above all

they depend upon the geo-political and economic context in which they were formulated. In relation to common ventures, national obligations depend increasingly on the internal organization of powers within each participant country, on the distribution of competences and the weight of political factors influencing the economic decision. For their part, Community institutions generally play a positive or negative role in the outcome, rarely that of a zero-sum game. When Europe is weak, or in a crisis, all the Community institutions, which in any case can be equated with the position taken by the Commission, become more reticent in order not to dissatisfy states and public opinion, the Council is more timid in order to defend national interests better, and even the European Court in Luxembourg rediscovers the virtues of subsidiarity. When Europe picks up momentum, the institutions vie with each other to set their seal of approval on the Community progress achieved.

3   The fusing of free market policies represents the constraints employed by member states of the European Union, especially the Latin nations (France, Italy and Spain), to reform their policies in protected sectors, where there may be either a strong trade union presence or political consensus prohibiting major changes. By doing so, governments have conferred real power on the Commission, which has been able to prove its ability to come up with and propose compromises. Brussels, perceived as a constraint mechanism, has thus progressively become a powerful lever towards modernization in spite of the resistance of concerned pressure groups. The statutory reforms of Telecom France, Bull and Air France strictly conform to this structure.

4   The power of the Commission is at its greatest when based on free market dynamics and prior agreement with the cartel of national bureaucracies. The case of European Monetary Union is a striking example of the cartel power of national administrations in a context which is delineated by an agreement between states, so much so that it conformed to geostrategic considerations.[32] HDTV is another case in point but from a different perspective.[33] The satellite television lobbies have bombarded the European HDTV project since its formal adoption by the Council.

5   Law and the market are the functional ideologies behind the Community machinery. This brings us back to the national level and has real effects, contributing to the acceleration of administrative redeployment within national bureaucracies. In this context the Commission, despite its right to take initiatives, being dependent on the Council and the cartel of national bureaucracies, tends to exceed the scope of the text of the Treaty as conceived by its drafters, and therefore tends to use law as a vector for applying pressure. This is the reason why we witness in the member states, particularly in France, the increased importance of legal

experts, in many cases coming from the Conseil d'Etat where engineers and management drawn from the country's technical and financial administrative elite (cf. the regulation of the telecommunications sector) hold sway. Again, the Community's influence develops on a terrain which has already been fenced off by a new national deal. The end of major state projects, the decline of the state as entrepreneur, and the trend towards privatization shift the deal to national level and contribute to a redefinition of the power hierarchy within national administrations.

6   Until now, states have transferred their competences, but they have not alienated their sovereign power. Not only do states preserve a 'way out' when their fundamental interests are challenged, but there has not been any irreversible evolution in terms of sovereignty in relation to matters concerning the economic order of monetary, fiscal of budgetary powers.

7   The analysis of the Community integration process turns more on a social policy of mediation (the role of the Commission, national administrations etc.) than on a theory of sovereignty. In the shaping of national public policies, European integration provides several resources which national actors are going to draw on to obtain their solutions: European law, intergovernmental negotiation, and the Commission's right of proposal. In trying to circumvent trade union powers, conservative elites, parliamentary powers, or even to cause problems for neighbouring administrations, sectoral actors have Community resources at their disposal.

8   What is particularly controversial about Brussels is that a directive, which is applied at national level, has been initiated by national bureaucrats with a view to circumventing national legislative and decision-making processes. What we consider as the proliferation of the European normative process is no other than the exported product of principles put forward by states, the rejection of positive policies and the ruses of national elites. Further still, this European norm is very susceptible to variation. The provision of services on networks held by state or private monopoly, which today constitutes the greatest single threat to the French public services, was initiated at the request of the French, who were not able to supply Portugal with electricity because Spain objected.

9   The Commission provides a permanent platform for negotiation, for bargaining and for the creation of block compromises. Each rejection of a specific measure masks the elements of a trade-off. The same measure is translated for public opinion on the basis of the prevailing rhetoric in each country (power in France, the free market in the United Kingdom, democratic principles for a small country, Europeanness for Germany, justice for a peripheral country).

10   The creation of a Europe with variable geometry can develop only outside the Community system, or within the framework of an extensively reformed system.[34] In fact, the institutional triangle was conceived for the functioning of the Twelve. Unless Europe takes a leap forward, and adopts Community institutional reform in 1996, Europe with variable geometry is impracticable. This leap must also be taken on the understanding that states which are reluctant to see a further integration are not able to prevent the motivated states from forging ahead. This institutional structure explains the Commission's inability to promote Community industrial projects such as Airbus, Ariane, which presuppose massive investment, with unequally distributed profits, integration in R&D and commercial yields, and aggressive protectionism.

11   Advocates of the Europe of States, and to that extent of national sovereignty, are at the same time those who denounce its weaknesses and the absence of Community political will. By undermining the strength of the Commission, extending intergovernmental decision-making, and putting national parliaments on a pedestal, they are exacerbating the tendency towards impotence, which moreover they denounce.

12   The Monnet method consisted in making politics out of economics. When economics becomes the central political issue, the shortcomings of the Community system can no longer be hidden away, the widespread but empty adhesion of opinion transforming into defiance. From that moment on, no single policy, institution or legal provision can escape criticism. The virtuous circle of integration is transformed into a vicious circle of involution.

CONCLUSION: THE COMMUNITY AS DECOMPRESSION CHAMBER

During the 1980s, all Western countries privatized, liberalized, deregulated. The phenomenon is therefore not particular to Europe. In this evolution towards a more liberal economic organization has there been any convergence of national intervention models? Has Europe played a particular role, especially the Commission? Our conclusion is that there is a plurality of ways of adapting to a more liberal organization of exchange; the European context was mobilized in order to allow national deregulation. The constraints which arose from globalization and the relative decline of European economies were absorbed by the European Community and retranslated into the criteria of a unified internal market. The necessary adaptation to the new international deal has been laid before national public opinion under two heads: on the one hand, the idea of a united Europe, engineered by national governments, as a force to be reckoned with globally, capable of becoming master of its own destiny; on the other hand, the bitter pill of modernization forcibly fed to us by Brussels and swallowed by those same governments. The Community therefore represented a decompression chamber before the great challenge of globalization. One can therefore understand that the Community was supported in periods of considerable growth, whilst it was no longer tolerated in periods of prolonged crisis. The current crisis of the European idea is the inevitable consequence of the resignation of national governments before their own incapacity to explain the conditions of modernization to public opinion.

NOTES

1 The European construction has always advanced in leaps, with renewed impetus after periods of immobility. For reference, ECSC +, CED –, Treaty of Rome +, Empty chair policy –, Accession of UK +, the freezing of the crisis –, EMS +, Departures from EMS –, Single Act +, After Maastricht Treaty –.
2 Michel Richonnier in his book *Les Métamorphoses de l'Europe de 1769 à 2001*, Paris, Flammarion, 1985, gives a good image of 'Le mal européen', pp. 177–219.
3 Elie Cohen, 'L'Europe ou comment construire un mythe nécessaire', *Médiapouvoirs*, fourth quarter 1988.
4 The disequilibrium is threefold: market policies exist, whereas industrial policies are absent or precarious, decision-making rules vary, depending upon the sectors of intervention, and finally the application of decisions taken varies according to sector. This fact is in itself worthy of further investigation. The chapter nevertheless compares the actions actually taken in the sectors in which the market logic can be identified, on the one hand, and development logic, on the other.
5 Extension of the principle stated in the ruling of the Court of Justice *Cassis de Dijon*.
6 The fact that the Community machinery is functioning remarkably well, with its 'comitology', its 'cartel of national bureaucracies', its integration with its pool of 'experts', is not tantamount to saying that the Commission has seized power in this period.
7 Hervé Dumez and Alain Jeunemaître, *La Concurrence en Europe*, Paris, Le Seuil, 1991, and for a summary in English of the main theses of the authors see 'Political Intervention versus l'Etat de droit économique: the Issue of Convergence of Competition Policies in Europe', Oxford Regulatory Policy Institute, *Essays in Regulation*, vol. 5, 1994.
8 The analysis by Peter Holmes does not challenge this observation. The limited and tightly structured opening of the automobile market is a prelude to the full opening without obstacles planned for 1999. The fact that, during the transition period, the Commission takes into consideration industrial and social problems means simply that time has been given to prepare for the reconversion.
9 The 'Terminals' directive was approved on the basis of Article 90-3 and reaffirmed by a judgement of the Court of Justice, confirming that it was not

necessary to use the Article 100a procedure according to Article 30 (elimination of quantitative restrictions between member states).

10 The French notion of *service public* is translated here as 'public service' rather than 'universal service' as in Brussels.

11 A devalued but not wholly insignificant sum, giving priority to research, is supplied by the Community budget. From a budget of ECU 70 billion, equivalent to 1.24 per cent of the Community GDP, only 3.4 per cent is devoted to R&D, against 51.7 per cent to agriculture and 31 per cent to regional development aid. The latest Community framework programme for research (1994–8) has risen to ECU 13 billion, 28 per cent of which is centred upon information technology.

12 These advances constituted up to 60 per cent of the total financing of the first aircraft, which today have been set at a ceiling of 33 per cent following the 1992 agreement between Airbus Industries Partners and the EU. Aid to finance R&D has a ceiling of 3 per cent of total turnover of the aerospace industries and 4 per cent of turnover of the undertaking concerned.

13 In his recent work, *Pompidou Capitaine d'Industrie*, Paris, Odile Jacob, 1994, Bernard Esambert gives an illuminating account of the role played by politics in the Airbus and CFM56 projects, drawing attention to the industrial and financial schemes, but above all to the role of industrial diplomacy in the joint project's successful outcome, the achievement of which is clearly left to industrialists.

14 For an evaluation of Esprit, I rely on the Community's statistics, notably the progress reports on the work of the team from Callon, Ecole des Mines (the role of the RTB) and the work of Lynn Krieger Mytelka (alliance strategies). Lynn Mytelka Krieger, 'Les alliances stratégiques au sein du programme européen ESPRIT', *Economie Prospective Internationale*, 1989, 37, and *Strategic Partnerships and the World Economy*, London, Pinter, 1991, and 'Dancing with Wolves: Global Oligopolies and Strategic Partnerships', intervention at the Merit Colloquium in Maastricht, December 1992.

15 Source: European Information Technology Observatory 1993.

16 Source: CEE 1991 Com. evaluation Esprit.

17 Cf. Elie Cohen in *Annales des Mines*, second quarter 1993.

18 Commission des Communautés Européennes, 'Croissance, Competitivité, Emploi: les défis et les pistes pour entrer dans le XXIième siècle', Livre Blanc, *Bulletin des CE*, Suppl. 6/93.

19 I have defended this thesis in a number of works since 1989, especially in *Colbertisme high tech*, Paris, Hachette, 1992.

20 Lester Thurow, *Head to Head*, New York, Morrow, 1992.

21 Cf. the *Lettre des européens*, edited by the Mouvement Européen in its January–February 1994 issue, which foresees a 'less liberal Europe' in which industrial policy and the cultural exception are the symbols for its new turning.

22 Martin Bangeman, *La Politique industrielle dans un environnement ouvert et concurrentiel*, communication of 16 November 1990. This communication was later edited in the form of a book.

23 L. Cartelier, 'Marché unique et système productif européen: les fondements d'une politique industrielle commune', *Revue française d'économie*, autumn 1991, vol. 6, pp. 177–226.

24 James Brander and Barbara Spencer, 'Export Subsidies and International Market Share Rivalry', *Journal of International Economics*, 1985, vol. 16,

pp. 83–100, and 'International R&D Rivalry and Industrial Strategy', *Review of Economic Studies*, 1983, vol. 50, pp. 707–22.

25 For a summary and discussion of these theses see Paul Krugman (ed.), *Strategic Trade Policy and the New International Economics*, Cambridge, Mass., MIT Press, 1986.

26 According to M. Porter, *The Competitive Advantage of Nations*, London, Macmillan, 1990.

27 For a summary of the author's arguments, cf. *The Age of Diminished Expectations*, Cambridge, Mass., MIT Press, 1992.

28 Andrew Moravcsik, 'Negotiating the Single European Act', *International Organization*, winter 1991, pp. 19–56, and 'Preferences and Power in the European Community: a Liberal Intergovernmentalist Approach', *Journal of Common Market Studies*, December 1993, vol. 31, 4, pp. 473–524, and, more generally, Robert O'Keohane and Stanley Hoffmann (eds), *The New European Community: Decision-making and Institutional Change*, Boulder, Westview, 1991.

29 J. Zynsman *et al.*, *The Highest Stakes: a Brie Project*, Oxford, Oxford University Press, 1992.

30 On the roles of the Commission and the Council, cf. the debate book edited by R. Keohane and S. Hoffmann, *The New European Community*, especially the contributions by Peter Ludlow (pp. 85–132) and Andrew Moravcsik (pp. 41–84).

31 The dynamics of globalization (deregulation, triadization, capitalism), of integration (anticipation of the consequences, importation of credibility, self-strengthening mechanisms) and of national policies (failure of the Keynesian solutions, crisis of the welfare state and difficulties of the national policies of adjustment).

32 Cf. Elie Cohen, 'Contrainte économique et action publique', *Pouvoirs*, 1994, 1, pp. 87–101.

33 Elie Cohen, *Le Colbertisme high tech*, pp. 307–51.

34 Cf. the French debate on the evolution of French institutions, Lamassoure (agreements between states) *v.* Rocard (European constitution).

9 The impact of Europe on national policies

Italian anti-trust policy

Giuliano Amato

ITALY: THE LATECOMER

Studies conducted today of the anti-trust laws of the various states in the European Union all arrive at a common conclusion. Italy has one of the best laws and the Italian Anti-trust Authority is one of the most independent, exercising highly effective powers of both investigation and sanction.

When the Treaty of Rome had already been in force for several years, the author of this chapter was invited to participate in a collective research project on anti-trust in Europe that was, at that time, being directed by Professor Harlan Blake of Columbia University. Its report was published in 1969. Unfortunately the work was much more laborious for Italy than for the other nations, for the only resource available to us was the Civil Code of 1942. The code stated simply that competition should take place 'in such a manner as not to prejudice the interests of the national economy' and, as such, regulated only those pacts which concerned non-competitiveness and unfair trade practices as well as regulations on consortiums. Elements which were seen not as restricting competition but rather as tools for strengthening the economy. Beyond the Civil Code there was nothing, only a few stalled Bills that had been dragging through parliament for ten years or more.

The Blake project effectively proved that the Civil Code was unfavourable to competition and, moreover, focused analysis upon many of the clauses of those bills which remained embroiled in the legislative process in parliament. In his preface Professor Blake was obliged to point out that 'the work was complicated by the fact that, unlike the other members of the European Community (with the exception of Luxembourg), Italy had not yet passed any general legislation on restrictive practices and monopolies'. It was this delay in the passage of general legislation, which effectively continued until 1990, that distinguished Italy from the other member states and it is the reasons for such legislative tardiness that requires explanation.

In the first half of this century competition had few champions in Europe. Indeed, cartels were considered to be an expression of freedom of association. Accordingly, the *Mißbrauch* principle (rather than the '*Verbot* principle') was deemed applicable to them, with the ensuing result that Fascist legislation on consortiums was no anomaly. However, consortiums, which had been formed with the express purpose of 'disciplining production and competition' among businesses operating in the same sector, were actually compulsory when requested by some 70 per cent of the companies involved.[1]

The explanations for Italian divergence may be found only somewhat later, emerging in the post-war period. They can be seen as intrinsic to the political concepts that prevailed during this period, as well as, more specifically, in the constitutional framework that was established for economic activity by the Constituent Assembly of 1946–8. Although monopolies and capitalist privileges were viewed as common enemies, they were not seen as adversaries of the concept of competition. Indeed, on one side of the post-war political debate was the Communist Party, implacable opponents of the market, who were committed to the global planning of the economy as the only way forward. On the other side of the political divide were the Christian Democrats, who were themselves, at best, wary of a free-market economy, even though they defended it in the name of the political freedom that, they believed, would have been engulfed by totalitarianism in the event of a communist victory. In their view a market economy would guarantee a non-communist economy and, consequently, state protection of small and medium-sized businesses, allied to control of what the Christian Democrats saw as the social benefits of investment, was a cornerstone of their policies. As a result, these activities were to be entrusted to the state and to the professional associations and trade unions that were allied to it.

Eventually the Italian constitution contained, and still contains, but a single clause on monopolies, Article 43, which provides for their nationalization if privately owned. Even when Luigi Einaudi, a great Liberal scholar who was to become President of the Republic, raised the problem of monopolies in the name of free competition he was told that Article 43 was 'sufficient' to solve the problem. Not even a man of Einaudi's professional, academic and political stature was able to challenge the primacy of statist thinking over this issue.

The central question remained: should monopolies be controlled by the state or through competition and the market? Although the Italian constitution left the question open, its clauses, and even more its early interpreters, seemed to favour the former. It is, therefore, hardly surprising that this pivotal question has remained open for so many years and that the primacy of the state has continued for so long to seem the only viable solution for Italy and Italians.

The first anti-trust Bills

It is a widely held belief that the first parliamentary attempts to safeguard competition were made in the 1950s. However, this is not exactly the case. Although the proposals that were put forward at that time were all opposed to monopolies, only a few of them were in any way concerned with or committed to safeguarding competition – for example, the bill brought forward by Giovanni Malagodi and Aldo Bozzi, Liberal Party deputies, and the one presented by Riccardo Lombardi and Ugo La Malfa.[2] Not specifically designed to safeguard competition was the Bill proposed by Giorgio Amendola, communist, which provided for various forms of public control over monopolies.

Nothing concrete resulted from these bills for many years and they might never have been taken into consideration by parliament had not the Treaty of Rome been approved in the meantime. Indeed, the Treaty made competition an issue, which, in turn, pushed the government into presenting a bill of its own in 1960. Even this initiative was insufficient to ensure any real movement on the issue. The Chamber of Deputies did set up a committee to examine the various proposals and it worked hard but it became bogged down and by the end of the legislative session had not achieved any concrete results. Moreover, even whilst the committee was working on the anti-trust proposals, a Committee of Inquiry was also established in parliament for the very purpose of investigating monopolies as well as the many other restrictions that were hampering competition in the Italian market. Thereafter, the Committee of Inquiry worked for some four years, from 1961 to 1965, and yet concluded in its final report that there were no major impediments to competition in Italy.

Three decades of state planning, state companies, state aid

The reasons for such an apparently surprising outcome were reasonably clear. The dominant policies of the times had been founded upon a contrasting doctrine which was firmly committed to state aid for small and medium-sized businesses; public investment in the underdeveloped south (through the auspices of a special agency) and, last but not least, public enterprise as a protective bulwark against possible abuse of dominant market positions by private enterprises. (Enrico Mattei's ENI brought this policy beyond national borders into competition with the so-called 'seven sisters' of the oil industry.) Principles such as these had guided the Christian Democrats in the Constituent Assembly and, after several years of their government, had become a *modus operandi* if not, indeed, a *modus vivendi*.

Furthermore, the Treaty of Rome brought about little change in either the policies or the instruments of the government. On the contrary, it led, instead, to even greater levels of state aid aimed at strengthening Italian businesses, which found themselves faced with the growing competition that membership of the common market had brought with it. What then followed could hardly be seen as in accordance with the wishes of the 'founding fathers' of Europe who had drafted the 1957 treaty, for instead of a gradual reduction in such aid there was a marked increase. This neat sleight of hand was achieved by simply placing such aid within the context of economic planning, seen as the great innovation of the 1960s.

Central economic planning was hailed as the most effective way in which to co-ordinate the massive subsidization of industry that was being carried out by the state, as well as direct public investment. In reality the final outcome turned out to be disappointing, resulting only in teaching investment planning and management to public administrators (which, at least, proved useful) and, of course, the many private businessmen who were naturally anxious to obtain state aid. The promotion of competition was not seen as an aim of the policy, nor, certainly, was it one of its results. Indeed, exclusive rights were granted to major players in the construction industry in the 1960s and grew even faster in the 1970s, when approval was granted by the planning authorities in cases in which they deemed that exclusive rights were the best way of promoting the public interest. Not only did competitive tendering effectively become useless as a result, but such exclusive rights frequently specified the company by name, which was, wherever possible, a state-owned or state-controlled company, to which public works, the management of airports or public services, etc., were to be assigned.

In this climate the attention focused on consortiums seemed to be minor, and, at that, much less restrictive to competition. Indeed, the Civil Code was actually amended in order to make business collaboration a necessary element of any consortium bid. As a result, state aid was renewed as well as being extended to the consortiums through membership of which small and medium-sized businesses strengthened their production capacity and/or their market position. Not surprisingly, even the new legislation failed to provide any controls to safeguard competition. When such legislation was finally enacted, in the latter half of the 1970s, the era of central planning was coming to an end. What is especially interesting is that such draconian tools were to remain in the armoury of the state, little different from those with which the state had wielded such omnipotent power in the 1950s.

UNDER THE PRESSURE OF THE EC, THE ANTI-TRUST LAW ARRIVES

It may possibly be an exaggeration to link such Italian 'persistence' with the centralist creed with the debilitating effects of 'Eurosclerosis' which increasingly infected the European Community. However, it remains a fact that principles of competition only managed to assert themselves in Italy after the renaissance of Community activity that was brought about by the now famous White Paper in 1984 and the Single Act of 1986 (i.e. the imperative created by the deadline for the introduction of the single market, which had then been set for the end of 1992). At first there were some important signs that a process of liberalization was under way which, ironically, derived from European directives that had been issued prior to 1984. The most remarkable change was in the banking sector, where the market crash of 1929–30 had led to the total disappearance of competition and which had become an administrated sector under the guidance of the Banca d'Italia. Finally, in spite of many delays and, indeed, with some inconsistency, the years between 1985 and 1990 saw the first EC banking directive (which dated from 1977) being implemented, with the result that the power of the Banca d'Italia over such mundane issues as the opening of branches was progressively eliminated, in favour of market decisions taken by the individual banks themselves.

The core issue, however, remained: the approval of a general law on competition. The White Paper had already addressed the 'fundamental role' of an 'active policy on competition'. Furthermore, the European Parliament, in a resolution that was passed on the *Sixteenth Report on Competition*, which had been submitted to it by the Commission, had noted that 'legislation concerning competition is not yet considered with sufficient seriousness by some member states, which have no national regulations'. In November 1986 the Minister of Industry had established a committee to study competition, headed by Professor Franco Romani, an eminent economist, who is also now a member of the Anti-trust Authority. The committee concluded its work in April 1988 and as a fitting conclusion to its efforts a bill was presented to parliament shortly thereafter. At the same time another bill was drawn up in the Senate following the parliamentary investigation into the 'internationalization of businesses and industrial mergers'. As a consequence, these two Bills became the basis of law No. 287/1990, 'Regulations for safeguarding competition and the market'.

'It was born in the lap of European Community regulations.' Thus, law 287 entered the legislative realm. Even those unaware of the pivotal influence that the Community had played in bringing to an end the long and involved saga of Italian anti-trust legislation were forced to conclude that law 287 was an intelligent Italian translation of EC regulations. Indeed, the law adapted EC directives to a legal system in which competition had to be viewed as an autonomous goal in its own right, rather than as merely part of a process towards the integration of the intra-European market. Moreover, progress in two other important areas was also achieved. First, responsibility for applying the law was conferred upon an independent authority of a quasi-judiciary type which was empowered to adjudicate.[3] Second, the authority was only given powers of exemption which were more limited than those of the commission and, although Article 4 provides for both individual and collective exemptions, the procedure established for exemption was clearly designed for individual cases only (individual exemptions being decided on the basis of reasonableness and not of policy. It was not by chance that exemptions in the national interest are also provided for in the law. Even though the relevant power had been conferred upon the Council of Ministers it had never been exercised). Thus, competition as an autonomous and self-sufficient principle, asserted purely through adjudication, has been confirmed and emphasized.

Restrictive trade agreements and the abuse of a dominant market position, have been subjected to the discipline inherent in the Treaty of Rome, while, it must be said, legal monopolies have been so subjected to a somewhat lesser degree. In addition, regulations now exist which govern mergers, which the Treaty did not contain, but which, however, faithfully reflect the intent of EC Regulation 4060 of 1989. As if such action were not enough, Article 1 of the law states that subsequent provisions must be interpreted 'in compliance with European Community principles'.

Thus, after some five years on the Italian statute book, European Community directives have not only been applied but their supremacy has been reconfirmed and their importance underlined. Thanks to the substantial similarity between the EC's provisions and those of Italian origin which the authority has had to apply, it has utilized European precedents as if they were its own. What is being constructed, therefore, as a result of these important precedents, is a conceptual framework that gives powerful meaning to the words of the law, through the European interpretation of the core concepts of 'business' that is subject to regulations on competition, of that of relevant market, the real meaning of concerted practice and of dominant market position, as well as the concept of abuse of such a position.

Article 1, of course, requires the law to be interpreted in compliance with EC principles. What the Anti-trust Authority has achieved has gone beyond this, for it has directly grafted its decisions on to those of the Commission and the Court of Justice. When it has been asked simply to respect the principles inherent in EC regulations, be they in the Treaty or in EC legislation, the Authority has instead made those principles and regulations its own, interpreting them in the same precise manner as European Community institutions, the Commission and the Court of Justice. As a result, the Authority has succeeded in duplicating in its decisions the legal reasoning of European institutions both as a general principle and through the application of the law in specific cases.

THE ANTI-TRUST AUTHORITY AND EEC PRECEDENTS

In May 1992 the Authority received a complaint from the Associazione Internazionale Classi Internazionale Vela d'Altura (Italian International Class Sailing Association) denouncing the FIV, the Italian Sailing Federation. The federation had adopted regulations stipulating only boats equipped with two particular tonnage-rating systems, of which the FIV itself was the exclusive licensee, could be admitted to official races. It was possible for other systems to be accepted but only after special authorization by the FIV. Moreover, the FIV had repeatedly discouraged the use of these different systems. Charges brought against the federation were based on these facts. Interesting though this case was, was it a matter that fell under the jurisdiction of the Authority? The behaviour of the FIV could, undoubtedly, have been viewed as discriminatory and as abusing the rules of competition. However, the rules of competition concerned the business world. The FIV was, by law, a body of the national Olympic Committee and was thereby charged with the statutory purpose of promoting, publicizing and defending the sport of sailing. Could it possibly be considered a business undertaking?

Had the Authority based its considerations purely upon the instruments available to it through the Italian Civil Code and its interpretations, the answer would undoubtedly have been negative. This was because no general agreement existed on the questions whether an entrepreneur controlled not only his own work but also that of others, whether it was essential for the profit motive to be involved or whether the activity simply had some intrinsic economic value. Such issues remain controversial aspects, under Article 2082 of the Civil Code. However, not even the most elastic interpretation of the law could reasonably encompass a sports federation.

Not intimidated by such reasoning, Authority chose to base its view of the case not upon national legislation but, rather, entirely upon the approach that had been pioneered by the European Community. First, the Authority pointed out the economic significance of yacht races, which are, after all, commercial events exploited by organizers and sponsors alike. In consequence the Authority then defined the FIV as an 'enterprise in a dominant position in the relevant market', directly quoting the words of the Court of Justice and the Commission. An enterprise was 'any entity engaged in economic activity regardless of its legal status or its modes of financing'[4] and economic activity, 'any activity which participates in economic exchange, regardless of profit-making'.[5]

No other decision, perhaps, more clearly shows the role that the Anti-trust Authority has assumed as an 'importer' of European Community principles and concepts into Italy. It is also a role which has enabled the Authority to broadly define the boundaries of its own jurisdiction (subsequent cases involved public organizations, boards and even professional associations, which were all, thereafter, treated as economic undertakings), whilst in other cases the Authority has sought to define the methods of exercising this jurisdiction, always, of course, on the basis of specific precedents.

The best way to illustrate this phenomenon would be to look at some of those cases which were pertinent to individual aspects of the anti-trust law. After the fundamental concept of business, the second basic concept of anti-trust discipline is that of the *relevant market*, since the restrictive effect of an agreement can be defined as 'substantial' and the position of an undertaking can be termed 'dominant' only when the boundaries of the market have been determined. For example, is the relevant market for Fiat Uno cars or for compact cars? Is the relevant market for airlines that of air travel or the individual routes? Whenever the Authority has had to answer these important questions, and has had EC precedents available, it has consistently based its decisions upon them.

In the case of *Assoutenti* v. *Alitalia*, which was adjudicated upon in 1994, the question at issue was whether or not Alitalia was abusing its dominant position on the Rome–Milan route. Naturally, Alitalia denied that its position was dominant, for two reasons. The first was that Rome and Milan are connected not only by an air route but also by high-speed trains and, consequently, the relevant market should be judged to include both. The second was that, within the sphere of air transport, it was appropriate to consider not only the Rome–Milan (Linate) route, but also the other routes that served passengers travelling to Milan, such as Rome–Milan (Malpensa) or Rome–Bergamo. The Authority accepted the more restricted concept of relevant markets, rejecting both of Alitalia's arguments on the basis of two EC precedents. First, that 'The interchangeability of air transport and rail transport is to be considered limited in consideration of the high value assigned by the primary category of users, that of businessmen, to speed and frequency of connection'.[6] Second, that 'The short distance between Rome and Milan and the brief duration of the flight exclude the possibility that an indirect connection, or a group of routes, could be considered a substitute for the direct connection'.[7]

The next point in question was the concept of a restrictive agreement. Should it have been taken to mean an agreement which actually produces a restrictive effect or is it sufficient that it has the purpose of so doing? When this problem arose the Authority issued a judgement in favour of the latter, basing its arguments upon the *All-Risk Insurance* case of 1994, as well as several other precedents. In particular, a sentence handed down by the Court of Justice, and two sentences of the Court of First Instance, as well as two decisions that had been taken by the Commission. Furthermore, immediately afterwards the Authority added that 'the validity of these principles has been reconfirmed by the TAR [the regional administrative tribunal] of Lazio' in two pronouncements that were issued in 1993 and 1994. First, EC jurisprudence took precedence, and then, and only then, Italian, which did not 'establish' but merely 'reconfirm' the EC interpretation. This was in accordance with a principle which, in the opinion of the Authority, was self-evident.

The concept of concerted practice, i.e. a restrictive trade agreement that had not formally been made public, was also based on EC precedents. Indeed, the key passage in the *Centro Italiano GPL* ruling of 1994 states:

> The adoption of a uniform contractual practice by the undertakings belonging to the Centro Italiano GPL constitutes concerted practice. Concerted practice is to be considered any form of co-operation in which the undertakings, even without arriving at an agreement proper, knowingly substitute for the risks of competition forms of mutual collaboration.[8]

Furthermore, are mere exchanges of information sufficient to produce an illicit agreement? This is a question that has prompted several different answers, depending, naturally, on the circumstances of the cases involved. The Authority has, in various cases, adopted the answers given in similar situations by the European Court of Justice. Specifically concerning insurance, the Authority stated that 'the limits within which forms of information-sharing among enterprises may take place have been indicated and clarified by the Court of Justice, which has deemed illicit those recommendations aimed at any collective increase in the price of the services offered by the companies involved' (*Ania* case, 1993). And again (in the *Restructuring of fuel distribution network* case, 1993):

The European Court of Justice has established that the need for independence prohibits any direct or indirect contact among the operators, having the purpose or the effect of influencing the behaviour on the market of a current or potential competitor, or revealing to a competitor the behaviour which the company itself has decided to adopt, or intends to adopt on the market'.[9]

It is not merely the general nature but also the specific contents of restrictive agreements which have been defined by the Authority through EC precedents. The same principle was also valid for price lists distributed by retailers' associations, which the Authority declared illegal 'in compliance with the orientation of EC authorities'.[10] Such was also the case with the agreement between the two airline companies, which was deemed not restrictive only after the respective governments had agreed not to allow a monopoly on the route which was subject to the agreement (the *Alitalia–Maleva* case, which was based entirely upon the EC case involving Air France and the Belgian airline, Sabena). The same applied to a minority shareholder who concluded a restrictive agreement (in the case of *Parmalat/Granarolo*, 1995):

> The principles of the EC regulations, as expressed both by the EC Court of Justice (Court of Justice, November 17, 1987, *BAT and Reynolds* v. *Commission*), and by the Commission (November 10, 1992, *Warner Lambert/Gillette and others*, *Bic/Gillette and others*), which were clearly taken into account by the Authority (*Titanus Distribuzione/ Cinema 5* and *Cernentir/Merone*) made it possible to ensure that the purchase by a company of a minority shareholding in a competitor company was not subject to the application of those regulations that safeguard competition *only* if the purchase was made *purely* as a financial investment. However, such a practice was prohibited whenever it could be proved that it constituted a suitable means of influencing the competitive behaviour of the businesses in question, in such a way as to restrict or falsify competitive activity in the market.

The exemption regulations that were adopted by the European Commission in accordance with Article 85 paragraph 3 of the Treaty were also the guidelines used by the Authority in order to interpret Italian regulations on agreements. In the case of *Associazione Bancaria Italiana* of 1994 the 'Unified Banking Regulations', i.e. the uniform conditions for a series of contracts and banking services, came under scrutiny. The Associazione Bancaria requested that the regulations should be considered non-restrictive or, at least, that they should be granted exemption in compliance with Article 4 of law 287, inasmuch as they were of benefit to the consumer. In the opinion of the Authority, as expressed to the Banca d'Italia, the second request was partially accepted, but those clauses which demanded a wholly uniform content for contracts were rejected. The conclusive argument of the Authority stated:

> It should also be stressed that evaluation of the above fully incorporates the most recent view of the Commission with regard to the stipulation of uniform conditions for other categories of contracts, insurance contracts in particular, for which the exemption regulations 3932/92 have been issued. In those regulations it is specified that the uniform insurance terms or clauses which have the advantage of offering the insured party a better comparison between offers and a greater uniformity of annual risks cannot lead to standardization of products or to restrictions on the customer.

The problem of dominant market position was focused upon in a manner that was very similar to that concerning concerted practice. Indeed, the wording of the EC ruling constituted, both directly and succinctly, the principal arguments of the Authority. In the case of *Tekal* v. *Italcementi* the Authority, having described the behaviour of Italcementi, concluded that the company itself had 'the power to determine the prices for a substantial portion of the products in question' and thus had 'the possibility of acting independently in regard to its competitors, its customers and, in the final analysis, the consumers'. These were the distinguishing features of the problem of dominant market position. Furthermore, the wording quoted to define the problem was not that of the Authority but, rather, that of the Commission and the Court of Justice.[11]

Is market share sufficient to define a market position as dominant? The answer is clearly no, by common (and now undisputed) consent. However, for the sake of consistency and clarity the Authority sought support from the European authorities. In the *Ignazio Messina* v. *Lloyd Triestino* case, Ignazio Messina, which holds 20 per cent to 30 per cent of the relevant market in maritime transport, accused Lloyd Triestino, which holds nearly 40 per cent, of abusing a dominant market position. However, the Authority responded that:

> The Court of Justice has stated that a market quota ranging from 40 per cent to 45 per cent is not sufficient to conclude that a business is unquestionably controlling the market. It should be evaluated in relation to the number and strength of the competitors (United Brands). The Commission has also recognized the validity of this principle, recalling the above-mentioned sentence in a case concerning maritime services and establishing that, in order to reach the conclusion that a dominant

position exists, it is necessary to evaluate the business's share of the market in relation to the number and strength of the competitors.

(Shipowners' Committee decision)

Having confirmed that an unreasonably dominant position existed, the Authority also turned to the Court of Justice and occasionally to the Commission, in order to define the meaning of abuse. In the *Tekal* v. *Italcementi* case the Authority took the view that the conduct of Italcementi was designed to restrict its competitors' entry into the market. The Authority immediately referred to EC jurisprudence, according to which:

> The concept of abuse is an objective concept, concerning the behaviour of a business in the dominant position aimed at influencing the structure of a market where, expressly due to the fact that said business is operating in it, the degree of competition is already diminished, the effect of which is to reduce still further the degree of competition still existing by recourse to means other than those pertinent to normal competition between products and services.

(Hoffman La Roche)

Again, as in the case of the yachting events, where it had been ascertained that the FIV, the Italian Sailing Federation, had prevented boats with rating systems other than its own from entering races, the Authority quoted the same verdict, from *Hoffmann La Roche*, and stressed, in particular, the parts of it in which abuse was seen as consisting of a series of obstacles to the 'development' of possible competition.

In the above-mentioned case of *Assoutenti* v. *Alitalia*, one of the defendants' arguments was that its flight schedules, and their variations, were submitted to the Ministry of Transport for approval. Such approval by a public authority, Alitalia argued, exonerated it from any charge that it had abused its dominant position in the domestic air travel market. Again, the response of the Authority was consistent, for it stated that: 'Also in the light of EC principles, a certain behaviour may be attributed to a business even where it has received subsequent administrative approval, which is to be considered a separate act not involving interference by the administrative authority in the company's autonomous decision-making processes'.[12] What has become abundantly clear is that European precedents, repeatedly and consistently, now take precedence over Italian jurisprudence.

Perhaps the sector in which EC influence has been most strongly felt has been that of legal monopolies. Indeed, within a purely Italian framework it would have been very difficult for the Authority to interpret legal monopolies as restrictive and abusive. It is quite possible that Article 8 of the law was written by parliament on the basis of reasoning that ran totally counter to that which lay behind Article 90 of the Treaty.[13]

Notwithstanding, Article 8 of Italian law was interpreted by the Authority according to the same principles that were applied by the EC authorities with regard to Article 90 of the Treaty. First, the similarity between the exercise of a legal monopoly and a dominant market position was confirmed, whenever the monopoly involved economic activity. For example, in the *Fremura* v. *State Railways* case, the Authority stated that:

> the dominant position of the State Railways in the rail transport of containers was a function of the company possessing an exclusive concession for railway freight service on the national network. In fact, the acknowledgment of exclusive rights to a company, even when such an acknowledgment emanates from a legal provision, constitutes a typical form of dominant market position.[14]

Based on this premise, therefore, and once again through the application of EC precedents, the Authority established that 'an enterprise having been assigned by law services of a general economic interest is exempt from compliance with national regulations safeguarding competition and the market *only* when the behaviour being evaluated is the only proven and possible means of achieving the institutional purposes of the body'.[15] Thus, UNIRE, another public institution which was charged by law with the promotion and improvement of bloodstock, was subjected to the rules that governed competition. UNIRE had always enjoyed exclusive rights in law to the organization of betting on horse racing and had exercised that right by choosing certain agencies and excluding others, in a manner that was purely arbitrary, i.e. without any competitive comparison of any kind. The Authority concluded that such behaviour 'was not indispensable to the fulfilment of the institutional aims of the body, nor did it appear connected with the exercise of its public function as attributed by law to the body'. As a consequence, this was adjudged to be abuse of a dominant market position.

This was, perhaps, the most far-reaching application for which the law on competition had ever been used because the judgement introduced the law into the public administration itself and struck at behaviour that had previously been covered only by administrative discretion. The Authority, however, proceeded with great caution. Only conduct that may appear to be irrational or restrictive is an abuse in its judgements concerning sectors which, it should never be forgotten, are now public only because they were so made as a result of Fascist legislation. It was typical of the 1930s to vest private associations with the gravitas and status of public institutions, thereby transforming public activities into those that, hitherto, had been purely private. Accordingly, the Authority merely undertakes what some might call the 'sacrosanct' mission of demolishing such false and outmoded premisses.

The strict application of Article 8 has led to another new departure within the Italian legal field, that of confining legal monopolies within the strict boundaries of their exclusive rights, both by preventing them from extending their dominant position to adjacent markets and by obliging them to ensure non-discriminatory treatment of those who have need of the essential facilities they manage. In *De Montis Catering* v. *Rome Airports* the airport company had claimed that its legal monopoly over the management of the airport also applied to the catering therein. The response of the Authority was important, for it represented a new zenith for the influence of EC precedents when it stated that 'The refusal by a business operating in a dominant position in a market to furnish a competitor, even a potential one, with services and products indispensable to its activity constitutes abusive behaviour'.[16] Consequently, a firm which possesses or manages and itself utilizes an essential facility cannot refuse access to that essential facility without objective justification.[17] This principle is applicable also to the case in which the competitor who claims access to the essential facility is a new entrant in a market.[18] In such a case, a company has to be allowed the benefit of fair and non-discriminatory conditions of access, in order to exploit a competitive opportunity in the market.

For example, in a similar case, Telecom had refused to disclose information it possessed, in its capacity as provider of telecommunications and information services. The Authority concluded that such conduct constitued behaviour that was an abuse of its position, on the basis of a sentence that had been handed down by the European Court of Justice some twenty days before, which also involved a case that had turned upon an exclusive claim to vital market information. The judgement in this case (*Sign* v. *Stet Sip*, 27 April 1995) stated that:

A business which possesses an essential resource and refuses other companies access to said resource without objective justification, or does not allow access under fair, reasonable and non-discriminatory conditions, is abusing its dominant position in so far as it tends to reserve to itself another market not assigned to it, excluding any competition on this market.[19]

Perhaps the best-known case of this type was *Telecom* v. *Telsystem* in February 1995. In that case the influence of the European Community was expressed by the Authority in a manner even more forceful and radical than ever. Telsystem had sought access to Telecom's network in order to organize closed groups of customers. However, Telecom had refused on the basis of Italian legislation, which continued to reserve any such service to Telecom itself. Telsystem, on the contrary, maintained that the service had been liberalized by Commission Directive 90/388, but that this directive, after more than four years, had still not been incorporated into Italian law. The Authority decided that the directive was, therefore, immediately and directly applicable and, moreover, that from the moment that it had entered into force national law had been nullified. In consequence the service was part of the free market and, therefore, Telsystem had the right of access to it. Such a conclusion was actually very simple legal reasoning which both upheld the principle of the supremacy of EC law and, on the basis of that principle, curtailed the sphere of a national monopoly.

THE REMAINING OBSTACLES

The Telsystem case provided a useful precedent with which to understand the context in which the Anti-trust Authority has worked in recent years, as well as the obstacles encountered by those EC principles that lie beyond the jurisdiction of the Authority. Why was it, for example, that after four years the directive liberalizing telecommunication services had not been implemented? Why was it necessary for the Authority to step in? The answers to these conundrums are, not surprisingly, complex and manifold. This is Italy! Not only does the strength of legal monopolies remain impressive, but the collective cultural background of Italians and of their political parties is much less pro-competition and market-oriented than that which is found among the members of the Anti-trust Authority. Within this context, the role of the Authority has been, and, indeed, still is, that of an *avant-garde* champion of competition, and for this reason it would be overoptimistic to evaluate the impact on Italy of EC competition principles on the strength of its decisions alone.

Italian legislation is still rife with concessions and exclusive rights. When a private economic activity interferes with a public interest – as frequently happens – the temptation remains strong (in the name of such interest) to plan the overall development of the activity, establishing by decree the limitations on the offer, the terms and even the sales price, for this iniquitous situation does not apply only to old laws and old disciplines. For example, service stations in Italy have never entered the free market and are still subject to public planning, thus establishing and controlling their number. This centralist tradition also applies to cinemas, as a result of a law that was enacted in 1994! The commercial sector is also disciplined in a similar manner, with regional governments being assigned responsibility for deciding upon the number of businesses allowed within the context of regional plans. The tradition of 'safeguarding' the consumer is strong, even at the expense of refusing him any freedom of choice, by protecting him from the risks of deciding. This results in fixed prices, high tariffs and barriers to market entrance remaining under the control of professional groups and associations.

Within this context, the Anti-trust Authority is the voice of the market and competition, and it is a voice which is heard not only in its rulings but also in the numerous 'recommendations' to the government and to parliament that it issues concerning laws or legislative initiatives that have the effect of distorting competition. Obviously, the recommendations are not binding, but they undoubtedly play a role in the cultural and political change which is slowly taking place. Indeed, the more they are based upon EC principles the more effective they are, which provides further evidence that Italian policy on competition is not only a child of European policy but still has constant need to turn to it for support.

THE GROWING ITALIAN CONSTITUENCY FOR ANTI-TRUST MEASURES

One thing is clear, a cultural change is under way. Proof is provided not solely by the activity of the Anti-trust Authority, for there is a political constituency for anti-trust, particularly on the left of the political spectrum (in accordance with the Western and liberal tradition of struggle against monopolies and economic power), while on the center-right the influence of the existing lobbies sometimes prevails. There is, also, a growing cultural constituency, embracing the mass media, scientific activity, and the professions. In Italian universities the economics of competition and competition law are now better understood and many of the academics who teach the two disciplines are drawn from industrial economics and commercial law. Intense research is now also being conducted to lay the foundations, not only European, but also Italian, of the principles of competition and to give them the most extensive practical application.

This work is, indeed, praiseworthy and, although it should undoubtedly be applauded, the scholars who are engaged in it should nevertheless be careful to avoid either excess or exaggeration. Excessive and exaggerated, for example, might well be a description of the claim that the Italian constitution contains a guarantee of the principles of competition which is more complete than that of the European Community and less contaminated by justification based upon reasons of economic efficiency that have opened the way to concentration and integration in recent decades. Indeed, it has even been suggested that Article 1 of the law on competition, in its respect for EC principles, may actually be unconstitutional. This represents a genuine paradox and an historical paradox at that, because in the constitution no policy of competition has ever, hitherto, been introduced. Competition policy began only when Italy adopted the principles of the EC. Equally, it also represents a legal paradox, since it distorts the constitution to the point where one could read into it a 'Sherman Act', which was rejected by the founding fathers.

In conclusion, I am satisfied that I can read the Italian constitution as a relatively neutral document with regard to the issue of competition, for it enables me to continue the struggle against monopolies, not only on the basis of Article 43 of the Italian constitution but also on that of the added armoury provided by Article 90 of the Treaty on European Union.

NOTES

1 Law No. 834 of 16 June 1932.
2 These Bills were the work of the great judge Tullio Ascarelli with the support of the Amici del Mondo association. The association was a real intellectual lobby in favour of a free market and its members, in many ways, echoed policies similar to those that had been espoused by Sherman in the United States at the turn of the century.
3 However, the Anti-trust Authority was not empowered to legislate, unlike the position within the Community, where the Commission has the power to do both and uses it for the express purpose of promoting market integration.
4 The precise wording of the Court of Justice in *Klaus Hoffner and Fritz Elsen* v. *Macroton GmbH*, 23 April 1991.
5 Words of the Court of Justice and of the Commission itself, cited by the Authority on several occasions in the FIV case.
6 Decision of the EEC Commission, 5 October 1992, Air France–Sabena.
7 Decision of the EEC Commission, 17 February 1993, British Airways–Dan Air.
8 See EEC Commission ruling of 23 April 1986, IV/31. 149 propylene, EEC Commission ruling of 19 December 1990, IV 33.133-A, Carbonato di Sodio Solvay, ICI, Court of Justice sentence of 16 December 1975, joint proceedings 40–8, 50, 54–6, 113 and 114/73, *European Sugar Cartel, Suiker Unie and others* v. *Commission.*
9 Court of Justice, 16 December 1975, 40/73, *Suiker Unie.*
10 Letter to Fipe, Fiepet and others dated 27 December 1994.
11 Commission, 19 October 1988. *Napier Brown–British Sugar*, Court of Justice, *Continental Can, Hoffman La Roche, United Brands.*
12 Court of Justice, 4 May 1988, *Bolson SA Pompes funèbres des régions libérées* v. *EEC Commission*, 30 June 1993. CNSD. See also Authority decisions of 17 March 1993, *IBAR–Rome Airports* and 18 March 1994, *IBAR–Società Esercizi Aeroportuali.*
13 Article 8 states that 'The provisions of the preceding articles do not apply to enterprises which, by law, manage services of general economic interest or operate as legal monopolies, as concerns all matters strictly linked with the

fulfilment of the specific tasks assigned to them'. Article 90 of the Treaty affirms the principle that the rules of competition are applicable to legal monopolies, apart from aspects relevant to their specific mission.

14 Court of Justice, 11 July 1985, *CBEM–CLT–IPB*; Court of Justice, 19 March 1991, *France* v. *Commission*.
15 Court of Justice, 23 April 1991, Hofner, 19 May 1991, Ert., 10 December 1991, Port of Genoa, 13 December 1991, *GM–INNO–BM*.
16 Court of Justice, 6 March 1974, *ICI* v. *Commission*, and 3 October 1985, *CMB –CLT–IPB*.
17 EC Commission, 21 December 1993, *Port of Roedby* v. *Denmark*.
18 EC Commission, 21 December 1993, *Sea Containers–Sea Link*.
19 Court of Justice, 6 April 1995, *Magill TV* case.

BIBLIOGRAPHY

Alessi, R. and Olivieri, G., *La disciplina della concorrenza e del mercato (Commento alla 1. 10 ottobre n. 287 ed al Regolamento CEE n. 4064/89 del 21 dicembre 1989)*, Turin, Giappichelli, 1991.
Amato, Giuliano, *Il governo dell'industria in Italia*, Bologna, Il Mulino, 1972.
—— 'Il mercato nella costituzione', *Quaderni Costituzionali*, 1992, vol. 7, 1, pp. 7–19.
Benedetelli, M. V., 'Sul rapporto fra diritto comunitario e diritto italiano della concorrenza (riflessioni in margine al disegno di legge n. 3755 ed al regolamento comunitario sulle concentrazioni)', *Foro italiano*, 1990, vol. IV, p. 235.
Blake, H. (ed.), *Business Regulation in the Common Market Nations*, New York, McGraw-Hill, 1969.
Cassese, Sabino, *Diritto pubblico dell'economia*, Bari, Laterza, 1995.
Chiti, M., 'Il Trattato sull'Unione europea e la sua influenza sulla Costituzione italiana', *Rivista italiana di diritto pubblico comunitario*, 1993, vol. 3, 3, p. 343.
Cocozza, F., 'Riflessioni sulla nozione di Costituzione economica', *Il diritto dell'economia*, vol. 34, 1992, p. 71.
Frignani, A., 'Ambito di applicazione e rapporti con l'ordinamento comunitario', *Diritto antitrust*, 1993, vol. I, p. 96.
Niro, R., *Profili costituzionali della disciplina antitrust*, Padua, Cedam, 1994.
Onida, M., 'I rapporti fra disciplina nazionale e disciplina comunitaria in tema di concorrenza', *Concorrenza e mercato*, 1993, vol. 1, p. 4.
Saja, F., 'L'Autorità Garante della concorrenza e del mercato: prime esperienze e prospettive di applicazione della legge', *Giurisprudenza commerciale*, 1991, vol. 1, p. 457.
Siragusa, M. and Scasselati Sforzolini, G., 'Il diritto delle concentrazioni a livello Cee: una prima analisi pratica delle decisioni della Commissione', *Foro italiano*, 1992, vol. IV, p. 252.
Zito, A., 'Mercato, regolazione del mercato e legislazione antitrust: profili costituzionali', in *Jus – Rivista di Scienze Giuridiche*, 1989, vol. 36, pp. 219–62.

Index